the New Reformation

the New Reformation

Returning the Ministry to the People of God

GREG OGDEN

Spring 2000
Ezra Sangjun Han

ZondervanPublishingHouse
Grand Rapids, Michigan

A Division of HarperCollinsPublishers

To my wife, Lily,
and daughter, Aimee,
whom I deeply love

The New Reformation
Copyright © 1990 by Greg Ogden

Requests for information should be addressed to:
Zondervan Publishing House
Grand Rapids, Michigan, 49530

Library of Congress Cataloging-in-Publication Data

Ogden, Greg.
    The new reformation : returning the ministry to the people of God / Greg Ogden.
       p.   cm.
    Includes bibliographical references.
    ISBN 0-310-31021-0
    1. Priesthood, Universal. 2. Clergy—Office. 3. Lay ministry. 4. Pastoral theology. I. Title.
BT767.5.O37   1990   89-29502
262'.15—dc20   CIP

Edited by James E. Ruark
Designed by Louise Bauer

Printed in the United States of America

Contents

Foreword

WHETHER WE KNOW it or not, almost all contemporary American Christians and churches have been deeply influenced by the great controversies, struggles, and new forms of church life that arose from the sixteenth century in what we now call the Protestant Reformation. In the decades and centuries following the dramatic nailing of Luther's Ninety-five Theses to the door of the castle church at Wittenberg, the Protestant Christian movement has claimed and cherished as the heart of its heritage the great assertions of "justification by faith alone," "the priesthood of all believers," and "sola Scriptura." New denominations came into being and moved across the Atlantic to find new forms and expression in the New World. Yet the great Reformation of Luther and Calvin left unfinished business.

There are serious matters on the unfinished agenda of the Reformation that demand urgent attention in our own day. One of the most critical of these is the theme of this book—the ministry of all believers, whether lay or ordained, male or female. If, as the Reformers agreed, priesthood is no longer limited to the hierarchical few but is intended as God's gift and God's intention for all believers, what is the situation in regard to Christian ministry or service? Is it possible that it too belongs to all believers and that our present structures and patterns actually inhibit God's intention for the way the work of the church is to be done?

Greg Ogden provides a valuable service in offering a thoughtful, biblically founded yet provocative review of the key issues involved in equipping God's people for ministry. Writing as part of the Reformed tradition, he stresses the importance of reenvisioning the church and its ministry so as to empower and enable all of its people as servants of God in the church and the world.

In the last twenty years or so, serious signs of strain have become increasingly visible in traditional American church life. While there is much evidence of spiritual vitality and growth in many parts of American Christianity, it is still true that mainline American denominations have lost close to one-fourth of all their members. In far too many congregations, overworked and stressed pastors worry about large numbers of inactive and passive members who look to the church for services in times of need, but who often give very little in the form of regular, committed service. While many factors are involved, I find it noticeable that many, if not most, fast-growing churches and younger denominations are growing, at least in part, because they have found ways to entrust significant ministries to nonordained people. The apostle Paul in 2 Corinthians 4:1 speaks of "ministry by the grace of God." To whom is ministry given?

As an experienced pastor who seeks to live out the insights in this book, Greg Ogden helps us to start thinking about a New Reformation. Enjoy the challenge!

Roberta Hestenes
President, Eastern College
St. Davids, Pennsylvania

Preface

YOU HAVE PROBABLY seen the wood carvings that outline the name JESUS. "What do you see?" someone asks with a knowing grin. Try as you might, you can find no discernible pattern in the raised outline. Then for some unknown reason, your eyes refocus on the background rather than the raised portion, and you "see" what was there all along.

The burden of this book is to help us "to see." I want us to see that the church of Jesus Christ looks very different according to the lens we use. The church viewed through the lens of "institution" is distorted. By contrast, the church seen through the lens of "organism" becomes clear. The shift of our gaze elicits an "Ah-hah! Now I see what the church was meant to be!"

This book is meant to be prophetic in a double sense. In the first instance, I have attempted something risky—to read the signs of our times. Trying to state what God is up to in our day may be presumptuous. I am not referring to the signs of world events that signal the end times, but to the signal that there is a gathering climate in the church that will make it possible to return the ministry to where it belongs—God's people. In the second sense, this book is prophetic as a prod. The reader is confronted by an urgent message: "Don't miss the opportune moment for a whole-body ministry."

I have self-consciously written in a style I like to call "accessible," or popular, theology. In other words, this is a theology written by a practitioner. I trust that the theological analysis and biblical exposition are academically respectable, but presented in a way that always moves toward implementation. Interwoven with the theological framework are illustrations from my experience as a pastor who is attempting to live his theology. It has been a burden of mine for some time that we pastors need to be guided by a clear theology of ministry in the daily practice of ministry. Too often we unconsciously live out other people's expectations of what a pastor is to be and what ministry is about, without a proactive theology that guides the overall implementation of our ministry.

This book contains my vision for ministry, some of which has been tried and tested, and some of which is before me as a lifelong agenda. Any ministry vision has needed a context in which the dreams become a reality. This book is only possible because of what I experienced as an associate pastor at St. John's Presbyterian Church in West Los Angeles. Before this congregation I "sang" my song ad nauseum that all God's people are called to ministry and that they needed to demand that their pastors equip them. They responded, not with patronizing smiles, but with motivated desire to be God's ministers. They affirmed my gifts and delighted in what I had to offer. St. John's also provided a context for staff ministry with my dearest friend, Darrell Johnson, the senior pastor, and with Joan Stock, fellow associate. This team relationship and responsive congregation provided the ideal environment for me to live out the vision.

My special thanks and appreciation go to Ellie Bima Lea for her free use of the red pencil. Shirley Knisley and Janet Anderson not only typed the manuscript, but were a source of encouragement. Gratitude goes to Michael Smith, editor of the Ministry Resources Library of Zondervan, who thought that I had something to say to the church. And finally, to my new church family, the Saratoga Federated Church, I am delighted that the visions contained here are matching the reality I am seeing in you.

Unfinished Business

WE LIVE IN THE GENERATION when the unfinished business of the Reformation may at last be completed. Nearly five hundred years ago, Martin Luther, John Calvin, and others unleashed a revolution that promised to liberate the church from a hierarchical priesthood by rediscovering "the priesthood of all believers." But the Reformation never fully delivered on its promise.

When Luther made such explosive statements as, "Everyone who has been baptized may claim that he already has been consecrated a priest, bishop or pope"[1] and "Let everyone, therefore, who knows himself to be a Christian be assured of this, and apply it to himself—that we are all priests, and there is no difference between us,"[2] he envisioned the priesthood of all believers on two fronts.

We are fully acquainted with the first aspect of the priesthood of all believers since it is a part of the church's fabric. All believers have direct access to God through Jesus Christ. The Reformation released us from the stultifying practice of going through a human mediator who pleaded our case before God. We are all priests in that we minister directly before God. The one high priest Jesus Christ has opened the way to God by presenting himself as the sacrifice for our sin, and he sits at God's right hand to make intercession for us continually. A special class of priests representing us to God and God to us is no longer needed. We are all drawn into the priesthood in that we represent ourselves before God through the covering of the mediator, Jesus Christ.

The unfinished business and the unkept promise that has the power to unleash a grass-roots revolution is the logical corollary to the priesthood of all believers. For not only are all believers priests before God, we also are all priests to each other and in the world. Wallace Alston captures the priestly role of our representing God to each other.

> The priesthood of all believers, therefore, does not only mean that each person is his or her priest. . . . In very personal terms, it means that the minister is your priest and that you are the minister's priest; that you are my priest and I am your priest; that we are God's representatives to each other, and that we are each other's representatives before God. It means that we are to speak to each other about God, calling each other to repentance and faith. It means that we are to speak to God about each other, interceding before God for each other, and seeking God's guidance and blessing. It means that we should try to become increasingly responsive to one another, tending to each other in God's name and offering each other practical and constructive help for Christ's sake.[3]

Nearly five hundred years after the Reformation there are rumblings in the church that appear to be creating a climate for something so powerful we can call it a New Reformation. *The New Reformation seeks nothing less than the radical transformation of the self-perception of all believers so we see ourselves as vital channels through whom God mediates his life to other members of the body of Christ and the world.* What are the rumblings of renewal in the church that now create the climate to complete the unfinished business of the Reformation? What has been occurring over the last three decades to transform people from being passive recipients of others' ministry to active ministers in Christ's name?

In this past generation we have experienced six important changes that provide the basis to unleash the ministry of the whole body. These changes have revolutionized our identity:

1. The Holy Spirit has been rediscovered as the means of direct encounter with the living God.
2. The Christian life is Christ in you.
3. The church is a living organism, the body of Christ.
4. All God's people are ministers.
5. An ecumenism of the Spirit transcends denominational loyalties.
6. Worship is the defining event in the church.

Let us look at each of these six signs of renewal and how they have reshaped our experience of the Christian life and the church.

1. The Holy Spirit Has Been Rediscovered as the Means of Direct Encounter With the Living God

The Holy Spirit as Hidden Member of the Trinity

Figure I.1

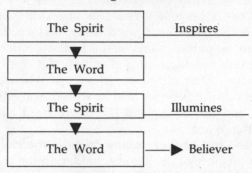

Over the last generation the Christian church and the nature of the Christian life have been deeply affected by a renewed understanding of the role of the Holy Spirit. As recently as the early seventies, when I was a seminary student I was taught what I would call a "rationalist" approach to the work of the Holy Spirit. The person of the Holy Spirit has little independent personality of his own and is hidden in the shadow of the written Word of God. According to the "rationalist" view, the Spirit has two roles to play in relationship to believers, both tied to the Word: (1) the Holy Spirit is the *inspirer* of the Word. The Word of God can be trusted as the measuring rod of faith because its source is the Holy Spirit; and (2) the Spirit is to take the written Word of God and apply it to our hearts. In Reformed theology we speak of the *illuminating* work of the Spirit. Our minds are perfectly able to grasp what the Word says, but our hearts need to be softened to receive the Word. So the Spirit both inspires and illumines the written word.

I call this the rationalist approach because in it the Christian life is conceived as the passionate study of and conformity to the Word of God. The Spirit's work is solely related to the Scriptures. Transformation occurs by filling our minds with Bible content. If we want to encounter God, we do so in his Word. The Holy Spirit's job is to point to the written text and create a love for the Word of God. In this scenario the Christian life comprises grasping propositional truth and assimilating sound doctrine. The mark of being an orthodox believer is holding to the historic truths of the faith.

The fear that lurks behind the rationalist approach is that religious experience apart from the Word of God can lead to doctrinal error. Therefore I was taught to distrust any emotional or spiritual experience because it could be the wide path to heresy. Nonrational occurrences such as dreams, visions, healing, and direct, inward impulses were suspect, the seedbed for false doctrine. The only reliable source of truth is the Word of God, but never experience. After all, how can we test whether an experience is true or false? It is better to stick with the objective standard of the Word and not go beyond it. All we need has been fully revealed in the Word.

So for me—and I believe many others—the Holy Spirit was the forgotten member of the Trinity, hidden in the shadow of the Word of God.

The Holy Spirit as Encounter With the Living God[4]

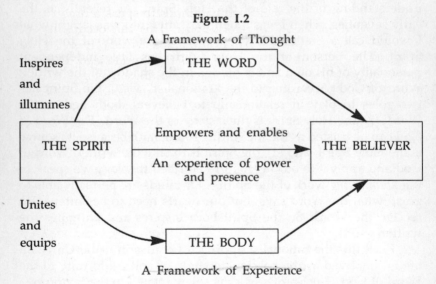

Figure I.2

A Framework of Thought

Inspires and illumines

THE WORD

THE SPIRIT

Empowers and enables

An experience of power and presence

THE BELIEVER

Unites and equips

THE BODY

A Framework of Experience

In recent years we have experienced a paradigm shift. The rationalist approach was not wrong; it was merely incomplete. Our recent understanding of the Holy Spirit incorporates everything the rationalists say is true, but goes beyond it. I affirm the inseparable connection of the Holy Spirit and the Word while at the same time asserting that the Holy Spirit has also a direct relationship with the church. I maintain that the Word is the objective standard by which we measure truth, and therefore it is the test of whether the claims of the Spirit's work are valid. But I also affirm that the Spirit speaks directly to the church today and not solely through the avenue of the written Word of God.

The rationalistic approach leaves God's people inwardly starved. It fills the mind but does not satisfy the heart. It creates a formal and distant relationship with Christ. Now we are rediscovering that the Holy Spirit is the means of an encounter with the living God. The work of the Spirit includes mediating the direct presence of God to the life of the believer. "What did the early believers experience that so fired them to action?" we ask. "How can we have the same reality of an inner filling?" The apostle Paul writes, "God's love has been poured into our hearts through the Holy Spirit which has been given to us" (Rom. 5:5). Paul is speaking of more than grasping propositional truth; he describes being grasped by the God who encounters us.

We are not only experiencing a revitalization of our faith, but also discovering today that God continues to speak a direct word to the church through the Holy Spirit. This can occur through inward impression or a word of guidance. When I prepare the order of worship for God's people, I ask the Lord to lead me in the proper way to honor him so that the community may be edified. I listen for the inner impulses and the life-generating thought that directs a proper focus for our worship experience.

God also speaks to the church through gifted people who are channels for the immediacy of the Holy Spirit. This ranges from those who have a prayer ministry for physical healing in Jesus' name to those who are led *by the Spirit* through inner healing prayer as Christ releases people from the debilitation of past hurt or sin; to prophets who speak a timely, confrontive message to a local body or to the church universal; to those with gifts of discernment who pray for those under the bondage of spiritual addiction or demonic oppression.

The Holy Spirit as Separated From the Word of God

Figure I.3

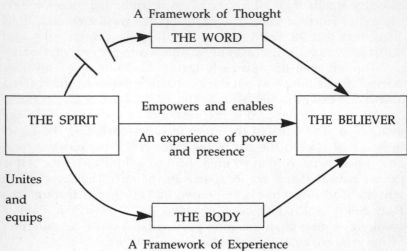

A Framework of Thought

THE WORD

THE SPIRIT

Empowers and enables

An experience of power
and presence

THE BELIEVER

Unites
and
equips

THE BODY

A Framework of Experience

Let me anticipate an objection. Isn't it possible for those who believe they have direct messages or leadings from God to be misled? Doesn't this contribute to the megalomania we have witnessed in some who set themselves up as mouthpieces of God? It certainly can—and does. The work of the Holy Spirit can be falsified and counterfeited. Therefore there must always be two tests in place:

a. *The Word of God must always be the ultimate test of truth.* We should be suspect whenever we hear people make claims such as, "The Holy Spirit is saying something different in our day than he has ever said before." This is separation of Word and Spirit. How can the Spirit who inspired the Word now say something contradictory to the very Word he brought into being? Whenever the Spirit is separated from the Word and not submissive to the Word, it is a sign of cultic activity.

b. *The Spirit of God is the Spirit of the community of believers.* The Holy Spirit in the New Testament almost without exception is portrayed as the One who indwells the corporate assembly of believers. The New Testament knows nothing of an individualized Spirit operating apart from community. Therefore anything spoken to an individual must be tested by the church. Autocratic leaders who claim to have a direct pipeline to God and set themselves up as spiritual potentates accountable to no one else are outside the New Testament view of the relationship between the Holy Spirit and the church.

This is all to say that in the last generation there has been an explosion in the numbers of people who have experienced the truth of being channels through which the Holy Spirit works. A faith that was distant and secondhand has now become personally engaging. The Spirit is directly available to and energizes all for service and witness to Jesus Christ. The expansive work of the Spirit creates the climate for the other specific signs that point to our generation as the one that will effect the return of the ministry to the people of God.

2. The Christian Life Is Christ in You

The Christian Life as Ethical Respectability

A generation ago the Christian life was conceived of as a life of ethical respectability expressed through the support of the institution of the church. During the decade after World War II, the United States witnessed a religious boom: build a church edifice, open the door, and watch the people stream in. A respectable family with three children and a station wagon would be found in church on a Sunday morning. What did this routine mean? It was the "right" thing to do. The church was seen as the disseminator of religious values for the family and society. Going to church was as American as apple pie, since the church provided the moral glue for the community and national spirit. Commenting on this 1950s faith, Joseph Triggs and William Sacks write,

> Loyalty to the churches seemed to be the natural complement to respect for the nation. President Dwight D. Eisenhower captured the spirit of the time when he said in 1954, "Our government makes no sense unless it is founded on a deeply felt religious faith—I don't care what it is."[5]

Will Herberg's landmark study *Protestant-Catholic-Jew* said that in the fifties, to be an American meant to identify with one of these religious traditions.

But being a part of the fifties church did not generally mean its people had a vital, living encounter with Christ. In fact, if you asked average churchgoers to explain the nature of their relationship with Christ, they would have been personally offended. The church was for respectable citizens, not broken, needy, or hurting people. Respectability meant distance. The idea of gathering face to face with other believers to discuss how following Christ intersects daily struggles was alien to the church atmosphere. People had a kind of institutional faith. They believed in what the church as an institution represented. The church was a moral pillar of the American way.

The Christian Life as Christ in You

In the 1950s Herberg identified a void in personal religious experience that was a clue to renewal. "The bland, homogenized force of secular American culture could not satisfy any genuine hunger for holiness."[6] Starved for an internal reality, the Christian life moved away from being defined in terms of the ethical norms that the institutional church represented and toward an encounter with the living Christ. Formerly the Christian life was characterized by acquiring behavior that was consistent with the way "a good Christian" acted. Ethical rectitude, dos and don'ts, and acting in a generous, loving manner made one a good Christian. Properly, being a Christian is seen not primarily as being good, but being alive—alive in Christ.

Though goodness and holiness are outward expressions of the Christian life, they are not its essence. Genuine faith means knowing God in Christ—repenting, receiving forgiveness, and beginning a new life under Christ's lordship. Triggs and Sacks describe "conversion" as the means of entry into a relationship with God: "It is dramatic, decisive, and individual, a conscious form of religious experience with the potential for far-reaching changes in a person's life."[7]

We put adjectives like "born again" or "Spirit-filled" before "Christian" as a way of saying that Christianity means knowing God. Each person can have a relationship with a loving God with whom to commune daily. We speak of "walking in the Spirit" or "abiding in Christ" as a way to capture the moment-by-moment, direct guidance of the Holy Spirit and the truth that God through Christ resides in our hearts.

We seek more than dry, institutional faith; we hunger for a God-reality at the center of our being. We are more than rational beings; we are also emotional and spiritual beings who need to be filled with God's presence, to encounter the living God, and to know and be known. And by God's grace, this relationship has become a transforming reality to many today.

3. The Church Is a Living Organism, the Body of Christ

The Church as Pastor-Focused

Historically the church has been entrapped in institutionalism. The institutional church resembles a corporation with the pastor as its head. Locked into a hierarchical structure, the clergy are ensconced at the pinnacle of the pyramid. They are the "experts" in religion. As a separated, elevated class, the clergy have acted as if only they are able to enter the realm of things spiritual. The clergy as a distinct caste have supposedly received a special unction and calling that enable them to have a closeness to God unattainable by ordinary church members. This theology of ministry has had more in common with the Old Testament priesthood than with New Testament peoplehood.

Appropriating another image, we can describe the pastor as performing a solo act on the theater stage while the church members are the audience, never fellow actors. Laypeople passively warm a pew and place money in the offering plate to create the context for pastors to perform their ministry.

The Church as People-Focused

As we rediscover the church as a living organism, the body of Christ, church members have been called out of the audience to become players on the stage. Everyone has a part in this play. Every believer is a necessary part of the drama that God is producing, the drama of salvation history. We are on stage together, pastors and people alike. There is no longer a select, professional union of actors. In the body of Christ, all the "actors" have a direct connection to the Producer, the Creator, and the Choreographer of History. The debilitating class distinction between clergy and laity is dashed. The pastor no longer plays all the parts, but like a director draws out the hidden talents of myriad actors and encourages them to perform according to their skills.

What has caused this shift to a people-focused ministry in our day is primarily the rediscovery of small groups. Small groups are a visible microcosm of the church as the body of Christ, working and sharing ministry together in face-to-face relationships. Here

Christians gather to encourage each other in spiritual growth, Scripture study, intercessory prayer, and neighborhood evangelization. All this occurs in the context of warmth and intimacy without dependence on or expectation of pastoral participation.

More than any other structure, small groups call people out of the audience and onto the stage to live together as the body of Christ. Small groups commonly proliferate when the church is being renewed. We can look at the first-century house churches, the Wesleyan class meetings, and the seemingly endless variations of cell groups today and affirm with Triggs and Sacks, "It is the small group experience, grounded in appreciation of the early church, that has been the most visible feature of spiritual movement today."[8]

4. All God's People Are Ministers

Ministry as Tasks Done for the Church

If the pastor is the star on center stage, what roles are left for God's people? In the institutional church there is a clear line of demarcation between spiritual and nonspiritual matters. The clergy are qualified to handle the spiritual (e.g., preaching, teaching) and people (e.g., pastoral care, counseling) ministries. The laity are left with odd jobs as stage hands, lighting technicians, and custodians. They carry out support or temporal functions so that the play can go on.

Laity too often perform tasks for the church, but are frequently not allowed to exercise ministry gifts to build up the body of Christ. They are given tasks such as overseeing budgets and devising systems for pledging, collecting, and accounting for the monies. For laity, maintaining the church facility consumes an inordinate amount of time, along with straightening up the pew racks and setting up and putting away the Communion elements. The only legitimate spiritual ministry generally entrusted to laity is the teaching of children in Sunday school—which somehow became included in these nonessential, temporal tasks. While we must not demean these tasks or deny them as legitimate areas of service, we have to recognize that they define a limited realm in which laity have heretofore been allowed to serve.

Ministry as an Expression of the Giftedness of the Body

As the reality of the church as an organism has been rediscovered, we are finding that in God's design all the people in the church are gifted for ministry. Ministry is not to be equated with what professional leaders do; ministry has been given to all God's people. So the pastor's role is not to guard ministry jealously for himself, but instead to turn the spotlight on this multigifted body. In the process, God's people are discovering that in fact they are gifted to act.

Christianity is essentially a lay movement. Over the past generation specialized parachurch ministries have arisen for the particular purpose of equipping laity to find their places in building up the body. A person can be trained today to provide pastoral care as an undershepherd; equipped to lead a small group of almost any kind; outfitted to be an evangelist; sensitized to be a lay counselor touching the hurts and wounds in people's lives; or prepared to be a teacher of adults. These parachurch groups fill a gap for training people in ministry that the church has long neglected.

We are also rediscovering that ministry is not confined to the church building. We are just beginning to see the church as a base of operations called to support and equip people to live out their Christian witness in the work environment. The broken world we live in needs a *called* army to address the enormous pain that is the result of our sin. Only people who know they are ministers can be compassionate tools of God's healing work.

To me, the clearest expression of body ministry's becoming a reality has been the influx of able and gifted women into service. When we begin to view ministry as what God performs through all persons, the doors are flung open to women. In the two thousand years since Christ affirmed the equality of all through the Cross, there has never been a time when the opportunities for women in ministry have been greater. And this has happened largely in the last twenty years. When I graduated from the largest interdenominational seminary in the country in 1973, there were no more than four women among the 350 students in the master of divinity program. Today about forty percent of that seminary's students are women. I believe one of the main reasons for this remarkable change is the realization that all God's people are ministers.

5. An Ecumenism of the Spirit Transcends Denominational Loyalties

Ecumenism as Structural Loyalty and Unity

In the face of decreasing support from the laity and local churches, mainline denominations have demanded greater loyalty to institutional programs. Sometimes denominational leaders have resorted to heavy-handed tactics that amount to "loyalty tests." "Loyal" congregations are expected to give a minimum of fifty percent of their mission monies to the denomination. Congregations that have participated in parachurch ministries or independent missions manifest a strong conviction to designate some mission funds to such groups in addition to the denomination's work. In response, church hierarchies have tended to reward the faithful and punish the errant. Where the reprimands were harshest, churches have fled the denomination.

Denominational mission agendas have become another "loyalty test," measured in terms of social and political action. Richard Hutcheson, at one time an official in the former Presbyterian Church U.S., says of such a loyalty test, "To continue to tell evangelicals that if they are loyal Methodists or Episcopalians they *must* give their money to fight multinational corporations in developing countries and institutional racism at home, and that they must do this because majorities of General Conferences have voted to support such activities is futile."[9]

Such loyalty tests signal a growing gulf over the last two decades between denominational direction at the top and life in the local church. The upper echelon has gotten out of touch with its constituents. Its hierarchy does not exist to serve the grass roots; rather, it has become a bureaucratic end in itself, expecting the local church to carry out the wishes of those in denominational headquarters. I am not saying that theological and ecclesiastical leadership is unimportant; it is. But when we place the stress on the institution, we tend to forget that any denominational structure is simply a historical and structurally visible expression of the one church of Jesus Christ. It has been created to enable the church to fulfill its call as disciples and servants of Jesus Christ.

A second concern of ecumenism in the mainline denominations is the effort toward structural union. For example, the Church of Christ Uniting was formed as a consultative body among many mainline churches with the goal of creating a megachurch. More recently these efforts have given way to attempts to restore schismatic groups within denominations, as in Presbyterianism and Lutheranism. Is it possible that, rather than indicating life and growth, these reunions are signs of dying institutions struggling to prolong their lives?

Ecumenism as Spiritual Unity

In contrast to organizational union, a sign of renewal in recent years has been an ecumenism of the Spirit that transcends denominational loyalties and has nothing to do with structures. Denominational distinctions become blurred when Christians connect with each other through the Spirit.

Many churchgoers today are not as loyal to institutions as they are to Christ. One negative result of this is that many people have little appreciation for a theological tradition and do not understand the high cost paid by martyrs and leaders to preserve a biblical faith. The positive side is a sense of being a part of God's kingdom work that can never be coterminous with church structure.

I experienced this ecumenism of the Spirit when I attended the Billy Graham Conference for Itinerant Evangelists in July 1986. As I was waiting to claim my luggage at the airport in Amsterdam, a contingent of forty black Africans arrived. They marched two abreast in a straight line and in delightful harmony sang choruses such as "He Is Lord" and indigenous African melodies. My spirit soared, and I thought, *These are members of my Christian family. These are soul brothers and sisters.* I had no knowledge of their denominational affiliation, and I didn't need to know it. I knew that they loved the same Lord.

So an ecumenism of the Spirit shifts our focus of loyalty. We are loyal first to the movement of God's Spirit, wherever his work is being accomplished, and loyal only secondarily to structures.

6. Worship Is the Defining Event in the Church

Our experience of worship has probably undergone more change since the 1950s than any other aspect of the church's ministry. This mark of renewal should perhaps be at the top of the list, because what happens in worship leaves its imprint on every other aspect of ministry.

Worship as Performance

The experience of worship in an institutional framework is something done to you, in front of you, or for you, but not *by* you. The congregants come as passive recipients subconsciously thinking, "I dare you to make this interesting." People having this frame of mind leave the sanctuary as unmoved as when they arrived. After all, pastors are paid to put together the order of worship, exude charisma, insert moving musical selections, and then preach a stirring message. Since the dynamic is essentially a performer-audience relationship, the worshipers are put in the position of being critics of the latest pastoral effort.

As a pastor I have often felt like an ice skater or a diver who immediately upon completing the routine receives scores from the judges of the competition. Somehow we don't think it unusual for the remarks at the door after a church service to focus on evaluating the morning message. This audience-performer mentality has become so much a part of our mindset that George Plagenz, who wrote a weekly column for a Cleveland newspaper, took to rating the quality of worship of whichever church he attended the previous Sunday.

There are a handful of pastoral superstars who know how to sustain the "show-biz" atmosphere from week to week. People go to Pastor So-and-So's church because he or she can orchestrate the best show in town. He or she can even create the impression that worship has occurred. With the right dynamics, the audience will get the feeling that something good has happened. So a leader with charisma can engineer a highly charged atmosphere and manipulate a response. Yet it may not be worship at all.

Worship as Participation

In contrast, there is found in many places today a people alive in Christ who come together ready to pour out their hearts to God. It matters little whether the worship is highly structured or spontaneous. The difference is that people are prepared to give of themselves in song, prayer, praise, and response to the Word of God. Worship is an expression of the community, not something done to the people by worship leaders. Søren Kierkegaard points us back to the image of the theater when he writes that in worship the people are the actors, the worship leaders are the prompters, and God is the audience.

I have been privileged to experience the electricity of a congregation that enters the sanctuary anticipating how God will meet it in a unique way. Worship there and elsewhere overflows with life in the Spirit. Charles Spurgeon, the great nineteenth-century British preacher, gives us an important reason why. When asked the secret of his powerful preaching, he replied that it lay in a people who continually prayed God's fullness into him. The staff of the church I serve gives high priority to planning a Spirit-led worship service, but it would mean little if people were not eager to enter into the particular way God would have us honor him.

Conclusion

Although this overview of the signs of renewal has been brief and selective, we get the impression that we live in a historical moment of enormous opportunity. The very foundation of the church of Jesus Christ is rumbling with renewal. *God is raising up at the grass roots a Spirit-filled people who see themselves as ministers, spiritually gifted ecumenists who see worship as the center.*

What appears to be the common element that gives sparkle to this multifaceted gem of renewal?

Simply put, from one viewpoint, we could say that we are rediscovering the ministry of the Holy Spirit. When this period of church history is written, it may well be labeled "the Age of the Holy Spirit." It may also be called "the New Reformation." Either way, through all these elements of renewal runs the radical transformation in the *self-perception* of every believer. Followers of Christ in this age will see themselves as Spirit-filled ministers who are a part of the ministry given to all Christians. In a word, Christians are priests ministering the presence of God on behalf of the people of God and the lost world.

These individual transformations are possible only because the church is again being perceived fundamentally as an organism. Only an organism can complete the unfinished business of the Reformation and return the ministry to the people of God.

This book is an attempt to sketch the shape of the sails of the church in order that we might catch the new winds sweeping over us. For us to skim the seas at full clip, the sails must be set. There are three sails that need to be hoisted for the church to be propelled by the gale of the New Reformation. In these pages I will attempt to shape a biblical view of these sails: the church, pastoral ministry, and leadership in the New Reformation.

NOTES

1. Martin Luther, "An Appeal to the Ruling Class (1520)," quoted in Lewis W. Spitz, *The Protestant Reformation* (Englewood Cliffs, N.J.: Prentice-Hall, 1966), 54.

2. Martin Luther, "The Babylonian Captivity of the Church," *Works of Martin Luther* (Philadelphia: Westminster, 1943), 282–83.

3. Wallace M. Alston, Jr., *Guides to the Reformed Tradition: The Church* (Atlanta: John Knox, 1979), 47.

4. Chart used by permission of William Tibert, associate pastor of Glendale (California) Presbyterian Church.

5. Joseph W. Triggs and William L. Sacks, *Of One Body: Renewal Movements in the Church* (Atlanta: John Knox, 1986), 11.

6. Quoted in Triggs and Sacks, *Of One Body*, 37.

7. Triggs and Sacks, *Of One Body*, 15.

8. Ibid., 43.

9. Richard G. Hutcheson, *Mainline Churches and the Evangelicals* (Atlanta: John Knox, 1981), 29.

PART 1

The Church in the New Reformation

CHAPTER 1

The Church as Organism

IN THE INTRODUCTION I made the bold assertion that we live in a moment of history when the ministry is potentially being returned to the people of God. To harvest the fruit that the Holy Spirit is producing, we must recapture a biblical vision of the fundamental nature of the church. We are in the midst of something as radical as a paradigm shift from the church as institution to the church as organism. The juxtaposition of these two concepts will serve as the framework for doing our theology of the church.

What do I mean by organism? By organism I mean that the church in its essence is nothing less than *a life-pulsating people who are animated by the indwelling presence of Jesus Christ.* There is a host of biblical images for the church that point to this reality. In the New Testament the church is described, among other things, as the household of God, the people of God, the bride of Christ, and a fellowship of the Holy Spirit. In fact, ninety-six word pictures have been identified.[1] But the image that dominates the New Testament and serves as an umbrella for all these is the image of the church as the body of Christ. I will use this metaphor to paint a picture of the church as organism.

Implicit in the phrase "body of Christ" are three questions, the answers to which provide the biblical substance for understanding who we are:

1. What is Christ's relationship to the church?
2. What is the church's relationship to Christ?
3. What is our relationship to each other?

To answer these questions I will draw on the *locus classicus* for Paul's image of the body—1 Corinthians 12—but not be restricted to it.

WHAT IS CHRIST'S RELATIONSHIP TO THE CHURCH?

The apostle Paul ingeniously selected the image of the human body to convey the organic manner in which the church is to function. We can examine the human body from two standpoints. The first views the body as a functional whole with all its parts under the central coordination of the head. But on closer examination we notice that the whole is made up of diverse parts, each with distinctive functions. The hands are for grasping, the eyes for seeing, the feet for walking, and so on. The body is the prototype for unity in diversity.

Paul uses the analogy of the human body to apply spiritual truths in an arresting fashion. Note the startling conclusion to 1 Corinthians 12:12: "For just as the body is one and has many members, and all the members of the body, though many, are one body, *so it is with Christ*." I have read this verse perhaps a thousand times and I still silently conclude, "so it is with the church." For Paul "the body of Christ" is not just a metaphor or helpful word picture, but points to the reality that Jesus dwells among his people and gives his life to them. "The body is a reality," writes Arnold Bittlinger. "Christians are not like members of any body but are according to their very nature members of a specific body, the body of Christ."[2]

The church is not a human organization that has contracted by common consent to keep alive the memory of a great man, Jesus Christ. On the contrary, the church is a divine organism mystically fused to the living and reigning Christ, who continues to reveal himself in a people whom he has drawn to himself. Ray Stedman puts it this way in his book *Body Life:* "The life of Jesus is still being manifest among people, but now no longer through an individual physical body, limited to one place on earth, but through a complex, corporate body called the church."[3]

The understanding of the church as organism was experientially true for the apostle Paul from the moment of his initial encounter with Christ. Saul, the firebrand and self-righteous protector of the Hebrew law against the perverters of Judaism called Christians, was on his way to Damascus, having received authority to arrest and bring them bound to Jerusalem. His plans were dramatically altered. A blinding light filled the sky and completely engulfed his field of vision. Thrown to the ground, he heard a voice, "Saul, Saul, why do you persecute *me*?" Saul replied, "Who are you, Lord?" The heavenly voice responded, "I am Jesus, whom you are persecuting" (Acts 9:5–6). But wait! Saul was not persecuting Jesus, but those who claimed to be his followers.

What is the relationship between Jesus and his followers? Jesus dwells in them; the church is the aggregate body to whom Jesus has given his life. If you touch Christians, you have touched Christ. Christians are a sacramental people. A sacrament is a means of grace; it is a symbol that mysteriously bears the presence of Christ and through which believers encounter Christ. It would then be fair to say that *the church is a sacramental people* who are corporately and individually the conduit of Christ.

The church as the living organism of Christ is further underscored in Paul's cosmic statement in Ephesians about the place of the church in God's eternal scheme. Paul concludes with a flourish: "and he [God] has put all things under his [Jesus'] feet and has made him [Jesus] the head over all things for *the church, which is his body, the fulness of him who fills all in all*" (Eph. 1:22–23).

What is the relationship of the phrase "fulness of him" to "his body"? Does Jesus fill the body, or does the body fill out Jesus? The Greek word *plērōma* (fullness) is most often used in an active sense in the New Testament to mean the content (body) that *fills* some container (in this case, Jesus). Likewise, the pieces of the loaves in the feeding of the five thousand are described as *filling* the baskets. In Ephesians 1:23 *plērōma* taken in the active sense would mean that the body fills Christ. In other words, the church as the body of Christ fills out, or completes, Christ. Christ is in some way incomplete without the church. Jesus is the head, but a head is no good without a body. Some theologians, such as Armitage Robinson, go so far as to say, "In some mysterious sense the church is that without which Christ is not complete, but with which He is and will be complete. Christ is waiting to find completion in His body."[4]

I believe it is more consistent with the message of the New Testament to interpret fullness in a passive sense: "that which is filled." *The church is the container, and Jesus is the one who fills it with his life.* Jesus is the content who indwells the form. Nowhere else in the New Testament are we given the sense that Jesus is incomplete. Jesus' existence and sufficiency do not rely on us for completion. Jesus gives his life to us, not out of an unfulfilled need, but out of his sovereign and gracious freedom. He wants to share his very being with the creatures he has made; he wants us to enjoy the love that overflows from the triune God.

What makes the church different from every other way humans have chosen to relate to each other? It is different because the church is not of human origin, but a divine creation. Thomas Oden has captured this uniqueness in writing,

> Christianity is distinctive as a religious faith in that it understands itself to be living as a continuing community through the living Christ. . . . Its uniqueness lies in its particular relationship with its founder. . . . It is the resurrected presence of the living Lord that continues to be the sole basis of the present reality of the church. Jesus is not merely the one who founded the community and left it, but rather the one who is present to the community now and in each historical period as the vital essence of the church.[5]

We do not understand the core nature of the church until we grasp the unspeakable truth that Jesus extends his life on earth through a corporate people that can literally be called "the body of Christ." Frank Laubach poignantly summarizes Christ's relationship to the church:

> When Christ was here on earth, He was limited to performing His ministry in one place and at one time. He was one man, walking beside one sea in one little corner of the earth. He healed whoever He touched, but His touch was necessarily limited by time and by space. Now, does it make sense that the Father would send His Son for this limited ministry? I don't think that is tenable. He made provision to carry on the work through the Holy Spirit: we are to complete His mission. We are His multiplied hands, His feet, His voice and compassionate heart. Imperfect and partial to be sure, but His healing Body just the same. And it is through the Holy Spirit (Christ's love which is everywhere at once) that we receive the power to carry on the work of the apostles. It is a challenging and sobering thought: when we receive the Holy Spirit into our lives, we receive the same urgent and life-giving force that led our Master.[6]

WHAT IS THE CHURCH'S RELATIONSHIP TO CHRIST?

Max Thurian helps us make a transition from Christ's relationship to the church to the church's relationship to Christ. He writes, "In our day, Jesus does nothing independently of the church *nor can the church do anything independently of Christ.*"[7] Just as the parts of the human body cannot function without the head, so the church is absolutely dependent on its head, Jesus Christ. The nature of the church's relationship to Christ is implicit in the expression that Jesus is "head over all things for the church" (Eph. 1:22). Biblically the word *head* in reference to Christ has two meanings: (1) life source, and (2) ultimate authority.

Life Source

We are totally reliant on Jesus as our life source. We commonly use *head* almost exclusively to refer to the one in charge, yet biblically it can also mean "origin." The Greeks spoke of the source of a river as its head, and in our parlance we speak of the headwaters of a river. Paul uses the unusual imagery of head as the source of nourishment for the church:

> Rather, speaking the truth in love, *we are to grow up in every way into him who is the head*, into Christ, from whom the whole body, joined and knit together by every joint with which it is supplied, when each part is working properly, makes bodily growth and upbuilds itself in love (Eph. 4:15–16).

Whoever heard of a body growing into its head? In this context Paul is exhorting the Ephesians toward "mature manhood," "the stature of the fulness of Christ," and growing up as opposed to being "children" (vv. 13–14). Paul reminds the Ephesians that (a) the only way to become spiritual adults is to recognize their absolute reliance on Jesus to supply their life, and (b) his likeness is the goal toward which they are growing. So Jesus is the head *into* whom and *from* whom we grow.

The church is absolutely dependent on Jesus Christ for its life. It has no life in itself. It is on life support. Like a patient clinging to life by tubes and machines, the church dies when its lifelines are disconnected. This is Jesus' point when he says that he is the true vine and we are the branches (John 15:1–11).

> Abide in me, and I in you. As the branch cannot bear fruit by itself, unless it abides in the vine, neither can you, unless you abide in me. I am the vine, you are the branches. He who abides in me, and I in him, he it is that bears much fruit, *for apart from me you can do nothing* (John 15:4–5).

Jesus does not say, "Apart from me you can do *a little*." Life flows only in one direction on the vine—from the source, the vine, to the branches. The branches have no inherent life. They live and die by their connection to the vine. So our responsibility as the church is to stay connected to the source.

Yet our witness is replete with testimonies of disconnected lifelines. Disconnection occurs subtly. Imperceptibly the church can become an organization for and in which we perform acts of service rather than a body where we are conscious of the indwelling Christ. For example, during a retreat with the leaders of my church, the elders had the opportunity to articulate their frustrations with their role. Almost all expressed dissatisfaction and irritation that the business of the church dominated their corporate time as elders. Symbolic of the organizational trivia was a forty-five minute discussion about the merits and demerits of the size and location of a wall unit. The frustration was heightened for these leaders because they intuitively understood the church fundamentally to be a people in whom Christ dwells, and when they gather they desire to attend to and foster their life in Christ. But for them and for us, when we move from abiding to business, we experience the church as organization, not organism.

How does the church remain attached to the vine? What are the lifelines that keep the church nourished? The regular disciplines of public and private worship are essential to tap the life in the vine. Healthy branches cannot rely on last year's sap. The sap must flow continually to keep the branches resilient. Therefore we must avail ourselves of regular communion with the Lord.

Public Worship

The corporate event that defines our position before God and reminds us of our absolute dependence on him is public worship. The church's basic reason for being is "to live for the praise of his [God's] glory" (Eph. 1:12). In worship we are reminded that we are not "the still point of the turning world," as T. S. Eliot put it. God is the center, and we find our proper place in orbit around him. We were made for him. Nevertheless, we must admit that worship can be an experience of dead institutionalism. We have all sat through church services where we sensed both pastor and people fulfilling a required routine.

For worship to be a life-giving experience, there must be a sense of awe among the people of God. Victor Hugo said of his bishop, "He did not discuss God; he was dazzled by Him." When worship is planned with the expectant question, "Lord, how can we honor you this week?" and the people privately prepare to encounter the living God in the dynamic of community, God will make his presence known to his people.

Private Worship

Jesus said, "Abide in me and I will abide in you." This is accomplished through private moments in quiet stillness. I like to look at a daily quiet time as an opportunity for my personal rendezvous with the Savior. Robert Munger in his popular sermon "My Heart, Christ's Home" paints the warm image of meeting with Jesus at his invitation in the living room of life. Sitting in an overstuffed chair in front of the fireplace, we are invited to share in daily communion with the One who wants to spend time with us. This is an opportunity for transparent dialogue. We speak to Christ in prayer, and he speaks to us through lingering meditation upon his written Word.

My personal practice in the daily rendezvous is to sing through the hymnbook and make notations in my journal using the ACTS formula for prayer: Adoration, Confession, Thanksgiving, and Supplication. This is the place in my heart where I can say to my Lord, "Search me, O God, and know my heart! Try me and know my thoughts! And see if there be any wicked way in me, and lead me in the way everlasting!" (Ps. 139:23–24).

For Jesus to be head means he is first of all the church's life source.

Ultimate Authority

For Jesus to be head means in the second place that the church is under his direct authority. The church's relationship to Christ is to accept obediently and fulfill faithfully the particular role that God has assigned to each of us through the Holy Spirit. To affirm the most basic confession, "Jesus is Lord" (1 Cor. 12:3), is far more than reciting a creed. In the context of Paul's image of the church as the body of Christ, the phrase "Jesus is Lord" describes a functional, operational reality.

Jesus as head of the church means that he arranges life in the body. Each member is directly connected to the Head and therefore able to receive signals from the head. Every member as a part of the body finds the role suggested by the spiritual gifts assigned to him or her. The Lord through the immediacy of the

Spirit determines each person's function. "But as it is, God arranged the organs in the body, each one of them, as he chose" (1 Cor. 12:18). Similarly, Paul writes, "All these [spiritual gifts] are inspired by one and the same Spirit, who apportions to each one individually as he wills" (1 Cor. 12:11).

The church functions as an organism when those who make up the body of Christ seek obediently to fulfill the role God has assigned to them. The analogy of the human body is very helpful in understanding the way the living organism of the church is to function. The human body is beautifully coordinated when each part functions according to its design. The central command post, the head, sends the signals through the nervous system, which activates the bodily parts. These bodily parts have no will of their own. The hands and feet, for example, only function in response to the head If the hand could act independently of the head, there would be chaos in the body. So the body of Christ harmonizes in perfect coordination with the head when each person seeks to exercise the gifts that have been assigned to him or her.

What is the church's relationship to Christ? Jesus Christ is the head of the church, his Body. This church is alive when it remains attached to its life source and is directly under his authority.

WHAT IS OUR RELATIONSHIP TO EACH OTHER?

If organism is the reality to characterize the essence of the church, then being in the church means sharing in divine life. Jesus lives in us. We have life only as we remain in him; our relationship to each other has to do with passing on the life he has placed in us. We can summarize Paul's description of our relationships of interdependence in three ways:

1. We belong to each other.
2. We need each other.
3. We affect each other.

We Belong to Each Other

Paul writes, "For by one Spirit we were baptized into one body—Jews or Greeks, slaves or free—and all were made to drink of one Spirit" (1 Cor. 12:13). This says that everyone, no matter who we are or what we have done, comes into the church by the same means. We all must come humbly on our knees, for we did not choose Christ; he chose us.

Someone has said that the ground is level at the foot of the cross. Though we try to live without God, his sovereign Spirit opens our hearts. We are drawn into a new life from above. We are picked up by the scruff of our neck and placed into his body, the church. The only thing we may have in common with the person in the pew next to us in worship is that we do not deserve to be there. God has wonderfully and gently come into our lives so that each of us has a story of our wooing to tell. What knits our hearts together is that we belong to Christ.

Therefore we have no choice about who our brothers and sisters are. God did not and will not consult with us on whom he brings into the body. Every other human organization can set its standards for membership and filter out those not to their liking. But by listing "Jews or Greeks, slaves or free," Paul declared that racial, ethnic, and religious heritage and station or class in life are meaningless categories of distinction in the church. He tells us to get out of our mind any nonsense that would allow us to think that we can be selective about our church family.

Through baptism in the Holy Spirit we enter into this divine body and therefore find ourselves with others who have also been chosen. Arnold Bittlinger catches Paul's intent in 1 Corinthians 12:13:

> Before people can participate in this Spirit, they are bound to national, cultural, social, and religious groups of all kinds. Participation in the one Spirit transcends these human ties and binds those who possess the Spirit in the body of Christ. This new relationship is stronger than all previous ties.[8]

Elizabeth O'Connor writes, "The church means staying locked into a concrete web of relationships until we come to know ourselves as belonging to one another and to the body of Jesus Christ."[9] From the world's viewpoint this can make for strange bedfellows. But when the most unlikely people are reconciled through Christ, then insurmountable earthly barriers are overcome. Charles Colson tells the moving story of a dinner gathering that included Harold Hughes, a former senator; Tommy Tarrant, a white racist; Eldridge Cleaver, a militant black activist, and Colson himself, a former White House official. Colson recounts the powerful experience that evening:

What a strange collection of people: the one-time Nixon loyalist, a recovered alcoholic and liberal Democratic senator from Iowa, a member of the Black Panther Party and an avowed Marxist revolutionary out on bail, and an ex-Ku Klux Klan terrorist doing 35 years in prison. Here were men who represented opposite poles culturally, politically, socially; it would be unthinkable in the world's eyes that they could come together for any purpose. Yet on this night they prayed together, wept together, and embraced—joined together by the power of the Holy Spirit in a fraternity that transcends all other.[10]

We belong to each other because we first belong to Christ.

We Need Each Other

According to Paul's body image, all the parts are interdependent and necessary for the body's health. Robert Banks says, "God has so designed things that the involvement of every person with his special contribution is necessary for the proper functioning of the community."[11] No individual part can function without a connection to the other parts. A hand disconnected from the wrist is useless. "For the body does not consist of one member, but of many" (1 Cor. 12:14).

Paul is concerned with two wrong attitudes that subvert the interdependence of the body: inferiority and superiority. The corrective is interreliance.

1. *Inferiority.* There are some who attempt to detach themselves from the body because they feel unimportant in the overall scheme. "If the foot should say, 'Because I am not a hand, I do not belong to the body,' that would not make it any less a part of the body. And if the ear should say, 'Because I am not an eye, I do not belong to the body,' that would not make it any less a part of the body" (1 Cor. 12:15–16). Some compare themselves with the highly gifted and conclude that they have nothing to offer. Again, Bittlinger says, "They say: 'I am only a foot'—now if I were a hand then I would be something. A hand is much better than a foot and much more useful to the body."[12]

Invariably, when we compare ourselves with others we come up second best and therefore fail to accept ourselves as the valuable persons God has made us. Comparison is really a self-focused coveting of gifts. I think of Vicki, who upon observing people with leadership abilities and communication skills was convinced she had been absent when God distributed the gifts.

Since her eyes were so focused on what she did not have, she failed to value the compassionate spirit that made her the first one to console troubled members of the body.

We suffer today from an epidemic of low self-image and lack of healthy self-importance. Yet the body functions in a healthy fashion when all are affirmed and valued for the contribution each has to make. Marriage Encounter has a saying, "God don't make no junk." The remedy to the disease of low self-esteem lies in helping each member discover the unique gifts given to him or her by the Spirit for building up the body. Gordon Cosby, pastor of the Church of the Savior in Washington, D.C., addresses inferiority in saying,

> Christ makes each of us something unlike any other creation fashioned by God—something wonderful, exciting, unique; something specifically needed in the total body of Christ. This uniqueness, this very self that is so hard to describe, this charismatic person is the gift of the Holy Spirit. It is the primary gift we bring to the Body, and without it the Body is immeasurably impoverished.[13]

2. *Superiority*. The second wrong attitude Paul describes is just as destructive as inferiority. There are some who believe they are complete in and of themselves and do not need the other parts of the church. "The eye cannot say to the hand, 'I have no need of you', nor again the head to the feet, 'I have no need of you'" (1 Cor. 12:21). The attitude of superiority is reflected in the belief that the church is on God's optional list. So we hear people say that "the church is helpful if you need it, but as for me, I can be as close to Christ in my rose garden or on the golf course as I can be with other Christians on Sunday morning."

The "I have no need of you" attitude is also expressed as the arrogance of gift projection, a form of superiority. It is psychologically true that we expect that everyone sees things as we do. We then project our perspective on others. This can apply to spiritual gifts and involves a failure to see the diversity of the body. George Mueller of Bristol, England, was a great Christian of the nineteenth century. What God accomplished through Mueller's faith was truly astounding. But Mueller had a blind spot in thinking that everyone had the gift of faith. He wrote, "Let not Satan deceive you in making you think you could not have the same faith, but that it is only for persons situated as I am. . . . I pray to the Lord and expect answers to my requests, and may not you do the same, dear believing readers?"[14] Faith was George Mueller's spiritual gift. Yet he expected it to be everyone's as if there was only one part to the body.

3. *Interreliance.* The middle ground between inferiority and superiority is interreliance. None of us is complete in and of oneself. We are whole only in relationship to other parts of the body. Jesus makes himself known more fully corporately than he does in isolated individuals. For example, evangelism done in the context of community is more powerful than individual witness. A small group within our church held a "discussion party" for friends and work associates. These people were invited into a permissive environment in which they could ask any question related to the Bible's perspective on matters of interest to them. The power of this approach was the opportunity for unbelievers to observe the qualitatively different way a group of Christians interacted with each other in contrast to the distancing and alienation they experienced in the world.

We are created for relationship. This was so from the beginning. The Lord told Adam before creating Eve, "It is not good that the man should be alone" (Gen. 2:18). None of the living creatures could be a "helper," or better yet, a "counterpart" to Adam. When the woman was presented to him, Adam exulted, "This at last is bone of my bones, and flesh of my flesh" (Gen. 2:23). He was no longer alone. The Hebrew language reflects this completion. Until the creation of woman, the word for "man" was *adam*, meaning "mankind." When woman was created, the word for man became *ish*, meaning "male" in contrast to *ishah*, "female." Man did not become male until there was female.

To be created in the image of God means to be created for relationship. "In the image of God he created him, male and female, he created them" (Gen. 1:27). But sin marred the image of God in man and thereby shattered relationship. The church of Jesus Christ is meant to be a reflection of the corporate restoration of the broken image. Christ, "the image of the invisible God" (Col. 1:15), called a people out who would be the visible expression of the image of God being restored. The church is not simply a good idea, convenient when it is needed. The church is essential to God's redemptive plan. Jesus reflects his presence to the world through an interreliant people. We need each other.

We Affect Each Other

We are called together to leave a holy imprint on each other's lives, and we do this in two ways: (a) in our ministry, and (b) in our relationships.

1. *In our ministry* (1 Cor. 12:4–8). Paul spells out what we have already alluded to: we all have ministries. "To each is given the manifestation of the Spirit for the common good" (1 Cor. 12:7). It is through our ministry that we contribute to the good of the whole. Our ministry is defined by the gifts God has given to us. Paul uses a variety of synonyms to capture what he means by spiritual gifts.

> Now there are varieties of *gifts*, but the same Spirit,
> and there are varieties of *service*, but the same Lord,
> and there are varieties of *working*, but it is the same God
> who inspires them all in every one (1 Cor. 12:4–6).

a. "Gifts" (1 Cor. 12:4). The Greek word for "gifts" is *charismata*, from which we get our word "charismatic." The root of *charismata* is *charis*, which means "grace." So charismata are literally "grace-gifts" that come with the package of salvation. I like to look at spiritual gifts as the tangible, manifest expression of the love of God for us. Each of us has a basic need to make a contribution, to know that our lives have added to the common good. The grace-gifts are the means God has provided for us to make this contribution.

b. "Service" (1 Cor. 12:5). The Greek word translated "service" is derived from *diakonia* from which we get the word "deacon." It could also be translated in 1 Corinthians 12 as "ministries." "Service" captures the attitude in which we make our contribution. Jesus is our model. He said, "I came not to be served, but to serve and to give my life as a ransom for many" (Mark 10:45). He not only said these words, but lived them. The way we give our lives away is through the proper stewardship of our gifts. We all have a service to give the body. For me, the best way I can serve the body is to be encouraged to take the time to properly prepare to teach.

Gifts are not for self-aggrandizement, but "for the common good." There was a time when I wanted to use my preaching gift for self-adulation. I wanted people to hang on my every word and adoringly say, "Wasn't that wonderful!" This motivation was the opposite of service; it was self-inflation.

c. "Working" (1 Cor. 12:6). The term "working" also has a familiar derivation, coming from the Greek word *energematon*, from which we get our word "energy." In other words, gifts energize, charge, or make a positive impact on the body. Each gift operates in its particular way to strengthen the body. Evangelists bring in new babes in Christ, pastors help create a nurturing atmosphere, mercies reach out in compassion, servers identify and meet basic needs, and so on. Each one strengthens in his own way. Therefore a spiritual gift is an ability to minister that is given by God to strengthen and upbuild the body of Christ.

2. *In our relationships.* Paul captures the rhythm of mutuality in the body when he writes, "If one member suffers, all suffer together; if one member is honored, all rejoice together" (1 Cor. 12:26).

In describing a mutuality of suffering Paul draws a lesson from our physical bodies. When one part of our body hurts, the rest of the body turns its attention to the hurting part. We don't say to ourselves, "I shouldn't be concerned about that throbbing toe. I should be glad that all the other parts of my body are functioning correctly." Of course not! Our entire attention is focused on relieving the pain of the sore toe. In the body of Christ, what happens to one member affects the whole. The Greek word translated "all suffer together" is *sympatheō*, which literally means to "suffer with" or "sympathize." Sympathy implies an identification with another's suffering to the degree that we enter into and carry another's pain as if it were our own. It is the image of getting next to a person and lifting the burden so that the weight is distributed on the shoulders of other people. Paul says that the suffering should be spread out so it is carried by the whole community.

The reverse of this concept is true as well. "If one member is honored, all rejoice together." It is deflating to have something wonderful happen to you and have no one with whom to share the joy. When I received the phone call that this book—my first— had been accepted for publication, my colleague in ministry, Joan, was gleefully eavesdropping on my conversation. We shed tears of joy together.

John Winthrop, the first governor of the Massachusetts Bay Colony, shared these words with his fellow colonists shortly before they set foot in the New World in 1630: "We must delight in each other, make other's conditions our own, rejoice together, mourn together, labor and suffer together, always having before our eyes our community as members of the same body."[15]

The purpose of this chapter has been to sketch in broad strokes the shape of the rediscovery of the biblical vision of the church as an organism. In summary, I have said that the church as organism means we are a people in whom Jesus invests his life; we are a people who remain connected and receive direct signals from the head; and we are a people through whom divine life is transmitted to one another. Paul has his own summary: "Now you are the body of Christ and individually members of it" (1 Cor. 12:27).

SNAPSHOTS OF ORGANISM

In conclusion let me share some snapshots from the photo album of St. John's Presbyterian Church in Los Angeles to illustrate the church as organism. The church's motto reflects organism: "We are people helping people become mature disciples of Christ."

- That motto is lived out in the counseling room as people receive healing for past hurts and release from sin in order to be freed for ministry.
- Discipling triads reflect organism as one person invites two others into a yearlong commitment to study, pray, and grow together. While studying the essentials of the Christian life these three people share life in a context of accountability and intimacy.
- The church is organism when people have their arms around each other, with heads bowed in prayer, taking some concern together to the Lord.
- When people gather in small groups for face-to-face sharing of their lives over Scripture, assisting each other in Christian nurture, they are the living organism of Christ.

The church is organism when a member starts a Bible study in his insurance agency for the purpose of leading others to Jesus Christ. When members gather in mission communities around a call to address human need and brokenness, they are extensions of Christ. When fifteen to twenty people return from a Monday night visit to a Youth Authority where they have ministered to juveniles from ages nine to fourteen, they are a life-pulsating people animated by the indwelling presence of Christ.

When the church is receiving the infusion of life from its head, its body grows organically. People are added to the body, ministry arises spontaneously, and it all takes on a sense that God is doing something that is bigger than the people and they had better not try to control it. The people are being led to see that the church is primarily and essentially defined as the living organism whose life is created by and dependent on the living Christ.

To say that it is primarily organism does not mean that the church is without order. There must be structure within the organism. In the next chapter we will look at the place of institution and see why the Reformation understanding of the church did not provide the context to deliver the ministry to all God's people.

NOTES

1. E. Best, *One Body in Christ* (London: SPCK, 1955).

2. Arnold Bittlinger, *Gifts and Graces* (Grand Rapids: Eerdmans, 1967), 55.

3. Ray C. Stedman, *Body Life* (Glendale, Calif.: Regal, 1972), 37.

4. J. Armitage Robinson, *St. Paul's Epistle to the Ephesians, With Exposition and Notes* (New York: Macmillan, 1903), 42–43; as quoted by John R. W. Stott, *The Message of Ephesians* (Downers Grove, Ill.: InterVarsity Press, 1979), 64.

5. Thomas C. Oden, *Agenda for Theology* (New York: Harper & Row, 1979), 117.

6. As quoted by Arnold Bittlinger, *Gifts and Graces*, 56.

7. Ibid.

8. Ibid., 57.

9. Elizabeth O'Connor, *Journey Inward, Journey Outward* (New York: Harper & Row, 1968), 27.

10. Charles Colson, *Life Sentence* (Lincoln, Va.: Chosen Books, 1979), 173.

11. Robert Banks, *Paul's Idea of Community: The Early House Churches in Their Historical Setting* (Grand Rapids: Eerdmans, 1980), 64.

12. Bittlinger, *Gifts and Graces*, 59.

13. Gordon Cosby, *Handbook for Mission Groups* (Waco, Tex.: Word Books, 1975), 72.

14. Peter Wagner, *Your Spiritual Gifts Can Help Your Church Grow* (Glendale, Calif.: Regal, 1979), 159.

15. John Winthrop, "A Model of Christian Charity," in *Puritan Political Ideas, 1558–1794*, ed. Edmund S. Morgan (Indianapolis: Bobbs-Merrill, 1965), 92.

CHAPTER 2

The Institutional Entrapment of the Church

HENDRIK HART LEVELS the following indictment against the church: "Even though the leaders of the Protestant Reformation sincerely intended to break with the traditional Roman Catholic conception of the church, nevertheless the tradition arising from the Reformation did not succeed in making the break."[1] The theme of this chapter is an explanation why the Reformation did not make a complete break from a hierarchical conception of ministry. Before we begin this analysis, however, let me provide the microscope through which we will view the church.

In chapter 1 I stated that for the ministry to return to the people of God, we must experience the church as organism. I boldly asserted that we are in the midst of a fundamental refocus that is so radical that we can call it a paradigm shift. We are moving from a view of the church as institution to that of the church as organism. The definition of the church as organism has as its starting point God's people indwelled with the presence of the living Christ.

I have already referred to "the church as institution" without clearly defining what I mean by that phrase. A clear definition is essential to an analysis of what undermined the Reformation's ability to fulfill its promise regarding the priesthood of all believers.

The term "institution" as applied to the church can be understood two ways: (1) The necessity of institution as order, that is, the need for organization within the organism of the body of Christ; and (2) institution that becomes institutionalism, that is, the ministry of the church defined from the top-down viewpoint of its official leaders as opposed to the bottom-up perspective of God's people.

THE NECESSITY OF INSTITUTION

So that I am not accused of wanting to dismantle all structure within the church, let me sketch the biblical basis for institution as order as distinct from the entrapment of the church in institutionalism.

Although the church as institution does not describe its essence, the church must have an institutional aspect. The human body illustrates the need for order within the organism. Within the human body are four life-support systems that are essential to its health. The *skeletal structure* serves as the frame on which all the vital organs hang, and it gives a shape distinctive to each person. The *nervous system* is the body's internal communications network that harmoniously integrates the whole. Running through every extremity are hundreds of miles of nerves that carry electrical impulses sent from the head to activate the individual body parts. The *digestive system* takes in food as fuel, breaks it down, and replenishes life for the body's survival. The *circulatory system* carries this fuel in the form of oxygen and nutrients to every cell and also cleanses the body's waste. The human body shows us a harmonious relationship between organism and order. Its internal structure provides the means for the proper flow of organic life.

To apply this analogy to the church, the institutional aspects should similarly serve the organism of the church to facilitate its life-flowing energy. It will come as no surprise, therefore, that in the same passage where Paul defines the essential nature of the church as organism, the body of Christ, he also affirms the necessity of institution or order. If 1 Corinthians 12 were read in isolation, we might conclude that there is no need for a defined leadership structure or policy guidelines within the church. After all, Jesus is the head of the body and thus arranges the members of the body directly through the impulses of the Holy Spirit.

But Paul makes it clear that there must be order in the organism. In 1 Corinthians 13 and 14 he outlines the principles of order to govern the chaos created by the Corinthians' abuse of freedom and mismanagement of spiritual gifts. For the Corinthians, the Christian community was turned into a stage to show off their gifts and build themselves up rather than an opportunity to edify the body. So the church became a platform for self-focused performance and "look-what-God-gave-me." Paul is compelled to remind the Corinthians that unless the gifts are motivated by love, they lose their value. "If I [fill in the gift], but have not love, I am nothing" (1 Cor. 13:2–3).

Paul continues in 1 Corinthians 14 to deal with two problems of the church that surfaced in the worship gatherings of the community. First, some were speaking in tongues without interpretation into the lingua franca. Paul previously had affirmed the value of addressing the mind with an intelligible word from God rather than speaking in an ecstatic manner in an unknown language. While underscoring the legitimacy of the gift of tongues, Paul stated that tongues in a public setting must be interpreted into a meaningful message. In this context Paul laid down an operational principle. "If any speak in a tongue, let there be only two or at most three, and each in turn; and let one interpret" (1 Cor. 14:27). This is the kind of statement that would be appropriate for the church bylaws.

The second problem related to governing prophecy. One way that the gift of prophecy expressed itself was through spontaneous messages under the prompting of the Holy Spirit. If more than one prophet at a time was speaking, there was cacophonous confusion. To bring control and restore order, Paul wrote, "Let two or three prophets speak, and let the others weigh what is said. If a revelation is made to another sitting by, let the first be silent. For you can all prophesy one by one, so that all may learn and all be encouraged; and the spirits of prophets are subject to prophets. For God is not a God of confusion but peace" (1 Cor. 14:29–33).

Paul concluded this section with a statement of his overall concern: "All things should be done decently and in order" (1 Cor. 14:40).

This is all to say that in spite of the absolute priority we must give to the church as organism, there is a real need for the institutional elements of leadership, policy, and structure.

THE ENTRAPMENT OF INSTITUTION

The primary way I have been and will be using the phrase "church as institution" is to see the church through the lens of institutionalism. My use of the phrase is pejorative. Institutionalism equates the ministry of the church primarily with its ordained leadership.

Ecclesiology has as its starting point a select group who represent the whole. Thomas Gillespie, president of Princeton Seminary, quotes from the *Form of Government* of the Presbyterian Church, U.S.A., in a paper entitled "Our Ministerial Roots." This denomination adopted the following statement as its understanding of ministry:

> The ministry is one, but specific forms of ministry may emphasize special tasks and skills such as proclamation, celebration, teaching, ordering, or deeds of love and justice.

It might seem that the statement "the ministry is one" could imply that the subject is body ministry and that the specific ministries listed belong to the body. But on further examination it becomes clear that ministry is associated with ordained offices. The ministries delineated are subsumed under one of three offices in the church.

> The ministry is characterized by an essential unity within a functional diversity. This diversity is honored, on the basis of a division of labor, in the ordering of the ministry into three church offices (the tasks of "proclamation, celebration, and teaching" being assigned primarily to the "ministers," the task of "ordering" [i.e., governance] being undertaken by the "ministers" and "ruling elders" conjointly, and the tasks of "deeds of love and justice" being the special responsibility of the "deacons").

The following is the telling conclusion:

> The three offices together constitute the *one ministry of the Church in its wholeness* (italics added).[2]

The conclusion is that ministry is accomplished through the set-apart, top-down leadership in the body. Therefore, when I use the term "institutionalism," it is akin to clericalism. Such a church is dominated by its leadership.

It was the institutionalism of the Roman Catholic Church that the Reformation attacked and attempted to change. The Reformers confronted a church that was hierarchical, sacerdotal, and clerical.

The rigid hierarchy of medieval Catholicism represented the embellishment of the threefold offices of bishop, presbyter, and deacon, which developed during the second and third centuries of the church. The stratified positions of status and honor were the seedbed for corruption during the Middle Ages as the church gained power equal to and often above the state. This dominance over people's lives was wedded to a theology that said that Christ had delegated to the church the right to dispense grace. Those in the hierarchy of the church therefore were in the powerful position of dispensing or withholding grace.

Priests, as the exclusive celebrants of the Lord's Supper, took on a sacerdotal function. The Mass was viewed as the reenactment of the sacrifice of Christ, the communion table was the altar, and the bishops or pastors were priests who exclusively had the privilege to preside at the altar as consecrated celebrants.

The sacerdotal interpretation of the priest's role led to an increasing bifurcation between the priesthood and people. It was generally assumed that there were two kinds of people, clergy and laity. Ordination was interpreted as a kind of second baptism that lifted the clergy into a superior stage of Christian achievement. Clerical garb symbolized their elevated status.

THE REFORMATION CONCEPTION OF MINISTRY

This clerical order was in place at the time of Luther's rediscovery of the evangelical gospel. So explosive was the doctrine of justification by faith that it held the promise of new wine bursting old wineskins and creating new ones. Luther's rediscovered gospel put all people on an equal footing: an individual is made right with God through a personal response to the saving grace of Christ. This marked a radical shift from the institutional church's being the dispenser of grace to the proclamation of the gospel as the means of salvation.

In principle, the doctrine of justification by faith was to have a marked effect on the view and practice of ministry. Ministry under Roman Catholicism was conceived in hierarchical terms because receiving grace and being within the realm of the church institution were one and the same. There was no grace apart from the church. This made those in leadership the dispensers of grace and the guardians of church order. The Reformation, by contrast, linked the reception of grace with the gospel message and the response of the individual to Christ. Being made right with God is not mediated through the church institution, but directly through Jesus Christ. Neither pastors, bishops, archbishops, cardinals, nor the pope can represent an individual before God; Jesus Christ alone has that function. A hierarchical conception of ministry is, therefore, undermined by the gospel.

The sacerdotal function of the priest also was eliminated in the Reformed understanding of the gospel. To the Reformers, the idea of the continuous sacrifice of Christ in the Mass was an abomination. Christ died for sinners once and for all and does not continue to be sacrificed. Therefore the priestly role of pastor is eliminated. Thomas Gillespie concludes, "For if the Lord's Supper is not a sacerdotal ('sacrificing') act, then those who administer it serve no sacerdotal function and they have no sacerdotal character or status. The ground was thus cut from beneath the ministry as a separate priestly office."[3]

The elimination of the clergy-laity bifurcation had the greatest potential to change a view of ministry. The rediscovery of the priesthood of all believers "signalled the end of the distinction within the Church between clergy and laity."[4] According to the universal doctrine of the priesthood of all believers, as articulated by Luther, every Christian should be a minister of the Word of God. Luther's conviction that every believer in the gospel is by nature a priest, a mediator, and intercessor between God and man had revolutionary potential for the conception of ministry.

Luther was deeply disturbed by the qualitative gulf that had arisen between those who pursued a monastic life as a "higher calling" and the ordinary Christian viewed as tainted by worldly-mindedness. Luther attacked this hierarchy of callings. Instead of there being a superior calling sanctioned by God, Luther said that because of the gospel, the call of God comes to us in our ordinary stations of life.

> God has placed his Church in the midst of the world among countless undertakings and *callings* in order that Christians should *not* be monks but live with one another in social fellowship and manifest among men the works and practices of faith.[5]

As a sign of the change from a sacerdotal and priestly conception of ministry, clerical vestments were replaced by the academic gown for preachers of the Word. The Reformation scholar Wilhelm Pauck has written, "Henceforth, the scholar's gown was the garment of the Protestant minister. It symbolizes all the changes that were wrought by the Reformation in the nature and work of the ministry."[6]

A Promise Unfulfilled

Although the rediscovery of the gospel promised a reversal of the Roman Catholic conception of ministry and in principle laid the ground for it, this has seldom been realized. In spite of the Reformation, clericalism has more often than not held sway. Pauck explains, "Clericalism tends to identify the church with the priestly-sacramental clergy to such an extent that it is no longer, in fact or conception, the people of God."[7] David Watson observes,

> Most Protestant denominations have been as priest-ridden as the Roman Catholics. It is the minister, vicar, or pastor who has dominated the whole proceedings. In other words, the clergy-laity divisions have continued in much the same way as in pre-Reformation times, and the doctrine of spiritual gifts and body ministry have been largely ignored.[8]

The question that screams for an answer is, Why didn't the new wine of the gospel produce the new wineskins of body ministry? What kept the Reformers from returning the ministry to the people of God?

The Reformed Church: Institutionally Bound

With the reclamation of the gospel came also a rediscovery of preaching. After all, the gospel released its power when it was proclaimed. "So faith comes from what is heard, and what is heard comes by the preaching of Christ" (Rom. 10:17). The seventh article of the Augsburg Confession captures this emphasis when it defines the church as "the congregation of the saints in which the gospel is rightly preached and the sacraments rightly administered." Calvin wrote, "Where the Word is heard with reverence and the sacraments are not neglected there we discover . . . an appearance of the true church."[9]

To the Reformers, the true church was distinguished by two qualities: (1) the Word of God rightly proclaimed, and (2) the sacraments rightly administered. The proclamation of the gospel was inspired by the watchwords of the Reformation, *sola Scriptura* (by Scripture alone), *sola gratia* (by grace alone), *sola fide* (by faith alone), and the priesthood of all believers. That is, the Reformers focused on the power of God to save based solely on the completed work of Christ as proclaimed in the gospel, not on the church as the repository of God's grace.

By "rightly administered," the Reformers meant at least two things. First, the number of sacraments was reduced from seven to two. Therefore a redefinition of what constituted a "means of grace" was of central concern. This was especially true since the church did not dispense grace. Second, the Mass was removed from the list of sacraments. The sacraments do not save; they are a means whereby we are nourished with the presence of Christ. It is Christ who saves through faith in him.

This discussion leads us to the question, Is the Reformers' view an organismic or an institutional definition of the church? Perhaps the way to answer that question is to ask another: Who carries out the functions according to the Reformed definition of the church? For the Reformed churches, it is the minister or pastor who has been given the responsibility to preserve the church's doctrine and the proper ordering of its sacramental life. Thus ministry in most circles is equated with ordination to "the ministry of Word and sacraments." So the church is defined by a select group of its leaders who have the role of carrying out the essence of the church.

Noticeably absent from this definition is an emphasis on God's people. What role are they to play? If the ordained ministry fulfills the functions of the true church, what is left for the unordained? Where does the Reformation doctrine of the priest-hood of all believers fit? *The Reformation was never fully able to realize the fullness of the priesthood of all believers because it attempted to wed this organismic doctrine to an institutional definition of the church.* So concerned were the Reformers to define the church in contrast to its apostate parent body that myopia set in.

Because the essential nature of the church in actuality was empowered by its top-down leadership, a priesthood within a priesthood was the outcome. Even Luther seemed to affirm the priesthood of all believers at one moment and then take it away the next. He wrote, "We are all priests insofar as we are Christians, *but* those whom we call priests are ministers selected from our midst to act in our name, and their priesthood is our ministry."[10] As long as leadership is conceived in mediatorial and representative terms—one group doing for another—then the doctrine of the priesthood of all believers is undermined. It was affirmed in theory and denied in practice. Actions always speak louder than words.

INSTITUTIONAL STRUCTURE

The Reformed definition of the church was quickly translated into its institutional elements. The understanding of the essential marks of the church had a direct bearing on a conception of ministry. Along with their zeal for the gospel of freedom, Reformation leaders tended to focus their attention on the appropriate leadership structure. This emphasis, combined with the sociological dynamics that intertwined church and state, created passivity among God's people.

The principles of Reformed church order can be traced to Ulrich Zwingli's introduction of the Reformation at Zurich, Switzerland. A fundamental principle of church government is that its purpose is to secure a sustaining, faithful obedience to Christ as the head of the church. In other words, structure should never have the effect of replacing Christ or in hierarchical fashion become the voice of Christ.

Church government, it must be remembered, was conceived in this Swiss context as a union of church and state, not the separation of the two we are accustomed to in North America. Ecclesiastical and governmental authority were completely intertwined. From the time of Constantine's rule over the Roman Empire at the turn of the fourth century to the ratification of the U.S. Constitution, it was an unchallenged assumption that the church needed the coercive power of the state to disseminate its teaching for there to be a stable social order. Therefore, Zwingli instituted in Zurich a new church order supported by the coercive power of public government. Every citizen and subject in Zurich was required by law to conform to this new, evangelical religion preached by Zwingli.

Wilhelm Pauck explains, "The evangelical churches were thus formed as territorial or state churches. Each of them became a closed unit, subject to the political authority of its own government, the prince, or the city council."[11] To be a part of the city or state was to submit to the established religion. The Protestant faith was often introduced to a city or new territory by a prince or dignitary. The emperor of a nation ruled by divine fiat in an "unholy alliance" with the religious power structure, known as "the vicar of God." Church and state were hopelessly intermarried. The catch phrase was "He who reigns, his religion."

Thus when church order was refined by Martin Bucer in Strasbourg and further refined by John Calvin in Geneva as consisting of four divinely appointed offices, ecclesiastical authority was interwoven with the city government. Calvin adopted in Geneva what he saw practiced in Strasbourg. He believed the Scriptures taught that there should be preachers, teachers, elders, and deacons. The function of pastors was to carry out the marks of the true church by preaching, teaching, and administering the sacraments. They shared the responsibility of enforcing church discipline with the city council, made up of twelve elders, who also had the authority to appoint and discipline its ministers.

Structuring church government into four ecclesiastical offices was intended to be the practice not only in Geneva, but in all Reformed communities. After Calvin returned from Strasbourg, the Geneva city council adopted his *Ecclesiastical Ordinance.*

> There are four orders of offices that our Lord instituted for the government of his church: first the pastors, then the teachers, after them the elders, and fourthly the deacons. Therefore if one would have the church well ordered and maintained in its entirety, we must observe that form of rule.[12]

By conceiving these offices as sacred law instituted by Christ, Calvin made this order of the church rigid and transferable.

This is all to say that even though the liberating doctrine of the priesthood of all believers was rediscovered and its radical implications at times clearly seen, yet the institutional definition of the church and subsequent obsession with proper church order blurred the vision and its expression. The whole focus of ministry was top down.

A NEW STARTING POINT

For ministry to be returned to the people of God, we must have a bottom-up view of the church. James Dunn calls for a reversal of our methodology and a new starting point.

> The attempt to graft a concept of ministry of the people of God onto the root of ordained ministry has not really worked. Now it is time to reaffirm the root of all ministry as the charismatic Spirit given variously to the members of the body, to recognize our starting point as the New Covenant of the Pentecostal Spirit, and not the old covenant of priesthood.[13]

An organism view of ministry begins with the people of God as the place where ministry resides, and it conceives of leadership from within the one body. In contrast, an institutional view of ministry defines the territory occupied by its ordained leadership and then attempts to tack on a role for lay ministry. The Reformation operated from an institutional mindset that tried to fuse an institutional conception of ministry with an organismic doctrine of the priesthood of all believers. It did not work.

Dunn asserts, "Now it is time to reaffirm the root of all

ministry is the charismatic spirit given variously to the members of the body." Why is *now* the right time? In addition to the signs of a fundamental shift in the view of the church that we identified in the introduction, the church in North America today is separate from the state and vice versa. The state allows the church freedom to function; that is freedom of religion. The church's authority is not derived from the state. The church is free from the coercive power of the state. This separation frees us to conceive of the church as a body under the authority of Christ. A case could be made that the relationship between church and society today is most like the position in the first century. The church's authority is derived from its servant Lord, who indwells his people. Thus the church is essentially organism, secondarily institution.

Before we examine the radical implications of viewing the church through the lens of organism, we must deepen our understanding of the institutional entrapment of the church. If a revolution is to be unleashed that sets God's people free, we must first see how thorough our bondage is to institutionalism. Liberation does not come easily. For the church to be unleashed, we must engage in spiritual warfare. In the next chapter we will assess the strength of the enemy.

NOTES

1. Hendrik Hart, *Will All the King's Men* . . . (Toronto: Wedge Publishing Foundation, 1972), 30.

2. Thomas Gillespie, "Our Ministerial Roots: The Historical Origins of the Presbyterian Doctrine of the Ministry" (Unpublished paper, Princeton Theological Seminary), 1.

3. Ibid., 5.

4. Ibid., 6.

5. Martin Luther, "On the Ordering of Divine Service in the Congregation," vol. 4, Weimar ed., *Luther's Works*, 62.

6. Quoted by Thomas Gillespie, "Our Ministerial Roots," 6.

7. Wilhelm Pauck, "The Ministry in the Time of the Continental Reformation," in *The Ministry in Historical Perspectives*, ed. Richard H. Niebuhr (New York: Harper & Row, 1963), 114.

8. David Watson, *I Believe in the Church* (Grand Rapids: Eerdmans, 1978), 253.

9. John Calvin, *Institutes of the Christian Religion* (Philadelphia: Westminster, 1936), 4.1.10.

10. *Luther's Works*, Weimar ed., 6:564.

11. Pauck, "The Ministry in the Time of the Continental Reformation," 121.

12. Gillespie, "Our Ministerial Roots," 10.

13. James Dunn, "Ministry and the Ministry: The Charismatic Renewal's Challenge to Traditional Ecclesiology" (Unpublished paper), 10.

CHAPTER 3

One People/One Ministry

BY COMPARING THE IMAGES of organism and institution, I have been suggesting the need for a new starting point in our concept of the church. The Reformation started something with radical implications, but failed to deliver fully on its promise. The doctrine of the priesthood of all believers held out the hope of returning the ministry to the people of God, but the Reformation could not bring this about, because an organism doctrine was wedded to an institutional theology of the church. Only a theology of the church perceived through the lens of organism can create the climate for a full-orbed priesthood of all believers.

For the people of God to enter fully into their ministry we must come to see that there is only one people and one ministry, not two peoples—clergy and laity—a view that inevitably leads to two ministries. In other words, what kind of lens we use to view the church will affect the kind of church we produce.

Figure 3.1 summarizes the argument to this point.

Figure 3.1

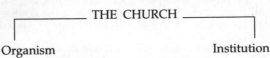

THE CHURCH

Organism	Institution
1. Starting point: The body of Christ. The church is the whole people of God in whom Christ dwells.	1. Starting point: Leadership offices in the church. The true church is found where (a) the Word of God is rightly proclaimed; (b) the sacraments are rightly administered.

2. Bottom-up: The church's ministry is shaped by the gifts and callings distributed by the Holy Spirit to the whole body of Christ.

2. Top-down: The ministry is the province of the ordained offices of the church.

3. All ministry is lay ministry.

3. Lay ministry supplements and is secondary to ordained ministry.

4. Conclusion: One people/one ministry.

4. Conclusion: Two people (clergy/laity)/two ministries.

I have come to the conclusion that the church has unwittingly adopted an institutional self-understanding that has led to a two people/two ministries structure. The clergy/laity split is alive and well. Our language reveals our thoroughgoing institutionalism and conventional mindset. We have taken biblical words that apply to the whole people of God and through the lens of *institution* have restricted them to apply only to a select group of people, primarily the ordained clergy.

This appropriation of language to institutional usage can be demonstrated in five commonly used terms. Each has been given a considerably narrower meaning than its biblical use. When we put these words back into their original setting, we can see how they identify the whole people of God. We must recapture each term as an organism reality if we are to return the ministry to the people of God.

SAINTS

We use the term *saint* in many ways, but common to each ascription is the idea of a person as being spiritually elite. "Saint" is most commonly used as a formal designation, a title. In the Protestant tradition, saints are the apostles or authors of Scripture, labeled "St. Mark," "St. Paul," and so on. The Roman Catholic Church expanded this list by canonizing selected exemplary Christians who meet certain criteria such as performing verifiable miracles.

In a less formal sense we consider people "saints" who have demonstrated their commitment by giving their lives to God in a religious order or "full-time Christian service." The implication is that these people are willing to forego worldly pleasure and enter into heroic work with little earthly reward. Mother Teresa is placed in the category of a saint because of her devotion to the poor and dying in the streets of Calcutta. Referring to someone who seems to be on a first-name basis with God or for whom self-giving is a way of life, we hear people say reverently, "Oh, she is a saint."

The most evident clue that we use "saint" in a restrictive sense is the personal embarrassment we experience when this term is applied to ourselves. "Me, a saint? Be serious!" Sainthood commonly means to have achieved a certain level of holiness or a standard of piety. In fact, we may not even desire to be called a saint, for it implies an other-worldliness that can be rather dull and unexciting.

The Biblical Usage of "Saints"

When we examine the biblical use of the term *saints*, we find the word always applied to the whole body of Christ, not to some select group that have achieved spiritual stardom. Saints (Greek, *hagios*) are the ordinary, garden-variety Christians in a particular time and place whose only distinction is that they are chosen by God, claimed by Jesus Christ, and convened by the Holy Spirit as the church.

It is instructive to note the apostle Paul's salutations to the churches with whom he corresponds. Paul always addressed the church as the whole, never in terms of a select leadership. The church is all the people of God, not a representative group such as pastors, elders, or deacons. In six of the nine letters addressed to churches, Paul's salutation is to the "saints" (Rom. 1:7; 1 Cor. 1:2; 2 Cor. 1:1; Eph. 1:1; Phil. 1:1; Col. 1:2). The term is used fifty-six times in the New Testament and never in the singular. It does not refer to an individual, but always to the entire body of believers.

The clearest indication of Paul's usage occurs in his greeting to the Corinthians:

> To the church of God which is at Corinth, to those sanctified in Christ Jesus, called to be *saints* together with all those who in every place call on the name of our Lord Jesus Christ, both their Lord and ours (1 Cor. 1:2).

Even though "saints," according to common usage, implies personal holiness, Paul's focus is not on our personal purity, but on God's holiness. To be saints means to be set apart and called out. To be a saint is to come within the realm of God's holiness. We are holy, not because of our purity, but because we have been made holy or declared right before God based on the work of Christ.

The phrase that precedes "called to be saints" is the key to the meaning of the word. We are saints because of what has been done for us—"sanctified by Jesus Christ." "Sanctified" means we are made holy by Christ and not through our own effort. The designation is all the more startling when we remember who are the recipients of this letter. The Corinthians would be the last congregation in the New Testament whom we would endow with sainthood if "saints" refers to keeping one's ways pure. The Corinthian church (1) was marked by party spirit (1 Cor. 1:12); (2) was described as carnal because the people were spiritually still drinking milk when they should have been eating meat (1 Cor. 3:2–3); (3) allowed the pagan immorality of a man consorting with his stepmother (1 Cor. 5:1); and (4) profaned the Lord's Supper because of the divisions between rich and poor (1 Cor. 11:27). But Paul can still describe the Corinthians as saints because Paul understood that God viewed them from the standpoint of the completed work of Christ on their behalf.

Paul demonstrates the all-encompassing scope of sainthood by calling the Corinthians "saints together with *all* those who *everywhere* call on the name of our Lord Jesus Christ (1 Cor. 1:2). You cannot get more inclusive than that. How far we have strayed from the biblical usage by narrowing saints to a restrictive group who supposedly excel in godliness!

We need to return to the Reformed doctrine of the communion of the saints, which views all God's people—past, present, and future—as a part of an eternal fellowship linked by our common life in Jesus Christ. The hymn "For All the Saints" by William H. How leads us in the right direction.

> For all the saints who from their labors rest,
> Who Thee by faith before the world confessed,
> Thy name, O Jesus, be forever blessed:
> Alleluia! Alleluia!
>
> O blest communion, fellowship divine!
> We feebly struggle, they in glory shine;
> Yet all are one in Thee, for all are Thine:
> Alleluia! Alleluia!

MINISTER

Who is a "minister"? A person who goes into *the* ministry. We all know for whom the ministry is reserved; it is reserved for people who have heard a call from God to enter into the ranks of the ordained. Our common usage tends very much toward a hierarchical, class distinction between those who have stepped behind the veil into the aura of holiness and those second-class citizens who have not attained to a "holy order." "Going into the ministry" is associated with a certain honor, and "leaving the ministry" is a badge of shame. We give titles such as "reverend" that set apart "ministers" into a spiritual realm unattainable by those who have chosen a "secular" way of life. Michael Green, an Anglican pastor, observes this tendency toward class distinction:

> One cannot but help feeling that the whole gamut of ecclesiastical courtesy titles, "The Venerable," "The Very Reverend," "The Most Reverend" and so on, are a hindrance rather than a help in the work of the ministry. They tend to build an invisible wall between their bearer and the world at large; much more important, they tend to make him just a little proud, just a little pleased with himself, just a little further removed than he was before from the role of servant.[1]

The Reformed tradition has expanded the definition of ministry beyond pastors to include elders and deacons. To be sure, each office has an assigned biblical role, but the whole ministry is defined only in terms of these functions.

Yet, if the ministry is associated with and summed up by the offices of the church, we must ask what is left for the whole people of God. If the ministry is for the initiated and ordained, by definition ministry is not for the rank and file. The laity are often viewed as those who supplement the ministry of the pastor because, after all, the pastor cannot do it all. Under this theology the people of God are at best adjuncts to the true ministers and have no real identity of their own. This restrictive view of ministry seen through the lens of institution leads directly to two people of God (clergy and laity) and two ministries (*the* ministry for first-class Christians; and what's left for second-class Christians).

The Biblical Usage of "Minister"

Nowhere does the term "ministry" or "minister" refer to a particular class of people set apart from the rest of the church. The noun *diakonia* is variously translated "service," "ministry," or "mission." The personal form of the noun, *diakonos* is translated "servants," "ministers," or "deacons," depending on its context.

It appears that these terms are used in the Bible in the following three ways:

1. "Service" or "ministry" captures the spirit in which our ministry is to be rendered on behalf of the whole body. Jesus embodied the model of servant when he said, "For the Son of man came not to be served but to serve, and to give his life as a ransom for many" (Mark 10:45). In Paul's description of the ministry, abilities have been distributed by the Holy Spirit to the entire body. One synonym for "spiritual gift" is "service" or "ministry." "And there are varieties of service [ministry], but the same Lord" (1 Cor. 12:5). "Service" captures the manner in which ministry is to be exercised. Ministry is to be performed for the common good (1 Cor. 12:7), not to promote the ego of the doer. Ministry inherently means giving one's life away on behalf of others.

2. Ministry is also the particular task or call we have been set apart to perform. Since the term "ministry" translated "service" is here a synonym for *charismata* (grace gifts), Paul wants us to understand that our gifts are also the means or channel through which we exercise our ministry. Paul evidently has the entire body in mind, not a select few, when he writes, "To each is given the manifestation of the Spirit for the common good" (1 Cor. 12:7).

Because the institutional mindset is pervasive, it is not surprising to find it infiltrating the translation of Scripture. From the Revised Standard Version's rendering of Acts 6:4, one might think that the apostles are the only ones set apart as a class by themselves to perform ministry. The apostles were drawn into a dispute between the Greek-speaking and Hebrew-speaking widows. The apostles were being deflected from their call, which was to "devote themselves to prayer and the *ministry* of the word" (Acts 6:4). Yet the exact same word translated "ministry" in Acts 6:4 is translated "distribution" in Acts 6:1. Distributing food to the widows was also a "ministry." The term "ministry" is used in two different senses in the space of a few verses. The apostles were called to a particular function of prayer and proclamation, whereas seven were appointed to give oversight to a ministry among the widows. Both are ministries without a qualitative distinction.

3. Ministry is the province of the entire body of believers. An unfortunate error in punctuation has sometimes been used as the basis for claiming that the Bible teaches a distinct class set apart for

ministry. The 1946 edition of the Revised Standard Version of Ephesians 4:11–12, inserts a comma after the word "saints," leading one to conclude that those with particular gifts are to do all the ministry. The passage read, "And his gifts were that some should be apostles, some prophets, some evangelists, and some pastors and teachers to equip the saints, for the works of ministry, for the building up of the body of Christ." With the comma included it would appear that these gifted individuals have three tasks: equip the saints, do the work of ministry, and build up the body of Christ.[2]

Almost all scholars agree that the comma after "saints" should be removed. This deletion changes the entire flavor of the statement. The passage now reads, "to equip the saints for the work of ministry, for the building up of the body of Christ" (RSV, 1971 edition). Ray Stedman illustrates the true impact of these verses in Figure 3.2.[3]

Figure 3.2

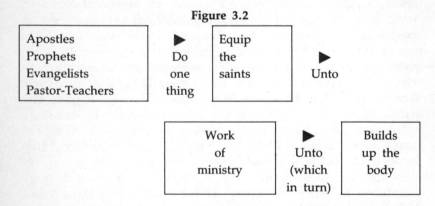

The saints (Paul's designation of all God's people) are to do the work of ministry under the tutelage of these particularly gifted people. Far from ministry being associated with a few, ministry is coterminous with the entire body. There is only one ministry—the ministry of the people of God.

PRIEST

With what do we associate the term "priest"? "Priest" is connected to the Roman Catholic designation for clergy who are qualified to represent people before God. The priest enters the realm of a holy order to be set apart through taking vows. The immediate association most of us make on hearing the word "priest" is a person, addressed as "Father," who is qualified to hear our confession and offer absolution.

Even in the Protestant tradition the minister has a priestly aura. Ministers are persons who, because of their office and ordination, carry with them the sacramental presence of Christ. Jesus is somehow more available or nearer to a minister than to ordinary Christians. Since it is assumed that the pastor's prayers have a more direct access to the ear of God, I as a pastor am often asked to pray for a particular need. All pastors have experienced a sense of being treated differently because of their priestly position. A Dutch colloquialism captures the holy aura of a pastor: When there is an awkward and uncomfortable lull in a social conversation, someone may interject the expression, "A minister walked by." The implication is that we cannot have our usual dialogue in the presence of a minister because of their priestly "purity." The same reality can be turned into a sense of privilege. Many times I have heard people pronounce themselves blessed because a pastor was sitting at their table for a meal.

I believe the function that reinforces more than any other the priestly role of a pastor is the administration of the sacrament of the Lord's Supper. As the Old Testament priest offered up sacrifices on behalf of God's people, so the contemporary priest stands behind the Communion table, breaking the bread and holding up the cup as the people's representative before God. James Dunn adapts Milton for our purposes: "Today's minister is but the old priesthood writ large!"[4]

The Biblical Usage of "Priest"

There is a startling contrast between the Old Testament and New Testament views of the priesthood. Under the old covenant there was a group clearly demarcated as priests and Levites, who were descendants of Aaron. They were so distinctively set apart that when the Israelites entered the Promised Land, the priests and Levites received no inheritance of land as the other eleven tribes did. They were to dedicate themselves to the service of the religious cult and be supported from the people's sacrifices, tithes, and offerings.

The priest's role under the old covenant was generally twofold: (1) He represented God to the people; he was a mediator of sorts who communicated the word of God to the people, for the people were considered holy only when they heard the Word and responded; and (2) he represented the people before God. Since the people could not come directly before a holy God because of their sin, the guilt of sin had to be dealt with through offering sacrifices. The role of the priest as the mediator for God's people is most clearly demonstrated in the high priest's entering the Holy of Holies annually on the Day of Atonement to offer an atoning substitute of a bull or lamb.

But there is a radical reorientation in the New Testament. The office of priest is eliminated as it pertains to a select group of people. This is based on the physical sacrifice of Christ, the ultimate high priest. Jesus fulfilled and completed the role of priest in his substitutionary death. "He [Jesus] has no need, like those high priests, to offer sacrifices daily, first for his own sins and then for those of the people; he did this once for all when he offered up himself" (Heb. 7:27).

Here we encounter a profoundly moving convergence of images. Not only is Jesus the high priest who *offers* the sacrifice, but he himself *becomes* the blameless, spotless sacrifice for our sin. Since Jesus' work is complete and he makes intercession for us continually before the Father, any human who claims for himself that priestly role would be denigrating the work of Christ. David Watson writes,

> [Jesus] is now the eternal high priest in the heavens. All earthly and human priesthood has now once for all been fulfilled and finished by that unique, final and unrepeatable sacrifice of our great high priest who "is a priest forever" (Heb. 7:24).
>
> The New Testament is absolutely consistent with itself. Since the priestly role is fulfilled in Jesus, the term priest is never used for someone who holds a distinct office in the church. Not once does it describe a class or caste of people separate from the laity of God.[5]

In fact, the New Testament idea of "priest" has so radically departed from the Old Testament that the entire body of believers is now described as by nature a priesthood (1 Peter 2:5). By ascribing to the church the images formerly applied to the nation of Israel, the apostle Peter makes it clear that the new priesthood is the church. "You are a chosen race, a royal priesthood, a holy nation, God's own people" (1 Peter 2:9).

The Reformers clearly understood the revolutionary implications of the transfer from the select Old Testament priestly office to the New Testament priesthood open to all believers. The first implication is that we all have direct access to God through Jesus Christ, the great high priest. Calvin wrote,

> "Now, Christ plays the priestly role, not only to render the Father favorable and propitious to us by an eternal law of reconciliation, but also to receive us as His companion in this great office (Rev. 1:6). For we are defiled in ourselves, yet are priests in Him, offer ourselves and our all to God, and freely enter the heavenly sanctuary that sacrifices of prayers and praise that we bring may be acceptable and sweet-smelling before God.[6]

This first aspect of the priesthood of all believers we have affirmed and incorporated into our Reformation practice.

The second aspect of the believers' priesthood is one which the Reformers clearly envisioned, but which we have yet to appropriate fully. Yet God is unleashing upon us in our day a power which I believe will usher in the New Reformation. We are priests to each other. We are God's representatives to each other. No one had keener insight into the logical conclusions of this doctrine than Luther himself. He foresaw the explosive possibilities of the doctrine of the priesthood of all believers. The return of the ministry to all of God's people was in sight. Commenting on 1 Peter 2:9, Luther wrote,

> Therefore we are all priests, as many as are Christians. . . . The priesthood is nothing but a ministry as we learn from 1 Corinthians 4, "Let a man so account of us as of the ministers of Christ, and the dispensers of the mysteries of God."[7]

Even though this truth never came to fruition in the Reformation, as we have seen it was captured in the theological vision of the Reformers.

CLERGY

"Clergy" is another term, along with "minister" and "priest," that formally designates a leadership caste. The word "clergy" is almost impossible to use without contrasting it to its counterpart. It has come to mean those who stand over against "laity." "Clergy" conjures up reverse collars and the institution of righteousness.

When someone introduces me as a member of the clergy, I immediately sense that I am like a third sex—there are men, women, and clergy. I have suddenly become a holy man who does not experience the struggles and temptations of the rest of the human race. As a pastor I take care of things spiritual, so the rest of the church can enjoy the temporal.

I fear that many participants in the church view their pastors as specialists in the things of God, so they need not be bothered with that realm. As a result, clergy are held in both respect and contempt. The laypeople's respect is derived from the clerical devotion of one's whole life to God—something the laity considers beyond their grasp. At the same time, however, there is contempt based on the clergy's cloistered lives, which separate them from the rough-and-tumble matters of the real world. The underlying assumption is that religion does not fully work where it matters.

Even though the Bible knows no distinction between clergy and laity, the separation of the classes developed relatively early in the history of the church. The first hint of a professional ministry that became synonymous with the ministry of the church occurred in the writings of Ignatius of Antioch (between A.D. 98 and 117). In some personal correspondence, Ignatius defined the church as "one eucharist, one body of the Lord, one cup, one altar, and *therefore one* bishop together with the presbyterium and the deacons, my fellow servants."[8]

The distinction between clergy and laity did not become full-blown until the fourth century, when the church adopted a secular model. In the Greco-Roman world, the Greek word *klēros* referred to municipal administrators and *laos* to those who were ruled. As the gulf between these two grew, the *klēros* in the church became associated with the sacred, the *laos* with the secular. Since the lives of the *laos* were consumed with temporal affairs, they were perceived to be on the low rung of the saintly ladder.

By the twelfth century, the partition between clergy and laity was fixed to the point where Hugo Grotius could speak of two kinds of Christians: the *klēros,* who have devoted themselves to the divine office, marked by contemplation and prayer with freedom from earthly things; and the rest, called "laity," who have compromised the authentic Christian life by marrying, possessing worldly goods, and making other concessions to human frailties.

The Biblical Usage of "Clergy"

How far all this has strayed from the New Testament meaning of *klēros!* The word *klēros* means "lot" or "inheritance." It can mean a share or a portion or that which is allotted. It is used in Acts 1:17 to refer to Judas: he "was allotted his share [*klēros*] in this ministry." The replacement for Judas was chosen by casting lots, and the lot (*klēros*) fell to Matthias (Acts 1:26).

Klēros more richly refers to the inheritance all the saints receive in Christ. Paul concluded his prayer for the Colossians with gratefulness, "giving thanks to the Father, who has qualified us to share in the inheritance [*klēros*] of the saints in light" (Col. 1:12). Recounting God's call to him to carry the message of the gospel to the Gentiles, Paul stated Christ's promise to them "that they may receive forgiveness of sins and a place [*klēros*] among those who are sanctified by faith in me" (Acts 26:18). Far from *klēros* ever carrying the distinction between an upper and lower class in the kingdom, the word conveys the full inclusion of the Gentiles as equal partners in the benefits of the gospel. But prevalently in the church we have taken an inclusive concept and transformed it through the lens of institution into something that conveys exclusion.

LAITY

To this point we have examined the terms "saints," "minister," "priest," and "clergy," which have all become associated with a particular, set-apart class, often designated as the ordained. On the other side of the ledger is "laity," used for the vast majority of the church. In common speech the words "layperson" and "laity" have largely negative connotation. The Oxford English Dictionary defines laity as "the body of people not in orders, as opposed to clergy." Kathleen Bliss captures this sense of nonentity of laity well: "For these [the laity] have a strong element of 'over-againstness' toward the clergy—the clergy are, the laity are *not*, the clergy do, the laity do *not*. Nobody wants to be an is *not*."[9] John Stott illustrates further how the word "lay" has been debased: " 'Lay' is often a synonym for 'amateur' as opposed to 'professional,' or 'unqualified' as opposed to 'expert.' "[10]

The Biblical Usage of "Laity"

The same term "laity" that in contemporary usage has a pejorative ring, is a word scripturally filled with dignity and honor. *Laos* exudes a sense of specialness. God designates Israel as his special people, selected from among all the peoples of the earth to be his possession. Speaking to the gathered nation, Moses conveyed God's covenant heart: "For you are a people holy to the LORD God. The LORD your God has chosen you to be a people for his own possession out of all the peoples that are on the face of the earth" (Deut. 7:6). God said, "I will be your God and you shall be my people" (Lev. 26:12).

As we have already noted, this special covenantal relationship is transferred to the church, which was purchased at the price of Jesus' blood. Peter said, "You are a people of God's own possession" (1 Peter 2:9). Out of all the peoples (*ethnos*) of the earth, there is a special people (*laos*) who are God's called-out people. The *laos* of God are nothing less than a new humanity, the vanguard of the future, the prototype of the kingdom of God not yet completed; a people of the future living in the present. Next time we hear someone say, "I'm just a layperson," we can say, "That's more than enough."

THE INSTITUTIONAL MINDSET

From this survey of the common biblical designations for leaders of the church, we can see that a thoroughly institutional mindset has been all too dominant in Christian history. The damage to the church of defining God's people from a top-down perspective has been catastrophic. Robert Munger writes,

> In our time it may well be that the greatest single bottleneck to the renewal and outreach of the church is the division of roles between clergy and laity that results in a hesitancy of the clergy to trust the laity with significant responsibility, and in turn a reluctance on the part of the laity to trust themselves as authentic ministers of Christ, either in the church or outside the church.[11]

The institutional model of the church leads us to a two peoples/ two ministries bifurcation. Richard Lovelace points to the very issue that the New Reformation addresses:

> It is still true that the model of congregational life in the minds of most clergy and laity is one in which the minister is the dominant pastoral superstar who specializes in the spiritual concerns of the Christian community, while the laity are spectators, critics, and recipients of pastoral care, free to go about their own business because the pastor is taking care of the business of the kingdom.[12]

This institutional legacy has quenched the release of the Spirit. But a new vision is arising in the church today of a living organism in whom Christ dwells. Therefore the whole people (*laos*) of God are called to the ministry, which means exercising their function as priests to each other and the broken world. When we come to realize that there is only one people and therefore one ministry, God's people will be released to fulfill their callings.

In the next chapter we will get specific about the radical changes the church will need to undergo if it is to experience an organism reality.

NOTES

1. Michael Green, *Called to Serve* (London: Hodder and Stoughton, 1976), 16.
2. John R. W. Stott, *The Message of Ephesians* (Downers Grove, Ill.: InterVarsity Press, 1979), 166.
3. Ray Stedman, *Body Life* (Glendale, Calif.: Regal, 1972), 81.
4. James D. G. Dunn, "Ministry and the Ministry: The Charismatic Renewal's Challenge to Traditional Ecclesiology" (Unpublished paper), 9.
5. David Watson, *I Believe in the Church* (Grand Rapids: Eerdmans, 1978), 248.
6. John Calvin, *Institutes of the Christian Religion* (Philadelphia: Westminster, 1960), 2.15.6.
7. Martin Luther, "An Open Letter to the Christian Nobility," *The Works of Martin Luther* (Philadelphia: Muhlenberg, 1941), 279.
8. Quoted by David Watson, *I Believe in the Church*, 275.
9. Kathleen Bliss, *We the People, A Book About Laity* (London: SCM Press, 1963), 69.
10. John R. W. Stott, *One People* (Downers Grove, Ill.: InterVarsity Press, 1968), 29.
11. Robert Munger, "Training the Laity for Ministry," *Theology News and Notes* (June 1973): 3.
12. Richard Lovelace, *Dynamics of Spiritual Life* (Downers Grove, Ill.: InterVarsity Press, 1979), 224.

CHAPTER 4

Implications of One People/One Ministry

THERE IS A FRESH WIND blowing in the church today that is being felt wherever the doors are thrown open to include all of God's people in ministry. We live in a day of a paradigm shift. We are on the verge of recapturing the biblical vision of the church as organism in contrast to the church as institution.

We have discovered thus far the following characteristics of an organismic ministry:

- The organism church defines itself from the bottom up as the whole people of God.

- This biblical perspective causes us to shift our starting point for defining ministry from the institutional view of the ordained clergy to the organism perspective of the body.

- The ministry of the people of God cannot be tacked onto the root of ordained ministry; ordained ministry must find its place within the people of God.

- Therefore, there is one ministry, the people's ministry that is derived from one people.

The question then becomes what shape the sails must take if we are to catch the new wind. What are the contours of the canvas in order for the ship of the church to skip through the high seas? Or to put it negatively, what old, tattered sails need to be discarded because they will only tear under the force of the new wind? Movements of the Holy Spirit are replete with opportunities seized and missed. We are presented with the choice of catching the gale and skimming the seas, or resisting and watching the sails tattered and torn by the force. As the mainline churches become further entrenched in their institutionalism, the breath of God passes them by while new structures develop that are more able to adapt to an organism reality. We are presented with a choice of ultimate proportion—life or death—when God's Spirit moves among us.

Is this not the choice that was presented to the Grand Inquisitor in Fyodor Dostoyevsky's masterpiece *The Brothers Karamazov*? Dostoyevsky paints the hideous picture of the church that has turned the body of Christ into a cruel ecclesiastical machine. The writer returns Jesus to the Spanish town of Seville in the sixteenth century. The faithful recognize the Christ immediately. He performs the same signs of life-giving power that he did during his first visit to the earth.

At the foot of the cathedral steps there unfolds the tragic scene of a funeral procession as a seven-year-old girl is carried in an open coffin. Amid this emotional setting the mother pleads for Jesus to raise her daughter. In compassion Jesus once again says, "Talitha cum." The young girl is presented alive to her mother. Enter the Grand Inquisitor. He is a tall, severe man in his nineties; his presence alone dampens the joy of the occasion. This religious kingpin has Jesus arrested. As night falls, the Grand Inquisitor visits Jesus in his cell. "It is you, you!" he says. The Grand Inquisitor lectures Jesus about the bargain the church made with the people: the people agreed to surrender their freedom to the church, and in return the church was to give them happiness. Jesus had no right to come and restore freedom to these people.

All along, Jesus sits in silence and offers no verbal response. Then suddenly he rises, comes to the old man, and kisses him "gently on his bloodless, aged cheeks." The old man does not respond.

Then Dostoyevsky levels his terrible indictment against the entrenched church: "The kiss glowed in his heart, but the old man sticks to his idea." May it not be so with us.

I see four radical choices before us that have the potential to revolutionize our understanding of the church and ministry. We can stick to our traditions and quench the spirit, or we can do what is necessary to unleash the sleeping giant and see the ministry returned to the people of God.

ORGANISM MINISTRY, NOT ORDAINED MINISTRY

The Reformers and the contemporary commentators on the implications of the Reformation speak with one voice. They all agree that the doctrine of the priesthood of all believers obliterates the caste distinction between clergy and laity. There is no qualitative difference between the two. Yet historically the gulf between them remains. Our stated theology is not informing our practice and mindset, for reasons that we will explore in the next chapter.

If in fact Robert Munger is correct that the clergy-laity bifurcation is the "greatest single bottleneck to the renewal and outreach of the church," then we must begin to take drastic steps. John Stott is more direct: "I do not hesitate to say that to interpret the church in terms of a privileged caste or a hierarchical structure is to destroy the New Testament doctrine of the church."[1]

What is required for us to begin moving toward a one people/one ministry New Testament church? In a word, repentance.

Biblically "repentance" means to change our minds, to have a second thought that corrects our first thought. It means to come to our senses, see ourselves for what we are, and change our way of thinking, which will in turn change our way of acting. "We have met the enemy and they are us."

We need a fundamental change in our vocabulary. A way to implement repentance is to use a different language. It is no accident that repentance pertains to our way of thinking. Language is the expression of our mindset. We might ask, "How is a change of language going to solve any problems?" One answer: "Language is not merely a means of communication; it is also an expression of shared assumptions. Language transmits implicit values and behavioral models to all the people who use it."[2]

I propose to remove the terms *clergy* and *laity* from our vocabulary. I say this because the words have become so corrupted as to be all but irretrievable. As I have said, "clergy" has become synonymous with "ministry" (and in fact is defined that way in the Oxford English Dictionary). When we think of clergy we mean a professional, religious person whose role it is to protect religious values in an institutional cast. The American Heritage Dictionary defines clergy as "a person authorized to perform religious functions in a church." By implication, then, laity are unauthorized. To not be clergy is not to have the ministry stamp of approval.

"Clergy" and "laity" have to come to have such an unhealthy connection that it is impossible to use one term without its opposite coming to mind. For this reason a perfectly beautiful word, "laity" has become associated exclusively with the negative. It has a pejorative ring. It has come to mean either what you are not or what you cannot. It means you are not clergy—"a member of a congregation as distinguished from the clergy." It also means you cannot—for "a layman is an unqualified, nonprofessional" who lacks the necessary training in an area requiring expertise. The clergy are the experts; the laymen are the "are not." Even if we speak as we do today of "lay" ministry in our attempts to move beyond the exclusive domain of professional ministry, we are creating a "separate and not equal" order. "Lay" ministry is still an attempt to tap ministry onto the root of ordained ("real") ministry.

Alma Graham sums up this dilemma:

> If you have a group half of whose number are As and half Bs. . . . if you call the group A, there is no way that the Bs can be equal to the As within it. The As will always be the real and the Bs will always be the exception—the sub group, the sub species, the outsiders.[3]

> A = Clergy = ministry
> B = Laity = lay ministry

Clergy do ministry; laymen do lay ministry.

In the place of *clergy* and *laity* let me offer a substitute. We need to use functional and not positional language. Organism stresses function, not titles and offices. The hierarchical, top-down orientation of the old, tattered sail of institutionalism will be torn by the new breeze. When our starting point is one people as the body of Christ, then functional language describes roles that people perform within that one body without attaching value to them. When we use the term "pastor" rather than "minister" or "clergy," we have moved from positional language to a description of what one does. I am particularly taken by Elton Trueblood's prophetic suggestion that the best modern image for pastor is "player-coach." I like it because it suggests an equipping model of ministry and also describes the role of pastor as a member of a team. This image stresses that there is one team with the pastor as an integral part of it. There are not two teams of differing value.

When we speak in organism terms, members of the team have particular roles to play according to their giftedness within the body. In my own Presbyterian tradition we have functional language that keeps everyone on the same team. The ordained offices of the church are threefold: "ministers of the Word" (and sacraments), "elders," and "deacons." This is institutional language, but functional language is also available. We speak of pastors as "teaching elders" who share ministry with "ruling elders." We must jettison the corrupted language of clergy-laity and in its place put functional language that reflects our ministry.

A word I believe is retrievable is "minister" or "ministry." Even though we have tended to equate ministry with the ordained, or have spoken of going into "the ministry" as referring to those who go into a profession, the word does not seem nearly so tainted. Evidence of the New Reformation has shown up on church bulletins in the form of "ministers: all the members of [church's name]." We are attempting to recapture this term from its institutional tone.

I have told the members of the church I serve that my goal is to redefine "minister" so completely that when they hear that word they will think of themselves and not those whom they pay to do ministry. One day I was almost caught in my own trap. I was visiting a deputation site where our high school youth were serving. At dinner that evening I was asked by a youth with whom our team worked, "How many ministers do you have at your church?" Eavesdropping on our conversation was one of the adult leaders serving as a counselor for the week. I was about to stumble into the traditional answer when Dave saved me: "Yes, Greg, how many ministers *do* we have?" Catching his tone and myself, I said, "We have close to six hundred." I came perilously close to reinforcing the old-wineskin perspective and thereby undermining the new vision that Dave and others had already adopted.

As long as we use "ministry" to mean what the Lord does through his entire body and not some limited portion of it, then the recaptured term can be an embodiment of the New Reformation. Modifiers before the term "ministry" such as "lay" or "ordained" get us right back into the "separate and unequal" mentality.

GIFTED PEOPLE, NOT GIFTED PASTOR

Churches have a penchant for wanting to find the leader who can "do it all." As a clergy-dominated institution the church seeks its "salvation" in the multitalented pastor. John Stott labels this the desire for "omnicompetence." Howard Snyder drips with satire when he writes, "We seek a pastor who handles Sunday morning better than a quiz master on weekday T.V. He is better with words than most political candidates. As a scholar he surpasses many seminary professors. No church social function would be complete without him."[4]

The trouble with this mentality is that because we want pastors who can do it all, they *will* do it all. The desire for "perfect" pastors creates a passivity in the congregation. People live out their lives vicariously through "Mr. Wonderful" as if his faith and abilities were theirs. The church member's role is to pay their dues so that the doors can be kept open and a context created for pastors to do their work. Howard Snyder characterizes this approach in these words: "If the pastor is a superstar, the church is an audience, not a body."[5]

Without denigrating the absolute necessity of leadership and its catalytic nature, the biblical emphasis is not on the "omnicompetent" pastor, but a "multigifted" body. Jesus Christ was the only fully gifted human, and when he ascended to his Father, he chose to create an interdependent, multifaceted, corporate body as the only entity that could contain his gifts. No individual was ever meant to show the fullness of Christ to the world. We are meant to do that through redeemed communities. The Holy Spirit is mentioned fifty-six times in Paul's letters, each instance referring to his indwelling the community, not simply an individual. If we want to see Jesus manifest on earth, it will be corporately through a community of people who lay down their lives for each other and build up each other through the gifts variously distributed throughout the body.

So the emphasis in our churches must be on the gifted community. The New Reformation allows us to discover experientially what the Bible teaches and demonstrates. We are all channels through whom the Holy Spirit works to bring strengthening grace to others in the body so that we grow together into Christlikeness.

The church is fundamentally a charismatic community, for the *charismata* (grace-gifts) have been distributed and assigned to all in Christ (1 Cor. 12:11, 18). This makes each person an initiating center for ministry. All are directly connected to Jesus, the head of the body. The signals for ministry are sent directly from the head to the parts. Initiative for ministry can be taken by any responsible person, whether or not they hold an office.

The bottom-up church is a bubble-up ministry. The body is

not passively waiting for or resisting the pastor's next move. Nor is the congregation reduced to an audience who applauds the solo performance of a multigifted pastor. On the contrary, the pastor in the bottom-up church must hustle to keep up with and encourage the ministry that spontaneously erupts out of the organism.

A SACRAMENTAL PEOPLE, NOT A SACRAMENTAL PASTOR

There is a common assumption among God's people that as a result of their calling, pastors have conferred on them the sacramental presence of Christ. The ordained are donned with a holy aura not attainable by ordinary, common believers. This myth has created a priesthood within a priesthood. Unwittingly the pastor assumes a mediatorial role, representing God's people before the Lord in a way that they could never do so for themselves. In other words, we have created a fiction that people of the cloth carry with them the mantle of Christ because of the holy order that they enter.

Even children are indoctrinated with a sense of separateness of pastors. I was talking to a young mother in the hallway of the church just before a worship service was to begin. Since I was to assist in leading worship, I was appropriately dressed in my black robe. As I stood talking to this woman, her shy, three-year-old daughter was playing peek-a-boo with me, using her mother's skirt as a curtain. After she had poked her head out a few times in discomfort, she pointed to me while catching her mother's eye and said, "Is that God?" That's a tough role to give up!

Associating the saintly, priestly role exclusively with those in a clergy caste is a hindrance to the full ministry of the body. As long as this myth is nurtured, "real" ministry will be performed by the ordained and the "real" presence of Christ will be seen as coming through the duly authorized.

Jerry Cook, a pastor in British Columbia, tells the story of a woman in the congregation he served who was angry with him because she had been in the hospital seven days and he had not found time to visit her. Upon her return home he planned to call her but decided first to investigate the number of visits she had received from church people. He discovered that during the seven days there had been an average of four visitors per day. The phone conversation went like this:

Pastor Cook: "Well, Mrs. White, how are you feeling?"

Mrs. White replied curtly, "Well, I'm fine *now*."

"I understand you have been in the hospital," Pastor Cook ignored the sharp tone.

"Well, it's a little late."

Playing dumb, Pastor Cook responded, "A little late for what?"

"I was there for seven days and nobody came."

Pastor Cook informed her that he was aware that she had many visitors during that time. Then she revealed her true convictions: "Yes, people from the church came, but *you* did not come."[6]

All those other people could not measure up to the pastor, for the pastor was viewed as someone special who bears the presence of Christ. The authentic ministry of the people of God could not be affirmed as equal value because the pastor was elevated to a cut above: pastors do "real" ministry. What a tragedy for Mrs. White to miss the real presence of Christ in those twenty-eight who stood at her bedside!

Unless we shift the priestly role from an elite core to the entire body of believers, the ministry cannot be returned to the people of God. The New Testament nowhere emphasizes a group of gifted people who uniquely mediate the presence of Christ. The focus is on a sacramental people, not a sacramental pastor.

To illustrate this biblically, let us walk through an Old and New Testament survey of the dwelling place of God. Where does the holiness of God reside? By tracing the imagery of tabernacle and temple through the Scriptures, we will see that the temple in whom God dwells is the whole people of God.

The old covenant introduces us to the images of tabernacle and temple. Coincidentally with the Mosaic covenant, God instructed Moses to build a tabernacle in the wilderness. What was this movable worship center's primary purpose? It was a visible, sacramental symbol that God was abiding with his people. "And let them make me a sanctuary, that I may dwell in their midst" (Ex. 25:8). Howard Snyder demonstrates in *The Problem of Wineskins* that this portable worship center transported during the wilderness wanderings was meant to be a permanent image: God's people are a pilgrim people. We are always to consider ourselves aliens and strangers in a foreign land. As the hymn says, "This world is not my home, I'm just a-passin' through."

The movable tabernacle was replaced by the permanent, immovable temple in Jerusalem. The request to build a temple first

came from King David, though God had never sought a permanent, ornate dwelling place (2 Sam. 7:5–7). The Lord agreed to
the request much as he did to Israel's pleas to have a king. The
Lord assured David that his throne would be established forever,
but David's son Solomon would be the one to build the temple. As
this magnificent edifice was being constructed, the Lord promised
Solomon that the temple would also represent his dwelling place
among his people: "And I will dwell among the children of Israel,
and will not forsake my people Israel" (1 Kings 6:13). At the
dedication ceremony of the temple, the Lord took up occupancy:
"And when the priests came out of the holy place, a cloud filled
the house of the LORD, so that the priests could not stand to
minister because of the cloud; for the glory of the LORD filled the
house of the LORD" (1 Kings 8:10–11). Under the old covenant,
God was represented as dwelling among his people in the
tabernacle and the temple.

The completion of the old covenant occurs in the coming of
the One whom the old covenant anticipated. It is no wonder that
Jesus is portrayed as the temple in whom God now dwells. The
cult of Israel is the foreshadowing of the One who was to come. So
the apostle John writes, "And the Word became flesh and dwelt
among us. . . . we have beheld his glory, glory as of the only Son
from the Father" (John 1:14).

Lest we miss John's intent, we could translate the word
"dwelt" as "tabernacled" or "pitched his tent." In John's day this
word had come to mean "settling down permanently in a place."
That John meant us to understand that Jesus is the fulfillment and
embodiment of the Old Testament dwelling place of God is
evident by his associating Jesus with the "glory" of the Father.
The *shekinah* glory in whose presence neither Moses (Ex. 40:34–35)
nor the priests (1 Kings 8:10–11) could abide is now resting on
and dwelling in the only Son of the Father. Where does God now
dwell among his people? In none other than the incarnate God—
Jesus Christ.

Jesus underscores this truth in referring to his body as the
temple that would be destroyed and in three days raised up (John
2:19–21). The place of the dwelling of the glory of God is the flesh
of Jesus. The transitory tabernacle and temple are now fulfilled
and superseded in the Word-made-flesh.

But where does Jesus dwell now? Where should we seek the
presence of the Incarnate One who reigns at the right hand of
God? Where does his sacramental presence reside? Jesus informed

us that he would come to us in the form of the Holy Spirit: "And I will pray the Father, and he will give you another Counselor, to be with you forever. . . . for he dwells with you and will be in you" (John 14:16–17). The Holy Spirit, the Spirit of Christ, will be the replacement for Christ and the one whose sole desire is to point to and give glory to Christ (John 16:14). Where does God now reside? Paul answers: "Do you not know that you are God's temple and that God's Spirit dwells in you?" (1 Cor. 3:16). God resides in his sacramental people, the church.

In chapter 1, I noted that Paul's favorite image for the church is "the body of Christ." Paul's second favorite image is a building. But Paul cannot think of a building simply in terms of an inanimate structure. He often fuses his understanding of the church as that life-animated body in whom Christ dwells with his image of building and comes up with the mixed metaphor of a "living building." Observe this mixture in Paul's pronouncement on the church as a new humanity: "So then you [Gentiles] are no longer strangers and sojourners, but you are fellow citizens with the saints and members of the *household* of God *built* upon the *foundation* of the apostles and prophets, Christ Jesus himself being the *cornerstone*, in whom the whole *structure* is *joined* together and *grows* into a holy [sacramental] *temple* in the Lord, in whom you also are *built* into it for a *dwelling place* of God in the Spirit" (Eph. 2:19–22).

We have robbed the church of its power by identifying sacramental presence with a few! Nowhere in the Bible can a priesthood within a priesthood be defended. The holy presence of Christ is in his whole body. Each one in whom Christ dwells is a channel through whom he mediates his presence. To lift up a few is to denigrate the whole. Each person bears a charism of God's action and all together make up the dwelling place of God.

COMMUNITY MEAL, NOT CLERGY MEAL

The last element in the one people/one ministry motif strikes at the most sacred stronghold of pastoral self-interest. Who has the right to preside at the Lord's Supper? It is my contention that the single greatest reinforcer of the pastor as priest is the exclusive right of the ordained to preside over the distribution of the elements of Communion. There is nothing that solidifies more in the minds of the people of God the priestly quality of the pastor than the sole right of the ordained to officiate at the table.

The visual image impressed on the consciousness of God's people gathered for worship is the pastor as priest, similar to the role that the priest played in offering sacrifice on behalf of the people under the old covenant. The communion table standing between the pastor and people represents the altar of sacrifice. The elements of bread and wine are the gifts of sacrifice broken and poured out upon the sacred table. The minister plays the role of the consecrated priest who alone has been set apart to this sacred role.

Thomas Torrance links ordination with the act of self-consecration, of presiding at the communion table:

> Those ordained are to be regarded as drawn in a special way within the sphere of Christ's self-consecration so that they can minister the word to others in His name. It is in this connection then that we have to see the relation of ordination to participation in the Lord's Supper, and see the Lord's Supper as the New Testament counterpart in which Aaron and his son participated at their consecration, a meal of thanksgiving and praise.[7]

The rites of ordination are not complete, according to Torrance, until the one ordained handles and dispenses the elements for the first time. "For it was when the gifts of bread and wine were put into his hands that the Lord Himself fulfilled this act of consecrating His servants to His ministry, as He consecrated the apostle-disciples at the Last Supper."[8] Torrance is influenced more by the Old Testament understanding of priesthood than by the New Testament conception of pastor. I am afraid in one degree or another any tradition that reserves serving the Communion elements to the ordained is more akin to Aaronic priesthood than to the priesthood of all believers.

In many traditions, especially Reformed, the elements of Communion cannot be served unless an ordained pastor is present. We speak of ordination to the "Ministry of the Word *and* Sacraments." It is assumed that the sacred trust of ordination is to protect the mystery of the Word made visible in the sacraments. Part of the stewardship of a pastor's call is to protect this sacred meal from abuse and to make sure it is rightly administered. The fear that Communion can be taken casually without proper reverence, or abused by subgroups in the church that may operate as a church unto themselves, has historical precedence. There is a legitimate concern that there be proper order to protect this means of grace.

Restricting the serving of Communion to the ordained is an

unfortunate way to solve a problem of order. Though John Stott believes the administration of the Word and sacraments should be reserved to the clergy, he makes it clear that this is a matter of church order, not doctrine.[9] In other words, there is nothing inherent in the call of pastors that gives them exclusive right to serve Communion. Giving pastors this right is a matter of expediency, not call.

It is noteworthy that nowhere in the New Testament is a special group set apart to protect and administer the sacraments. Leadership does not have an exclusive role in liturgy or worship. This is especially surprising since Paul had to correct the Corinthian church's abuse of Communion. The Corinthians had not discerned the mystery of the unity of the body of Christ implicit in the elements of bread and wine, and as they came together for this meal they displayed a horrendous party spirit, the rich lording it over the poor. In some of the harshest language in the New Testament Paul warns the Corinthians that abuse of the sacred meal brings judgment on themselves (1 Cor. 11:29).

What solution does Paul propose to this problem? Does he offer an institutional remedy? Does he lay down laws or rules to be followed? Does he establish a group in the church to supervise the meal? That he does none of these is curious, since the discussion of the Lord's Table (chap. 11) is immediately followed by an exposition of spiritual gifts (chap. 12). Nowhere does Paul mention a charism given to persons having a special call to protect this meal.

The Lord's Supper is a community meal, and Paul expects the community to act consistent with the sacrificial death of Jesus displayed in these elements as the purchase price of the new community. To put the meal into the hands of a few would destroy the community sense that all participate in the sacrifice of Christ. James Dunn writes,

> If we accept that presiding at the Eucharist is not a charism (gift) distinct from the rest, that God's Spirit brings grace to expression through all believers, then we should insist as a fundamental theological expression of the body of Christ that *conduct of holy communion must not be confined to a particular group within the diverse ministries of the community of faith.* . . . this single step of allowing the sacrament of the Lord's Supper once again to be the natural expression of fellowship wherever groups of believers come together, even when "the minister" is not present, could be one of the liberating steps in renewal and growth.[10]

The sails that will catch the wind of the Spirit will be
fashioned from the cloth of organism ministry, gifted and
sacramental people, and a community meal. While issuing the
challenge of one people/one ministry we have called into question
the priestly overtones connected to pastors. If you are a pastor you
might well be asking, "What is left for me? You have taken it all
away." In the next section we will examine the changing role for
pastors in the ministry of the New Reformation.

NOTES

1. John R. W. Stott, *One People* (Downers Grove, Ill.: InterVarsity Press, 1968),
19.

2. Casey Miller and Kate Swift, *Words and Women: New Language for New Times*
(New York: Anchor, 1976), iii.

3. Ibid., 32.

4. Howard Snyder, *The Problem of Wineskins* (Downers Grove, Ill.: InterVarsity
Press, 1975), 81.

5. Ibid., 83.

6. Jerry Cook, *Love, Acceptance, and Forgiveness* (Glendale, Calif.: Regal, 1979),
102.

7. Thomas Torrance, in *Theological Foundations for Ministry*, ed. Ray S.
Anderson (Grand Rapids: Eerdmans, 1979), 426, 419.

8. Ibid., 420.

9. Stott, *One People*, 42.

10. James D. G. Dunn, "Ministry and the Ministry: The Charismatic Renewal's
Challenge to Traditional Ecclesiology" (Unpublished paper), 26.

PART 2

The Pastor in the New Reformation

CHAPTER 5

Dependency:
A Counterproductive
Model of Ministry

TO THIS POINT I have been highly critical of the traditional role of pastor as defined from the institutional perspective. In this section I will examine the changes that are required in the role of pastor according to the New Reformation. These changes are grounded in a radical change in expectations—both what pastors expect of themselves and what congregations look for in calling a pastor. A reconfiguration of the relationship between pastor and people is necessary if the church is to become conformed to the biblical description of ministry.

My basic assumption is that the key to unlocking the New Reformation is a transformation of the pastor's posture. A congregation tends to assimilate the personality, stance, and approach of its pastor and reflect that identity as a mirror image. There is a reactive dynamic or interplay between the pastor and congregation. For example, if the pastor's basic approach to God's people is as scholar-teacher, the people will tend to become students-learners. If the pastor views the church and his role as social activist, the church will become a center from which to trumpet causes of justice. If the pastor projects the image of a father-mother, the people will view themselves as dependent children. But if the church is to be a ministering community, the pastor must be an equipper who empowers God's people to fullness of service.

There are many images of pastoral roles (e.g., shepherd and bishop) but I believe most pastors tend to conduct their ministry in one of two ways. We foster either a *dependency* (traditional) model of ministry or an *interdependency* (equipping) model. I am aware that pastors fall along a continuum. But for clarity and vision, seeing things in black and white will be a helpful way to diagnose where we are and how far we have yet to go.

In this chapter I will demonstrate how the dependency model is an expression of the church as institution and is counterproductive to the New Reformation. In chapters 6 and 7 I will delineate the interdependency model of ministry and the practical steps that can be taken to implement this model.

It has become fashionable for pastors to appeal to the often-quoted phrases in Ephesians 4:11–12 as the essence of the job description of a pastor. Pastoral candidates so often describe their role as "equipping the saints for the work of ministry" that search committees are likely to skip right over it from repetition. It is also fashionable for church bulletins, instead of listing "ministers" followed by names of paid staff, to announce, "Ministers: All the members of the congregation." There is much use of the language of equipping, but too often it is only lip service.

The reality is that the dependency model of ministry is firmly in place in the minds of most pastors and congregations. What is this model? *Pastors do the ministry, while the people are the grateful (or not so grateful) recipients of their professional care.* Pastors are construed to be experts in things spiritual, while the people view themselves as objects receiving what they are not qualified to give one another. The experts take care of the uninitiated. In a different image, pastors are the all-knowing parent figures who provide the protection and nurture for their dependent children. But in this family, the children never grow up.

The roles that pastor and people have learned to play are difficult to change, for they are replete with entrenched and unspoken expectations. Pastors are locked into a role that fosters dependency, because there are personal expectations for the role that have become integral to their identity. These expectations are then reinforced by a congregation who are so used to a pedestal view of the pastor that they cannot imagine any other role. Let us look at these role expectations from the angle of the pastor and then of the congregation.

THE PASTOR'S VIEW OF THE DEPENDENCY MODEL

Omnicompetent
"I must be good at everything."

As stated earlier, John Stott uses the word "omnicompetence" to describe the pressure many pastors place on themselves. There are certainly many demands made on pastors. Within a matter of moments in a typical day, a pastor may be called to exercise vastly different skills.

The pastor is in the study attempting in scholarly fashion to call forth the nuances of the biblical text in preparation for a sermon; his secretary buzzes on the phone, "Pastor, there is a man here with his son. They look deeply disturbed, and are in tears. Can you see them?" From the introspective task of study, the pastor attempts to come out of himself in order to make sense of a critical moment in these two lives. After the counseling session is concluded, the secretary reminds him that a decision still needs to be made as to which bulletin to order for the special Sundays of the year.

At noon it is time for the pastor's weekly discipling time with two businessmen who are key leaders in the church. He shifts gears to get his mind into their world and onto the relevant biblical subject matter for the day. Upon return from lunch the women's association has asked him to stop by and see the items being created for the fund-raising bazaar. The rest of the afternoon he must fit in a trip to the hospital to console a dear member before major surgery, followed by a premarital counseling appointment.

After a brief time with the family at dinner, the pastor will attend a special finance committee meeting, called because the current receipts are lagging behind the budget. In the space of one day the pastor has been called to be scholar, reconciler, administrative decision maker, discipler, pastoral showpiece, comforter, counselor, and expert fund-raiser.

The problem is compounded for average two-talent pastors when they compare themselves with the five-talent superstars in "megachurches" who seem to operate well-oiled machines. These people appear to be equally comfortable as the master of ceremonies on a Sunday morning and as the chief executive officer during the week. Ordinary pastors feel the pressure to be as gifted in the multiple demands of their position. Therefore pastors become "seminar junkies," pursuing the latest "how to," such as being a multistaff pastor, church planter, time manager, premarital counselor, and so on. Since the pastor does the ministry, the many facets of ministry must be a part of his portfolio so his church can "count itself fortunate."

Distrustful
"I am the paid professional."

Robert Munger has been previously quoted as saying that perhaps the greatest single bottleneck to renewal is "the hesitancy of clergy to *trust* the laity with significant responsibility." "Significant responsibility" usually means those duties that have been traditionally connected with the priestly functions of pastors. In other words, pastors are reluctant to entrust the laity with the spiritual welfare of people's lives. As the trained professionals, pastors are the only ones qualified to counsel, teach (adults, not children), visit in the hospitals, or even lead someone to Christ. One pastor told me he could have only two home Bible studies in his congregation. When I asked why, he said, "Because that's all I have time to lead."

Though we are seeing many good signs that the New Reformation is taking hold in various places, this complaint from a parishioner is still true: "Too often our pastors seem to treat us only as fund-raisers (pastors don't want to be too closely associated with filthy lucre) or cooks or office equipment operators . . . when our hearts are crying out for a meaningful ministry."[1]

This lack of entrusting to God's people both responsibility and authority for authentic ministry betrays the priestly view of the pastoral role. Pastors—perhaps unconsciously—have accepted the view that God's presence is borne by them to a higher degree, so by implication others cannot be full channels of God's activity. Pastors' distrust becomes an obstacle to equipping those who may be more gifted than they to carry out certain kinds of ministry. For how can the professional trust the untrained with people's lives? If you want it done right, you must do it yourself.

Ego-Enhancing
"Someone needs me."

When pastors operate out of a priestly self-perception, they are placed in a category of "specialness." Church communities become dependently attached when their pastors are viewed as wearing a priestly mantle that sets them apart. Being needed is addictive. To be fussed over and paid deference to at a social function is extremely ego-gratifying. To be seen as people's surrogate connection to God is a difficult role to surrender. People communicate in words and action, "I do not know what we would do without you." As a result pastors get to the point where they believe in their own self-importance. When this occurs, a psychological corner has been turned toward a sick pursuit of affirmation. It is intoxicating to be perched on the pinnacle, to be the person atop the church pyramid. How does one divest himself of the desire to be the centerpiece?

A chief reason why the dependency model of ministry is still dominant is that many pastors' sense of worth and value is derived from being a benevolent lord reigning over the little fiefdom. From a psychological view we would be appalled at parents who assert their authority by keeping their children dependent on them even though they are adults. Yet we do not evidence the same disgust at anemic churches made up of perennial spiritual children who are not allowed by their parent pastors to grow up. Underlying the dependency model of ministry is a distorted and unhealthy means of seeking value. Pastor and people are co-conspirators denying the addiction and fostering the sickness.

Motivated by Guilt
"What if people think I am lazy?"

Pastors have often been characterized as having as many bosses as there are members in the congregation. The unwritten job description in the minds of most pastors is the composite of the myriad voices of the people they serve, who freely express their expectation of pastors' responsibilities. As pastors we can begin with a sincere desire to serve people's needs, but end up being slaves to people's varied expectations. The voices are rarely still. In sermon preparation we try to satisfy the person who states, "You are too scholarly," at the same time someone else is telling us, "Give us more meat from the biblical text." We know the voices. A parishioner calls at 9:00 A.M., saying, "I hope I didn't wake you." Implicit in that comment is the idea that the pastor's life is not as strenuous as others'. It also indicates that the lifestyle of pastors is invisible to the people we serve, and therefore we must continually be proving we are not lazy by attempting to cover all the bases.

Dependency model pastors, manipulated by guilt, tend to be reactors rather than initiators. Pastors are expected to respond to the urgent or needy. Being responders means allowing others' needs to set the agenda. As you examine your datebook, do you find the names on your appointment calendar are people who have requested time, or are they ones you have sought out because of your agenda to develop ministry? I suspect that most pastors allow their agenda to be set for them, which means spending a considerable time with those who are problem-focused and therefore inherently draining. An inordinate amount of time is spent with emotionally dependent people, and minimal attention is given to stronger, more mature believers who could be motivated and trained for ministering to those in need. As long as pastors are available to all comers, rather than strategically using their time to build up and deploy people in ministry, the body will remain dependent.

Activity-Oriented
"Don't just sit there, do something."

Closely associated with motivation by guilt is the strong pull to be an activist. In his book *Clergy in the Cross Fire*, Donald Smith identifies the scholar-activist polarity as a source of great inner tension for pastors.[2] It is difficult for many pastors to see the quiescent aspect of their job as "real" ministry. After any long period of prayer or study an inner voice wells up, "I should *do* something worthwhile." "Real" ministry is viewed as activity that is directly related to program development or people involvement. Prayer and study are activities we do on our own time—whatever that is. Hilary of Tours called this "a blasphemous anxiety to do God's work for Him."[3] Busyness and activity then become a measure of success in ministry as well as a determinant of worth. Actually, busyness becomes another means by which the congregation is dependent on us. Have you ever felt like the entertainer who runs frantically to and fro keeping the plates spinning on the top of a wavering spindle?

Ineffectual in Leadership
"Propose and execute all plans."

Those who operate out of a dependency model of ministry are marked by two styles of leadership. One extreme is what has been called the *laissez-faire*, or nondirectional, approach. This style is marked by being so available and therefore reactive that we are directionless. Ministry means meeting needs and allowing others to set the agenda. We have no particular agenda of our own. We allow to happen whatever happens, and we are the ones who stamp out fires as they arise.

The other extreme, just as reinforcing to the dependency model, is *authoritarian* leadership. Since the congregation is dependent on the pastor, the pastor must be highly directive; dependent children must be told what to do.

This style dominated my subconscious for the first few years of my ministry. I would come to our board meeting with detailed plans, complete with my arsenal of reasons for implementing this great idea, its projected impact two or three years down the road, with a cost analysis attached. In my mind the leader must have it all worked out and then sell it to the board. I could not understand why the elders were not hailing me as the latest "messiah." I finally came to realize that I left them with two alternatives; they could say yes or no. They had no ownership in the decision. Even when they said yes, I realized, it was totally up to me to implement the action because others had not been part of the process to shape the direction. "Fine, whatever you want, pastor" was the response; the implicit message was, "Don't ask us to carry it out. It wasn't our idea!"

The dependency model remains the dominant pattern because pastoral self-expectations foster it. I have attempted to peer into the mindset and perhaps unconscious assumptions that control pastors' stance vis-à-vis congregations. This is where the battle is fought. Paul admonishes us to be "transformed by the renewal of your minds" (Rom. 12:2), because our minds contain our perception of reality, the worldview through which we see things. The New Reformation is a spiritual battle bent on replacing our old thinking patterns, which have crippled the church, with a new set of pastoral expectations that can empower God's people for ministry.

THE CONGREGATION'S VIEW OF THE DEPENDENCY MODEL

Congregational expectations that reinforce pastors' self-perception are another major stronghold that needs to be torn down. Many pastors revert to the dependency model because there is too great a price to be paid for becoming an equipping pastor. The path of least resistance is to succumb to the pressures of congregational wants rather than to go through the painful process of reeducation. What does a traditional congregation want from its pastor?

The Ubiquitous Pastor
"We count ourselves fortunate. Our pastor can do everything."

The desire for the pastor to be Jesus reincarnate is most clearly expressed when the pastoral search committee puts together the composite of their ideal candidate. This subject lends itself readily to satire, and the following is a magnificent example of unknown origin:

> Dear Church Member,
>
> This chain letter is meant to bring happiness to you. Unlike other chain letters, it does not cost money. Simply send a copy of this letter to six other churches who are tired of their pastors. Then bundle up your pastor and send him to the church at the bottom of the list. In one week you will receive 16,436 pastors and one of them should be a dandy! Have faith in this letter. One church broke the chain and got their old pastor back.

As outrageous as this sounds, this gag was born out of the frustrating desire for a pastor who can do it all. Why is this? When a winsome, charismatic figure is our leader, we can live his energy. There is a certain transference of value. We feel good about ourselves because we are attracted to a representative and figurehead who embodies a corporate personality. This in turn places little personal responsibility on us, and therefore a minimum of personal initiative is required. The leader covers the bases for us. The role of the congregational member is to be an enthusiastic supporter through verbal adulation and financial contributions. But the same dynamic remains in place: a few are doing for the many.

The Resident Expert
"I'm waiting for the pastor to come."

If pastors bear the presence of Christ in a way that an ordinary believer cannot, then the ministry of the members of the body will be disparaged and not fully received. I encounter this attitude all the time. Integral to my implementation of equipping ministry is a discipling network that is meant to move from one generation to another throughout our congregation. But since I have had the vision and more experience than others, I am viewed as the chief discipler. I am the resident expert. To be invited into a discipling relationship by me is seen by others as an honor, because I know how to do it "right." I have yet to be turned down. But as the discipling chain moves away from me into the second and third generations, the luster fades; it is not considered to be as high an honor to be discipled by an average church member. Some who have been asked have even intimated that they are waiting for an available slot in my discipling schedule. O how far we have to go! Yet I can still taste the firstfruits of the New Reformation.

The Inspirational Bandage
"Give me something inspirational to get through another week."

Donald Smith suggests that the people of God and the pastor often have differing perspectives about the aim of worship.[4] God's people come to worship as a place of escape from the troubles of everyday life. Worship is a moment of quiet, an island of tranquillity in the tumultuous and demanding sea of life. By contrast, an equipping pastor with a sense of mission views worship as the time to confront the hard realities of a broken world; he sees God's people as agents of reconciliation. The sermon is the means of outfitting God's people with substantive biblical content so there is enough ammunition to wage war against a world under the domination of the Evil One.

Frequently what God's people want is an inspirational Band-Aid that can be applied to the bumps and bruises of life. A spine-tingling message that will get people through another week is sufficient. Worship is one time when some ray of hope can break through the gloom of sagging spirits. At heart, people want to leave worship with a good feeling. Therefore the pastor should embody optimism and an upbeat attitude.

The Church as Possession
"I go to Pastor Ogden's church."

So accepted is the dependency model in the consciousness of most people that we do not think it strange to speak of the church in the possessive. The language of God's people is peppered with "that's Pastor So-and-So's church." Pastors are also heard to say "my church" instead of "the church I serve." That is a small thing, you say. But I assert again that our language is additional evidence of how thoroughly debilitating the identification of the church with its leadership can be. The pastor is not the possessor of the church, but one called to give his life away so that the ministry of God's people may thrive.

There is an interesting reverse twist on the pastor as the possessor of the church, and that is, there is also a sense in which people like to possess the pastor. People speak of "having a pastor" in the same way they "have a family doctor." The pastor is part of the package connected to life insurance. The pastor will be available in time of need and will provide comfort and make all the proper arrangements when death occurs. To have a pastor we can call our own is all a part of making sure things are set in order.

The Professional Minister
"After all, that is what we pay him for."

When a pastor does not live up to the traditional expectation of a congregation, we can hear people say, "Well, what do we pay him for?" God's people often see themselves as the ones who pay the bills and handle the administrative and organizational machinery to create the context for the pastor to do the ministry. When people do not get what they want or disagree with the way the pastor is carrying out his duties, what is one of the first ways they convey their discontent? They withhold their money. Giving money is the means to express approval, and withholding money is the way to "send a message."

CONCLUSION

Admittedly, these may be somewhat extreme characterizations of the dependency model of ministry—even caricatures. Yet I believe the overall picture of a church as a dependent child mired in a sickly attachment to pastors is a fair one. The church in general remains stunted, with only a small percentage of God's people having grown up with a view of themselves as authentic ministers. The dependency model fosters emotionally sick pastors who need a reliant church because they need to be needed. God's people are starved for responsible ministry, but are unable to break free from the hierarchical model.

A far healthier model views the pastor, not as the caretaker of those who can't fend for themselves, but as the equipper who encourages and provides a context to train all God's people for ministry. In the next chapter we will explore the biblical image of equipper as the fundamental posture of the pastor in relationship to God's people. Then in chapter 7 I will delineate a model for implementing the pastor as equipper around new pastoral and congregational expectations.

NOTES

1. John R. W. Stott, *One People* (Downers Grove, Ill.: InterVarsity Press, 1968), 31.

2. Donald Smith, *Clergy in the Cross Fire* (Philadelphia: Westminster, 1974), 48.

3. Quoted by Eugene Peterson, "The Unbusy Pastor," *Leadership* (Summer 1981): 70.

4. Smith, *Clergy in the Cross Fire*, 35.

CHAPTER 6

The Pastor as Equipper
for Ministry

IF IT IS TRUE THAT a New Reformation is taking place and the ministry is being returned to all God's people, then a fundamental shift of the pastor's role is required vis-à-vis the people of God. If we as pastors are no longer the ones on whom a local body of believers focuses its attention, then what role do we have in the New Reformation?

If the ministry is "for all who are called to share in Christ's life,"[1] then what is *the* pastor supposed to do? The New Reformation creates a crisis of identity for the pastor that can be very unsettling. If the pastor's identity can no longer be viewed as the center of a wheel from which the rest of the church radiates as spokes, then what is the New Reformation's vision of the pastoral role?

A second, related question needs to be answered. All those roles that we have come to associate with pastors—are they outmoded? Will pastors no longer serve as ambassadors, stewards, or teachers? What will we do with the identity of "pastor" as expressed in many churches' polity? The *Book of Order* (1982–83) of the United Presbyterian Church, U.S.A., is representative:

> When a minister is called to labor as a pastor, it belongs to that office to *pray* to God for and with the flock; to *feed* the flock, by *reading, expounding, teaching,* and *preaching* the Word; to *cultivate* in the congregation the *singing* of the praises of God; to *administer* the *sacraments;* to *instruct* the children and youth, and to *lead* in the educational program of the church; to *visit* the people, devoting special attention to the poor, the sick, the afflicted, and the dying; and with the ruling elders to *exercise* the joint power of government (italics added).[2]

These actions have described the traditional domain of pastoral ministry. But are any of these roles the exclusive province of those who have completed a seminary curriculum and passed the trials of ordination? Pastors know there are people within their congregations who, in fact, surpass them in ability in particular areas. When we describe the ministries often aligned with the pastorate, we are describing ministry that can and should be carried out by the entire body of believers.

Then what is a pastor to do? Trueblood has said it best: "The ministry is for all who are called to share in Christ's life, *the pastorate is for those who possess the peculiar gift of being able to help other men and women to practice any ministry to which they are called"* (italics added).[3] In other words, the reason for a pastor's professional training is to use this knowledge *to equip and deploy God's people in ministry*. What is wholly absent in the *Book of Order* is the empowering of the body for ministry. Equipping pastors are committed to giving the ministry away.

Let me anticipate some questions: Is not equipping simply one function among many that a pastor performs? Aren't some pastors especially gifted in equipping ministry? There is a trend of hiring a "Director of Equipping Ministries." This implies that equipping is a specialized ministry of certain people with certain skills. When I was called as the Pastor for Leadership Development and Discipleship at St. John's, I was perceived as the one having the responsibility to handle equipping ministry. The other two ordained pastors covered the terrain traditionally connected with a pastor's role—preaching, pastoral care (hospital visitation), and counseling. My duties included devising a way for the members of the body to discover their spiritual gifts and be deployed accordingly; training small-group leaders as undershepherds; setting up a discipling network; overseeing the adult education classes to deepen people's biblical knowledge and wield the truth in the pressures of Southern California life. The impression I received from the other staff and our elders was that "equipping has now been taken care of; Greg is doing the job."

I became increasingly uncomfortable treating equipping as a specialty in pastoral ministry. Equipping is not to be the latest fad in ministry; it is not something a few are called to do. It is a fundamental approach that needs to be integral to the identity of anyone who is a pastor. The role of a pastor is "to help men and women practice any ministry to which they are called." The New Reformation returns pastors to their proper role in relationship to

God's people: equipping them for ministry. The raison d'être of pastors is to die to self so that members of the body can come alive to their ministry. So the rediscovered role of pastors in our day is not to do ministry for those who are passive recipients of their care, but to empower the body through the avenues of the pastors' individual gifts and to call forth every person's potential for ministry.

We came to realize at St. John's that pastors are equippers in the areas where they have a particular heart for ministry. So the teaching-preaching pastor equips the people by clearly and passionately expounding the Scripture so there is sufficient food and fuel to drive the engine of the spirit to carry out ministry. And the pastor for pastoral care and counseling trains a pastoral care team to watch over those in the hospital and see them through to recovery; equips paracounselors to share the load of a felt-need ministry; and encourages the gifts of those with special sensitivity to healing ministry to pray in the name of Jesus for the sick and emotionally damaged.

The shift to an equipping model raises the question, How do we measure ministry effectiveness? In the dependency model, pastors are often asked to report to the church board on the number of visits made to the homes of members and the number of committees attended during the past month. That is the official report. The unofficial report is, Has there been a steady increase in giving and does the graph show a consistent rise in attendance? The equipping ministry, however, entails a different measure of success. The measurement of success is the ability to identify, train, support, and deploy an increasing number of people who will take responsibility for the spiritual welfare of God's people or to make a significant impact through their witness to Christ in the world in word and deed. An equipper's job is to build in people a belief that God has called them to ministry and to help them function in accordance with their identified call and giftedness.

Ray Stedman's helpful pictorial representation of Ephesians 4:11–12, which you will recall from chapter 3 (fig. 3.2), clearly captures the role pastors are to play in relationship to God's people.[4]

BIBLICAL OVERVIEW OF EQUIPPING

The Greek word *katartismos* (Eph. 4:12) is variously translated as "equip" (RSV), "perfect" (KJV), or "prepare" (NIV). An examination of how *katartismos* and its related family of words are used in Scripture will help us grasp the scope of equipping ministry and therefore the environment that equipping pastors are to cultivate in a local church.

Biblical Terminology of Equipping

1. *Artios*—The root of the better-known *katartismos* (Eph. 4:12) can be translated as a predicate adjective ("he is *complete*"). *Artios* conveys the goals of equipping for either an individual disciple or the whole body of Christ. It covers the range of meanings of suitable, complete, filled out, operating appropriately, meeting requirements, filling a particular situation, capable," and "sound." This term is found only in 2 Timothy 3:17.

2. *Katartizō*—This verb is by far the most common form in the Septuagint and the New Testament. It is found nineteen times in the Old Testament and is translated by no less than seven different Hebrew verbs. In the New Testament it is used thirteen times in a variety of contexts.

3. *Katartismos*—This well-known participle is used only in Ephesians 4:12 and can be translated "preparing" or "equipping."

4. *Katartisis*—In 2 Corinthians 13:9, Paul prays for the church's "improvement," which can also be translated "restoration, completion," or "being put in proper order."

5. *Exartizō*—Used only once, in conjunction with the singular use of *artios* in 2 Timothy 3:17, this verb means that the Word of God is able to fill out, finish, complete, or equip.

Selected Old Testament Passages

Note the wide variety of translations of "equip" and the images they invoke. During the celebration of Yahweh's triumph over the Egyptian army at the Red Sea, God's people are assured that the Lord will plant them on the holy mountain as their sure abode and *establish* a sanctuary by the Lord's hand at the same place (Ex. 15:17). Upon return from exile, Nehemiah found the walls of Jerusalem in disrepair; he received permission to *finish* the walls and repair the foundations (Ezra 4:12, 16; 5:3, 9, 11; 6:14). The Lord's glory is written into the wonders of the heavens and chanted by the mouths of babes. For those who don't acknowledge this glory, the Lord "has *founded* a bulwark" against his foes

(Ps. 8:2). During a time of testing by his enemies, David claimed "my steps have *held fast* to thy paths" (Ps. 17:5). The psalmist reviews the faithfulness of God from the Exodus on, and he describes the Lord as *restoring* the heritage of Israel by providing water in the wilderness (Ps. 68:9). Finally, the unshakable tone of the word "equip" is captured as God is said to have *established* the fixed courses of the moon, sun, and stars (Pss. 74:16; 89:37).

Selected New Testament Passages

The same breadth of meanings for "equip" can be found in the New Testament. When Jesus calls James and John to be disciples, they are *mending* their nets (Matt. 4:21; Mark 1:19). A disciple will be fully *taught* when he is like his teacher (Luke 6:40). God has *prepared beforehand* vessels that are the objects of his mercy (Rom. 9:23). Addressing the division at Corinth, Paul urges the congregation to "be *united* in the same mind" (1 Cor. 1:10). He prays for the *improvement* of the Corinthians and exhorts them to *mend* their ways (2 Cor. 13:9, 11). Christians are to intervene in the lives of those who have stumbled by *restoring* them in a spirit of gentleness (Gal. 6:1). Paul hopes to come to the Thessalonians to *supply* what is lacking in their faith (1 Thess. 3:10). Of Christ's incarnation, Hebrews 10:5 states, "A body was *prepared* for him." By the word of God the world was *created* (Heb. 11:3). Christ is sufficient to *equip* us for every good work (Heb. 13:21) and to *establish* us in our faith after a trial (1 Peter 5:10).

In summary, we find three ways "equip" can be categorized overall:

Mend/Restore

> Ezra 4:12, 16; 5:3, 9, 11; 6:14
> Psalm 68:9
> Matthew 4:21; Mark 1:19
> 1 Corinthians 1:10; 13:9, 11
> Galatians 6:1
> 1 Thessalonians 3:10

Establish/Lay Foundations

> Exodus 15:17
> Psalms 8:2; 17:5; 74:16; 89:37
> Luke 6:40
> Hebrews 11:5; 13:21
> 1 Peter 5:10

Prepare/Train

> Romans 9:23
> Ephesians 4:12
> Hebrews 10:5

After surveying the contexts of the various forms of the word associated with "equipping," a complete picture of a full-orbed, well-balanced ministry of the body emerges. "Equip" conveys both a style of ministry and the content of that ministry.

To simplify what appears to be complex, we can depict the images of equipping as clustered around these three foci and all with the ultimate purpose of deploying the entire body for ministry.

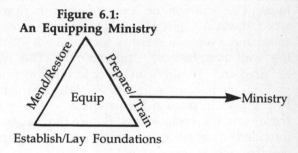

Figure 6.1:
An Equipping Ministry

Establish/Lay Foundations

MEND/RESTORE

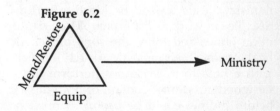

Figure 6.2

In the secularized Greek society of the biblical era, the word "equip" was used in a medical context. When a limb was broken, doctors "equipped" their ailing patients by putting the fractured bone back into proper alignment. A limb pulled out of joint was equipped by being returned to its proper place so that it could be restored to its appropriate function. Thus, the secular meaning entails restoring what was broken and correcting what was out of place so that it can return to its original, intended function. There are three different nuances derived from *Mend/Restore:*

Fix what is broken;

Bring back into proper alignment;

Supply what is lacking.

1. To mend and restore means *to fix what is broken*. R. Paul Stevens says in his book *Liberating the Laity* that the equipper in the church is like a "stone mason." Six times in the book of Ezra (4:12, 16; 5:3, 9, 11; 6:14) the Septuagint uses the verb *katartizō*, which is translated "finish." Upon return from the Babylonian exile, Ezra and Nehemiah discovered their beloved city of Jerusalem in a state of ruin and disrepair. The walls that enclosed the city were marred by gaping holes, and in some places stones were heaped in piles where the enemy had broken them down and left them to gather moss. The wall was no longer able to perform the function for which it was designed. Erected to provide protection from warring tribes and a sense of security for those who took refuge behind it, the wall had become dysfunctional. The wall needed to be repaired and "finished" in order to fulfill its purpose. It could not perform its function in its broken state. So the fallen stones had to be put back in place and new stones cut in order to fill in where there were no replacements. Before the walls could perform their intended function they needed to be equipped by someone *mending* and *restoring* them.

The New Testament conveys a similar nuance through a different image (Mark 1:19; Matt. 4:21). Early in his public ministry, Jesus walked beside the Sea of Galilee and met future disciples at work as fishermen. The Scripture says that Jesus came upon James and John, the sons of Zebedee, "who were in their boat *mending* their nets" (Mark 1:19). A fishing net is not much use with a hole in it. It cannot perform the function for which it is designed if it cannot contain or hold the fish it is meant to trap. So before the net could be useful, it must be equipped. James and John were getting the net ready to return to action, to be restored to service. But they had to undo the damage *before* its utility could return.

2. To mend and restore means *to bring back into proper alignment*. Psalm 68:9 states, "Rain in abundance, O God, thou didst shed abroad; thou didst *restore* thy heritage as it languished." Referring to the Exodus experience of wandering in the wilderness, the covenant people were restored to their heritage under the direct, protective care of Yahweh. For four hundred years they cried out under their Egyptian oppressors, feeling cut

off and abandoned by the God of their fathers. As God through Moses led them through the wilderness to the Promised Land, there was a sense that they had been realigned with their heritage. They were once more in the steam and flow of God, who was working out his plan through a chosen people.

In Galatians 6:1 Paul uses the word "equip" in the sense of *bring back into proper alignment:* "Brethren, if anyone is overtaken in any trespass, you who are spiritual should *restore* him in a spirit of gentleness. Look to yourself lest you too be tempted." Paul addresses our responsibility to those "overtaken" by trespass. The word "overtaken" suggests a member of the body of Christ who has unknowingly and unwittingly violated a law of God and has therefore put himself out of proper alignment with both God and his church. What is our responsibility? "You who are spiritual are to *restore* him in a spirit of gentleness," writes Paul. The secular, medical image serves here as the appropriate backdrop for "restore." As a doctor would gently realign a broken bone or a limb that is out of joint, so we are to sensitively help a brother or sister be realigned with God and restored to fellowship in the body.

In 1 Corinthians 1:10 Paul confronts the party spirit that has torn apart the Corinthian fellowship. The people are polarized to the point where subgroups are defending their own views of the truth based on a cult of personality—"I am of Paul, I am of Apollos." Paul exhorts these factions, "I appeal to you, brethren, in the name of our Lord Jesus Christ, that you all agree, . . . that you be *united* in the same mind and the same judgment." Instead of being disjointed and disconnected, be *united.* Line up with the same mind and judgment. Fix your broken and flawed thinking and become whole through agreement.

3. The third emphasis in the mending/restoring phase of equipping is *to supply what is lacking.* Paul tenderly relays to the Thessalonians that he and his colleagues, Silvanus and Timothy, are "praying earnestly night and day that we may see you face to face and *supply* what is lacking in your faith" (1 Thess. 3:10). The Revised Standard Version uses the verb "supply" to translate *katartizō.* The meaning of "supply" here is to complete what is incomplete, make up for what is deficient, and add what is missing. There is a deficit that must be made up if the Thessalonians are to minister at full capacity.

This same sense is conveyed to the Corinthians when Paul writes, "What we pray for is your *improvement*" (2 Cor. 13:9).

"Improvement" translates *katartisis,* which in this context focuses on improvement in one's understanding and experience of the faith. Paul is fighting a battle for the Corinthians' affection. They have been attracted to "super apostles," who don't seem to accept the weakness shown in a crucified Savior. When Paul modeled the way of the Cross, it looked to the Corinthians like weakness, because he had "decided to know nothing among you except Jesus Christ and him crucified" (1 Cor. 2:2). *What was lacking* in the Corinthians' faith was the knowledge that the power of God is released when we realize we have nothing in ourselves to commend. So Paul concludes with the exhortation, "Mend [*katartizesthe*] your ways" (2 Cor. 13:11). He wants them to understand that at the heart of our faith is the weakness of the Cross, which is the power of God. He calls them to be people of the Cross, because such people are by nature humble and therefore can "agree with one another" (2 Cor. 13:11).

So the equipping ministry of mending and restoring entails (1) fixing what is broken, (2) bringing back into proper alignment, and (3) supplying what is lacking.

The Equipping Ministry of Mending/Restoring

What might the mending/restoring phase of equipping ministry look like in the local church? The church is to be a therapeutic community. It is a place where broken, struggling people can become well and whole. The atmosphere of a therapeutic community immersed in grace says to those who enter, "We take you as you are." Bruce Larson years ago chided pastors when he said that the local bar often communicates a more accepting atmosphere than the church. In the midst of a casualty-creating world, the church needs to be a place where we come with wounds exposed and hear loud and clear, "Grace dispensed here."

Any equipping ministry begins with the assumption that we are all broken people because of our own self-destructive sin or having been victimized by the sin of others. Paul writes, "We have this truth [the Gospel] in earthen vessels" (2 Cor. 4:7). In other words, we are all "cracked pots." As broken people we "leak" the presence of the Holy Spirit. The mending/restoring ministry pays attention to our cracks so that we may better contain the presence of Christ in us. Therefore an equipping ministry makes provision for restoring all who bear the damage of physical, spiritual, and emotional brokenness. Our ministry will be only as effective as we are whole in Christ.

1. *Fixing what is broken.* To fix what is broken means to be committed to healing ministry. I use "healing" in the broad sense of seeking wholeness in Christ on the levels of body, mind, and spirit. Healing covers a wide spectrum, from prayer for the restoration of physical health to the full employment of healing tools to mend damaged emotions or spirit. This means, therefore, that the healing ministry of the church will assume many forms. There will be opportunity for public healing in the context of the prayerful and expectant faith of the gathered community. There will also be opportunities for long-term care by trained counselors who can apply the healing salve of the Holy Spirit. The tender care of nonjudgmental listening will allow fearful and traumatized people to expose hurts and pain long buried from conscious recognition. Memories are healed and the guilt of past sins released through the forgiveness of Jesus Christ as he is embodied in healing agents.

The church I serve offers several insights into how the various dimensions of a healing ministry function. Sunday evening "body life" services have been the context for a public healing ministry. After some time for refreshing worship through praise in song and prayer, we invite people to bring personal needs before the Lord. These may involve some spiritual blockage, broken relationships, besetting sin, or the need for physical healing. Those who have been identified with gifts of healing and sensitivity to the Holy Spirit's leading in prayer, all enhanced by careful training, are stationed in pairs as prayer teams along the front of the sanctuary. As space is available, people bring their concerns to the team and are powerfully prayed for in the name of Christ. The public setting creates an air of expectancy as the congregation enters into the faith-enhancing prayer.

Most healing is not instantaneous, but long-term. Traumas from the past are deeply buried and have multiple ramifications. Often the public setting is simply an impetus to the long-term process of fixing what is broken. This long-term care has taken different forms in the congregation. First, those gifted in inner-healing prayer make a commitment to take a person through the levels of pain to get at the roots of troubling behavior that is evidenced as sin. This kind of prayer is often described as "healing of the memories." Deeply hurtful experiences, long buried, are uncovered through Holy Spirit-guided prayer. These occasions of prayer can be wrenching experiences as veiled traumas are brought into the light; often spiritual darkness is encountered head-on. Secondly, those who have been the victims of similar kinds of painful backgrounds gather for support as they share a common journey toward wholeness. Two support groups exist for the adult children of alcoholics, who find great comfort in knowing that their story is not unique.

All of us have something broken that needs to be fixed if we are to be whole people.

2. *Bringing back into proper alignment.* The second aspect of mending/restoring implies that a relationship which was once solid is now in a state of disrepair. The disciple has done something to put himself out of alignment with Christ. Therefore a mending/restoring ministry exercises discipline. Grace is balanced by truth. A therapeutic community accepts people as they are, but loves them enough not to allow them to remain that way. Love without teeth is sentimentality. We do no one a favor by allowing him to hurt himself in his sin. Paul writes that "you who are spiritual should *restore* them in a spirit of gentleness" (Gal. 6:1). This means that the spiritual leaders who share oversight with pastors must be equipped in their role to protect the spiritual health of the body. This will require intervention into lives where people, knowingly or unknowingly, live self-destructively. The body of believers will need to be structured (as by small groups) and the community equipped to call people back to Christ when they are living contrary to the Lord's will.

Discipline requires a context of intimacy and accountability. I have deliberately included these two ingredients in discipling relationships. I encourage a triad, in which one person invites two others into an intense journey together toward maturity. A covenant is mutually negotiated that establishes the disciplines to which the parties will be mutually accountable. Explicit permission is given to each member to raise concerns whenever we see something in another's life that is a blind spot to his faithfulness in Christ. In one discipling triad we spent considerable time on one person's inability to manage his employees in a tone that was consistent with the way Christ would treat people. This person was consciously aware that his volatile outbursts were not honoring to the Lord. He needed a means to be called on it and to be encouraged to see transformation.

A more critical form of intervention is needed when someone is out of alignment with Christ as a result of demonic activity.

Some people in the body have gifts of discerning spirits, intercessory prayer, and wisdom. These can form prayer teams for a deliverance ministry when it is clear that every other attempt to break the bondage of sin has pointed to a force of darkness that is not the result of damaged emotions or willful sin, but the foothold of the Evil One. An equipping ministry recognizes the need for deliverance from the powers of darkness.

We cannot be fit for ministry unless we are released and realigned with the One who calls us to ministry.

3. *Supplying what is lacking.* When the circumstances of life shift around us, we need our faith to be built up through the encouragement of others. This building up takes many forms. Ministries traditionally associated with pastoral care—hospital visitation, bereavement counseling, and crisis intervention—are all focused on supplying what is lacking.

An anxious member is riddled with fear while awaiting surgery. The equipper—faith builder and hope creator—supplies faith by pointing him to the loving God, who is present and who gave his life for him. People who have lost a beloved one need to know they are not alone and have not been abandoned by God. The equipper is the sacramental presence of Christ conveying that they will never be left or forsaken. For example, the person whose world has been torn apart by divorce needs the stabilizing hope that says there is life beyond this pain. Hope is incarnated when we say, "I'll stay with you and see you through this." At St. John's this ministry is not simply carried out by a pastor designated to cover all these bases; rather, he has equipped a pastoral care team. This team intervenes at the point of trauma, and then stays with that person to either full restoration or, tragically, death.

The ministries associated with mending and restoring have traditionally been the province of ordained pastors. Churches have hired pastors to take care of them as if this ministry were an end in itself; the pastor has been to the church what a doctor is to a hospital. But we must realize that this ministry is not that. The focus should be on wholeness so that people can become effective ministers. People are put back together again so that they can be useful channels in God's service. We are not trying simply to create *happy* people who feel better about themselves, but *whole* people who build up the body of Christ and bring the message of salvation and the witness of compassion to a broken world.

Mending/restoring is to the end of body ministry, not simply a context where pastors feel useful.

ESTABLISH/LAY FOUNDATIONS

Figure 6.3

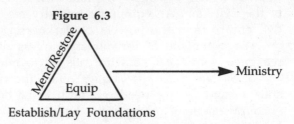

Establish/Lay Foundations

The second major focus of equipping concerns laying solid foundations in Christ. The biblical images related to laying foundations evoke strength: fixed, immovable, established, unshakable, solid, not tossed to and fro, unwavering, and firmly planted. The Psalms convey these images through nature, military might, and unswerving faith. The heavenly lights remain *fixed* and *established* in their place, therefore day and night are predictable daily events (Ps. 74:16). God erects a protective wall against the enemies of Israel, for "he has *founded* a bulwark [impregnable wall] because of thy foes" (Ps. 8:2). David describes his unswerving confidence in God even in the midst of violent people who have no regard for his God: "My steps have *held fast* to thy paths, my feet have not slipped" (Ps. 17:5).

1. *Jesus Christ, the True Foundation.* It should not surprise us that when we come to lay firm foundations, Jesus Christ himself is described as the Head Equipper. In the benediction to the book of Hebrews, Jesus Christ is presented as the One who directly equips and provides the resources necessary to do his will. "Now may the God of peace, who brought again from the dead our Lord Jesus . . . *equip* you with everything good that you may do his will, working in you that which is pleasing in his sight, through Jesus Christ" (Heb. 13:20–21). Christ himself, who dwells in us and mediates his life through us, prepares and makes us suitable to accomplish the particular will he has for us. This invokes the prevalent New Testament theme that there is only *one foundation* that can be laid in our lives, "which is Jesus Christ" (1 Cor. 3:11). So Christ is both our foundation and our equipper.

Peter makes a related point when he writes to Christians

suffering terrible persecution. They are living under a reign of terror to the point where the Devil is described as a "roaring lion ready to devour." When the ground shakes, our feet can easily slip. So Peter comforts the believers with these words: "And after you have suffered a little while, the God of all grace who has called you to his eternal glory in Christ, will himself *restore*, establish and strengthen you" (1 Peter 5:10). It is God himself through Christ who will set his people on their feet and strengthen them for service.

This raises the question, what is the relationship of human equippers to Jesus Christ, the Head Equipper and the only sufficient and sure foundation? How can pastors and Jesus Christ both be equippers at the same time? I like the answer that R. Paul Stevens gives in his book *Liberating the Laity*.

> Their [human equippers'] major function is not to make people dependent upon the leaders but dependent upon the Head. This is the highest possible calling. It requires the strongest possible leadership in the church to lead people in such a way that they do not become dependent on the human leaders. . . . Equipping, directing people to find their life and future in Christ Himself, makes the highest claim on leadership.[5]

The equippers God gives to the body must constantly be pointing to the all-sufficient Christ, to whom each member of the body is directly connected. It is appropriate to review one aspect of the church as organism. "Christ is the Head of the church" is not a theological platitude; it is the only way the church can be the church. Each member of the body is directly connected to the Head and therefore receives orders directly from the Head. Stevens notes, "The head does not tell the hand to tell the foot what to do. The head is directly connected to the foot."[6] So every part needs to stay connected to the Head. Every part must take full responsibility for its proper functioning. The role of human equippers is to promote that connectedness with the Head and consequently with the rest of the body, the church.

2. *The Word of God, Inherent Power.* Along with Jesus Christ as both our foundation and the builder on it, the written Word of God is fundamentally connected to establishing and laying foundations in a believer's life. Scripture in fact has an essential role in the equipping ministry generally, as we discover in the well-known New Testament passage on the inspiration and authority of Scripture, 2 Timothy 3:16–17: "All Scripture is inspired by God and profitable for teaching, for reproof, for

correction, and for training in righteousness, that the person of God may be complete [*artios*], equipped [*exertismenos*] for every good work." As a friend has said, "The Word of God not only informs, it performs." The Word of God plays a vital part in equipping in several ways:

a. Teaching—Creating a new worldview rooted in the new reality of the death and resurrection of Jesus Christ. (Laying foundations)

b. Reproof—Confronting the sinfulness in our lives and setting us on the right course. (Mending/Restoring)

c. Correction—Exposing false teaching and reestablishing the only foundation, Jesus Christ. (Mending/Restoring)

d. Training in righteousness—Walking morally upright with heart, mind, and spirit harnessed in devotion to God. (Laying foundations)

The goal or outcome of this work of God's Word is to make us "complete" so that we are "equipped for every good work." "Complete" does not convey "perfection" (KJV), but merely the suitable requirement for the task, readiness for the job. "Complete" means that we are prepared or enabled to do the ministry (good works) God has for us. The use of the perfect passive tense (*exertismenos*) means that the Word of God acts upon us at a point in the past and continues to affect us in the present, empowering us for every good deed.

Just as we asked the question, What is the human equipper's relationship to the Head Equipper, Jesus Christ, we need to ask, What is the human equipper's relationship to the inspired Word? When we examine the four gifted ones who are to equip the saints for ministry in Ephesians 4:11, note that they have in common the different ways they wield the word of God. The use of God's Word varies according to the particular equipper's function. Ray Stedman proposes that the role of these gifted individuals is analogous to a life support system of the human body.[7]

a. The *apostles* are to the church what the skeletal system is to the human body. The human body needs a frame on which to hang all its parts; otherwise there is no structure, but a mass of quivering organs. So the apostles spoke revelation that became the framework of truth recorded in the New Testament.

b. The *prophet's* message is meant to quicken and activate the body to faithfulness, just as electrical impulses are passed through the nervous system to stimulate each bodily part to act appropriately.

c. The *evangelist* can be compared to the digestive system, since it is the responsibility of evangelism to take in new life (food) and change it into a form that renews the body. The evangelist's passion is to carry the word of the gospel to those who are perishing and to see lives redirected to Christ and incorporated into the body.

d. The *pastor-teacher* is akin to the circulatory system, since his call is to make sure food and oxygen get to all the cells of the body and waste is removed. The pastor-teacher helps feed and cleanse the body by accurately teaching God's Word and by providing such an atmosphere of love for God's Word that God's people feed themselves through their own study.

3. *Modeling, the Incarnational Way.* Human beings are the filter through which the Word of God incarnate and the Word of God written come to us. People are the ongoing embodiment of Christ and the written Word. In God's design, the means by which he affects people's lives is fallible models. God's approach is fundamentally incarnational. He showed himself in a person. He continues to show himself through the vehicle of people in whom he dwells.

We can say, therefore, that the Lord's basic teaching method is modeling. "A disciple is not above his teacher, but everyone when he is fully *taught* [equipped] will be like his teacher" (Luke 6:40). Christian maturity does not result from the accumulation of head knowledge. Reflecting the rabbinic educational model, Jesus believed that a teacher's role was to model, or be an example in his life of what the students were expected to learn. A rabbi was said to be "the living Torah." Students were to copy every aspect of a rabbi's life. The extremes of a student's attempt to model his teaching could get humorous. An overzealous disciple was caught under the bed of his rabbi as he settled in with his wife for the evening. We imitate (model) Jesus Christ by being living letters of the Word of God.

The three aspects of establishing and laying solid foundations are (1) Jesus Christ, the true foundation, (2) the Word of God, inherent power, and (3) modeling, the incarnational way. Let's now go back through each of these categories in order to see how they translate into specific ministries of equipping.

Jesus Christ, the True Foundation

At the heart of an equipping church is worship. Worship defines the church's reason for being and is the constant reminder that every member is directly connected to the Head. The depth of the people's sense of call to ministry will be in direct proportion to their encounter with the Head of the church each time the church gathers. It is the responsibility of the worship leaders to uphold the living, reigning Christ. It is the responsibility of God's people to get themselves ready each Sunday to exalt Christ, place their lives at his disposal through confession, and be open to the Word proclaimed so that they are invigorated for ministry. The equipping congregation will put a high priority on a thoughtful, prayerfully planned, and focused worship experience where the Word of God is clearly and powerfully expounded and applied to the particular needs and challenges to discipleship facing the particular congregation and community.

Planning the order of worship has a high priority on my weekly schedule. Each service is carefully crafted around a one-sentence theme statement and an attribute of God closely related to the theme. For example, as I write this chapter, the worship service now being planned is organized around the truth that "the church is to reflect the oneness that exists already between the members of the Godhead." The attribute of God that serves as our focal point is "we worship the Triune God—the model of unity."

Each week I present a rough draft of the service to a planning group made of the pastoral staff and music leaders. We then creatively shape the service through broad discussion and prayerfully recruit worship leaders based on our knowledge of what they particularly have to contribute to the unique experience of this worship event. Each worship experience has a distinctive flavor. This creates a sense of newness and anticipation in the worshipers. Also provided a week ahead is a devotional guide that is the preaching content for next week's service. God's people come prepared with the scriptural focus already on their hearts. Worship is not pulled out of people, but it flows out because people have already put something in.

The Word of God, Inherent Power

The written Word of God that points to Jesus Christ is central to both formal and informal gatherings of God's people. Formally, it is right to make provision for people to "sit under" the teaching and proclamation of the Word. God has gifted and set apart prophets whose passion for truth energizes the body to faithfulness. Prophetic preachers keep a community of believers stirred up, having to confront truth in the context of the spirit of the times.

There must also be formal structures for teachers to explain and fill in the whys and wherefores of the breadth of the biblical message. In the image of an orchestra, prophets have been compared to the trumpeters who sound a clear note, whereas teachers are analogous to the violin section that fills out the sound. Teachers who can open the Word and make it live need a place to exercise their gift among hungry people. The teaching ministry of the equipping church is never satisfied with mere information, but teaches for transformation in Christ. Larry Richards says, "We don't want a truth system, but a reality system approach."[8]

Informally, foundations are laid in God's Word as people "sit around" the Word of God. The Bible in Protestant tradition is the "book of the people." It is sufficiently clear for people to gather around it and seek to understand and discern its message individually and corporately. A basic structure for equipping is the small group, allowing face-to-face encounter before the Word of God. Often the method of study in these types of groups is inductive, meaning that people are guided through a mutual investigative process by a series of questions that unlock the meaning of the passage and then apply this meaning in specific ways to their lives.

Those who equip by establishing and laying foundations hold the person of Christ before the community. They have a facility and passion to feed people with God's Word. Paul's letter to the Galatians expresses the equipper's heart: "My little children, for whom I am again in the pains of childbirth until Christ is formed in you, how I wish I could be with you now" (Gal. 4:19–20 NIV).

Modeling, the Incarnational Way

Another approach to laying foundations that I believe is fundamental to people's coming to full stature in Christ is *discipling*. I am using "discipling" in a narrow and technical sense. I have written elsewhere, "Discipling is the process of intentional modeling whereby God uses us to exhort, correct and build up a disciple(s) in love in order to produce maturity in Christ. This includes equipping the disciple to do the same unto a third generation."

One essential way to see solid foundations laid is through long-term investment of life into life. Ninety percent of believers have never had someone take them under their wing and make sure that the basic disciplines, doctrines, character qualities, or ministry issues have been inculcated in their lives. This occurs when someone invests himself in the life of another to guide him into the breadth of the new life in Christ.[9]

PREPARE/TRAIN

Figure 6.4

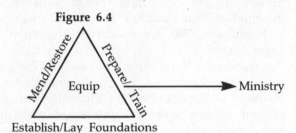

Establish/Lay Foundations

To examine the last leg of the triangle it will be helpful for us to recall the Greek secular use of the term "equip." We have already seen that "equip" was used in a medical context to refer to the setting of a broken limb or realigning a limb wrenched out of joint. In relation to artistry and craftsmanship, "to equip" meant to work with the hands to produce something useful or beautiful. Ephesians 4:12 has a product in mind. Those with support gifts are to "equip the saints for the work of ministry." In other words, people are to find out what their aptitudes and abilities are for ministry as the equippers exercise their gifts. This implies that particular training will be needed to prepare people to exercise ministry in the body and to the world. Refining skills and practicing tools will be essential for a prepared ministry.

This leads us back to an opening thought of the chapter. Why do pastors attend seminary and receive professional training? Is it so they can be set apart as a class and then exercise their gifts on a passive body? No! The professional training is to be given away to the body so that people can be empowered to carry out the body's ministry. Pastors are equipped in seminary so they can give away the ministry. If it is true that all ministry is body ministry, then every area traditionally associated with pastoral ministry—with the possible exception of preaching—can be performed by duly gifted and called members of the body. The pastor's role, therefore, is not to do the body's ministry, but to build teams of people to share the ministry in the different aspects of the pastor's giftedness.

1. *Spiritual gifts-oriented church.* All people have been given ministry abilities by the Holy Spirit, but few know what they are. Therefore the church needs to provide ongoing opportunities for the members of the body to discover their ministries and receive training in the specialized skills to carry them out. For the body to operate under the leadership of Christ, people need a spiritual gifts consciousness. Only when people are self-motivated caretakers of their gifts will the body have the dynamism of an organism under the direct supervision of Jesus Christ.

2. *Call.* All Christians have not only spiritual gifts, but also particular spheres toward which they are directed to focus their gifts. For example, a person with the gift of administration does not automatically know what should be the sphere in which this gift operates. Finding the particular context for the exercise of the gift is the call of God upon his life at this time. This concept is addressed at greater length in chapter 10.

3. *Specialized training.* An equipping church is a training center. Just as small, untrained children will not be able to read without instruction, people should not just be told to do ministry, but be given training in the particular skills. For example, in St. John's, small-group leaders function as pastors for five to twelve people. To be a small-group leader, a certain, minimum amount of formal and practical training is required.

In summary, what do we mean when we say that a pastor's fundamental role is to be an equipper? T. H. Thayer notes that equipping is "to make one what one ought to be."[10] Ray Stedman in contemporary terms says that equippers are to "shape up the saints."[11] In other words, equippers prepare, complete, put in order, and make ready for service the people of God.

What image best captures this new role for the pastor? Elton Trueblood poses a number of options while stating the limitations of each:[12]

1. *Minister?* No, we have already said this is a term for the whole body, not a few.

2. *Elder?* This term narrowly focuses on the position of rule and oversight, neglecting the equipping function.

3. *Pastor?* This image certainly captures the tender, protective, shepherding relationship, but also misses the equipping role.

Some twenty years ago Trueblood proposed that we view the role of pastor as equipper through the accessible, modern image of "player-coach."[13] This image suggests immediately that there is one team of which we are all a part, and the pastor has the role of helping people know and develop their places on the team. "The glory of the coach," writes Trueblood, "is that of being the discoverer, the developer, and the trainer of the powers of others." But as coach he is not just on the sidelines shouting instructions. As "player-coach" he is in the fray along with God's people.

John Stott sums up well the burden of this chapter. On the significance of Ephesians 4:11–12, he writes,

> The New Testament concept of the pastor is not of a person who jealously guards all ministry in his own hands, and successfully squashes all lay initiatives, but of one who helps and encourages all of God's people to discover, develop and exercise their gifts. His teaching and training are directed to this end, to enable the people of God to be a servant people, ministering actively but humbly according to their gifts in a world of alienation and pain. Thus, instead of monopolizing all ministry himself, he actually multiplies ministries.[14]

NOTES

1. Elton Trueblood, *The Incendiary Fellowship* (New York: Harper & Row, 1967), 41.

2. *Book of Order*, published by United Presbyterian Church in the U.S.A.: 1982–83.

3. Trueblood, *The Incendiary Fellowship*, 41.

4. Ray Stedman, *Body Life* (Glendale, Calif.: Regal, 1972), 81.

5. R. Paul Stevens, *Liberating the Laity* (Downers Grove, Ill.: InterVarsity Press, 1985), 37.

6. Ibid., 36.

7. Stedman, *Body Life*, 70ff.

8. Lawrence D. Richards, *Creative Bible Teaching* (Chicago: Moody Press, 1970), 51.

9. Greg Ogden, *A Disciple's Guide for Today* (Self-published, 1987), 15.

10. T. H. Thayer, as quoted by Ray Stedman in *Body Life*, 82.

11. Stedman, *Body Life*, 82.

12. Trueblood, *The Incendiary Fellowship*, 42.

13. Ibid., 43.

14. John R. W. Stott, *The Message of Ephesians* (Downers Grove, Ill.: InterVarsity Press, 1979), 167.

CHAPTER 7

Implementing the Equipping Model of Ministry

IN DEFINING THE ROLE of the pastor in the New Reformation, I have compared the dependency model of ministry with the equipping, or interdependency, model. The dependency model views pastors as the performers who enact "real" ministry, while God's people are the audience who passively write reviews of the actors' efforts. This model is the natural extension of an institutional theology of the church that defines ministry from the starting point of its ordained, or set-apart, leadership. But if we begin with the church as organism and view ministry as what the whole body is called to do, then the pastor is not the only one who does "real" ministry; instead, he readies the body for full service. This makes the pastor's role intrinsically dignifying, according to Elton Trueblood. The pastor as equipper is "to watch for underdeveloped powers, to draw them out, to bring potency to actuality in human lives."[1]

To implement this model will require a transformation in a pastor's self-understanding and in the same degree a different set of congregational expectations of the pastor's function and of itself. In this chapter I will follow the same format I used in chapter 5, defining the equipping model under two headings: (1) the pastor's view of self, and (2) the congregation's view of the pastor.

THE PASTOR'S VIEW OF SELF

Personal Issues Facing the Equipping Pastor

1. *Be willing to pay the price of change.* Fear of the price to be paid is often the reason we are long on talk and short on substance

in implementing the equipping ministry. The changes I advocate in the pastoral role will move a pastor into behavior that is generally contrary to the congregation's expectations. Confronting these expectations will precipitate scrutiny of a pastor's motivation for ministry.

As public figures, we pastors have learned to receive our strokes by accommodating the expectations of *our* people. We frantically attempt to cover all the bases by getting to the hospital, social functions, and committee meetings because we do not want to disappoint people. We dread congregational murmurings: "He's not doing the job." "She's lazy." "What do we pay him for?" As long as we are controlled by a motivation to please those whose expectations have been nurtured by the dependency model, the equipping ministry will be reduced to nice platitudes.

Because as I have stated, God's people find their place in relation to the projected role model of the pastor, it must be the pastor who leads the congregation into equipping ministry. Because people resist change, the pastor needs to be prepared to take the brunt of resistance and criticism. Criticism such as "why doesn't the pastor do more home visitation?" or "why didn't he attend our committee meeting?" must be seen up front as a price to be paid. Are we willing to experience short-term pain for long-term gain in ministry? The truth is, we cannot be equipping pastors and dependency pastors at the same time. We cannot simultaneously invest ourselves in developing the ministry of a few and keep all the plates spinning. We must decide what we believe: are we convinced that for the sake of the long-term health of the church of Jesus Christ, interdependency is the right model?

If our answer is yes, then the word "no" will become an important part of our vocabulary. It will be a no said graciously and winsomely, but a no nonetheless. This no is said to requests to fulfill the expectations of the dependency model of ministry in order to say yes to efforts that multiply the ministry of the body. The events related in Acts 6:1–6 illustrate this no to dependency ministry. A quarrel arose in the early church between the Hebrew- and Greek-speaking widows. The Jews of the Diaspora who were in Jerusalem on the Day of Pentecost responded to the gospel proclaimed in their regional tongues. These Hellenist converts remained in Jerusalem as an integral part of the new community. Ethnic tensions arose. The Greek-speaking widows felt they were being slighted in the daily distribution of the food supply in comparison with the Hebrew women.

This dispute was brought to the attention of the apostles. The apostles were no doubt tempted to handle the problem by adding the supervision of the daily distribution to their job description. They might have thought, "What better way to exemplify our Lord's model of servanthood than to wait on tables?" But that was not their solution. They realized that as meaningful a role as this was, it lay outside the particular realm in which they were called to serve the body. The apostles said a gracious no. "It is *not* right that we should give up preaching the word of God to serve tables. . . . But we will devote ourselves to prayer and to the ministry of the word" (Acts 6:2, 4). Serving tables was not beneath them. But this service did not best use their gifts. They were called to preach the Word of God and to pray for the body. Others in the body were called to serve the widows, just as others today need to be called to serve and thus multiply ministry.

The apostles' solution to the dispute enlarged the ministry of the church. The apostles did not keep it all for themselves. Instead, they called forth others within the body appropriately qualified to handle this important function of serving tables. "Therefore, brethren, pick out from among you seven men of good repute, full of the Spirit and of wisdom, whom we may appoint to this duty" (Acts 6:3). The apostles dignified ordinary members of the body with significant ministry and fully believed God would empower them to carry it out. This also became a way of affirming those who were ethnically disenfranchised in that the community selected people with Greek names to supervise the daily distribution of food (Acts 6:5).

This action left the apostles wide open to accusations that they were not doing their duty. But they were willing to pay the price of criticism. And what could have been a cause for fallout was actually received as the wisdom of God. "And what they [the apostles] said pleased the whole multitude" (Acts 6:5). The only thing the early church knew was ministry of the whole body.

At this point you may be thinking, "Yes, but—. " In your mind's eye you may be seeing Mrs. Walker complaining, "Pastor, how come you do not come to see me very often?" or the finance committee informing you of its next meeting. The underlying message is that your presence is essential. "Too many people will be disappointed," you think.

Let me suggest a starting point that I believe will decrease your loneliness and win converts to your side. If I were going into a new church or wanting to shift a model of ministry, I would begin the change with the leadership board of the church. The leadership body is the entity to which the pastor is directly accountable, and it shares with the pastor the care and oversight of the congregation.

Before you shift to an equipping model of ministry, enlist your leadership as members of the team who share your vision. Lay out a plan of a yearlong biblical and theological study and dialogue with the governing body on the nature of the equipping model. Special attention should be given to the changing role of pastor in relation to God's people. The leadership body should be fully prepared to act as a buffer for the pastor when criticism arises from the congregation. The leaders of the church then have the role of supporting and interpreting the pastor's ministry to the congregation.

Almost from the first day of my ministry at St. John's I began to share with Grant, a leader on the board of elders, my heartfelt conviction that all God's people are called to ministry. Weekly meetings cemented a bond between us. I watched Grant catch my vision for an equipped and released people. Out of the hours we invested in each other came a number of opportunities to be partners in ministry. In November 1985 we offered a sermon together entitled "Called to the Ministry." I will never forget his words of encouragement and exhortation as I strode to the pulpit: "Greg, preach the New Reformation!" A jolt of energy surged through my body. It truly felt as if the Holy Spirit were ushering in a new day and we were simply tools in his life-giving work.

Another result of our time together was Grant's initiative to create the Laos (Greek for "people of God") Commission. This commission was charged with the responsibility to be a steward of the New Reformation vision and to provide for the proper use of the human resources in the church. One event this commission has sponsored is an annual "Minister's Faire." On this day the whole body celebrates its ministry by each component displaying its work out in the church yard. In a festive atmosphere people have an opportunity to find out where they fit in ministry.

So there is a price to be paid by pastors in changing to interdependent ministry. First, pastors must be prepared for the accusation that they are not doing their job. Second, they must invest themselves in the church leadership and share the vision of equipping ministry with them. And third, they need to reinforce repeatedly from the pulpit the essentials of what they are committed to in ministry. One Sunday as I introduced my sermon topic, I jested with the congregation, "You know I have only one tune that I sing. Today's sermon is simply verse ten of the same song." We laughed together, and people immediately understood that this morning was going to be a further variation on the theme of an all-people ministry and the pastor's empowering role.

These are some of the costs. Before we begin, we must ask ourselves, "What price am I willing to pay?" Pastors will revert to the traditional pastoral role if they are not prepared to resist the forces that keep the church an anemic, top-heavy body.

2. *Accept limitations in giftedness as a blessing from God.* I have urged that pastors reflect with their church leadership on the biblical and theological foundations for equipping. One practical and liberating result of this reflection could be to write a job description for the pastor or pastors that would define the equipping role. This will require that the leadership body have a realistic understanding of the extent and limitations of the giftedness of the pastors. But there is a prior step before the leaders can be good stewards of their gifts; that is, pastors must make a sober self-assessment of their gifts.

Equipping pastors are good to themselves. They have given themselves permission not to have to be able "to do it all." Even the superstars who run the megachurches with seeming ease have learned to play to their strengths and remain focused there. One of the most freeing things pastors can do for themselves is to accept their limitations.

We need to allow ourselves to be finite. I have had to accept the fact that counseling and its related dimensions of healing ministry are simply not a part of my gift profile. Much of the ministry associated with mending and restoring does not match what motivates me. Moreover, I have not been given the commensurate gifts to carry out these activities. I could waste a lot of energy going to seminars and workshops to make me passable in these dimensions. Or I can simply admit to our leadership board that God passed me by as he was distributing these aspects of ministry to others.

When the leaders know the passions of the pastor's heart and the specific tools—the spiritual gifts—God has given to fulfill these passions, then a job description can be written that sets pastors free to pursue "calling." I certainly cannot equip people in every area of a church's ministry. For me to train paracounselors would be about as appropriate as my teaching someone skydiving. But I can help people discover their spiritual gifts and be deployed accordingly; I can also be an instrument to see that solid foundations are laid in discipling relationships and communicate a vision for a transgenerational discipling network; and I can teach and preach from Scripture effectively so that the Word stretches people to take the next steps of growth in discipleship.

So a job description should cover what the pastor's focus of equipping ministry will be. In some circumstances, especially in a solo pastorate, it would also be important to state what the pastor will not do. By delineating the areas of ministry outside the pastor's call, the leadership has a clear agenda for the ministry of the whole body of believers. Jerry Cook writes, "The pastor should be working all the time toward giving away everything that is peripheral to his/her own personal calling."[2]

What is freeing about accepting one's limitations in giftedness is that pastors build their ministry around their strengths. The leadership body will benefit from knowing the particular profile of the pastor so they can be stewards on behalf of God's people. The authoritative impact of one's ministry occurs when people recognize a congruence between a person's gifts and call that is underscored by the character of Jesus Christ evident in that person's life. The body of Christ intuitively "makes room" or confirms the call, as we shall see further in chapter 8.

Accepting limitations in giftedness runs counter to the institutional approach to ministry. In that approach, while urging the members of the church to act as a body of Christ and operate according to their giftedness, we do not allow the same privilege for pastors. Often a pastor's distinctive gifts are not recognized because they are expected to fit into a preconstructed box. The senior pastor's box comes complete with a whole set of expectations. To fit the box one must be a commanding preacher, a visionary leader, an able administrator, the chief pastoral caregiver, and a sensitive counselor. Pastors whose gift mix may only partially fit this box may become terribly overburdened trying to be what they are not. This in turn does not allow God's people to enjoy the actual gifts this pastor brings to them, because he is being judged and disabled by stereotyped expectations. Distortion and frustration are the by-products.

I am persuaded that a job description should be a liberating document, tailored to the unique personalities and strengths of the person who occupies a position. This all begins with a pastor's coming to terms with the limitations of his giftedness and joyfully accepting himself as God has created him. Just as the apostles defined their limits as prayer and preaching and thereby expanded the body's ministry, so pastors' clear statements of their parameters can help the rest of the body know how much they are needed. Consequently the leadership board can share in the ministry and serve as a buffer from criticism that equipping pastors are "not doing their job."

3. *Trust God's people as full partners in ministry.* Trust is an attitude. I have referred to the pastor-friend who told me he could have only two small group Bible studies in the church "because that's all I have time to lead." He explained that he believed laypeople could not be entrusted with the responsibility to "pastor" those in a home Bible study and also that he was fearful of what might take place in the groups if he was not present to assert control. Distrust leads to the need to control.

To trust means to believe in. To trust people with full participation in the ministry means to believe that God's people are worthy of the trust. Trust is rooted in one's theology. I convey to the people with whom I share ministry that I have full confidence in them because I am convinced that they have full access to the Holy Spirit just as I do. One function of an equipping pastor is to help people believe in and seek the Holy Spirit's empowerment for their ministry. People will rise to the level of expectations and begin to view themselves through the eyes of the person who believes in them.

Eric was a Christian young man whom I had invited into a discipling relationship. When we began our weekly meetings with Karl, Eric's attention was divided. He was two years out of college and very much enamored of the business world and the pleasures his salary could bring. He also had an active social life. Yet there remained the tug of Jesus Christ.

After a few months, Eric began to talk of quitting his job in order to travel and "see the world" while he was still young. He had dreamed for some time of a six-to-eight-month excursion through Europe or elsewhere. I challenged him to settle in one place for at least a month and to link up with some Christian mission in a cross-cultural setting. As we talked over the next few weeks, I watched Eric move from seeing this trip as a narcissistic adventure to wanting to commit the entire summer to mission work. Eventually he gave up his vagabond ambitions and joined the summer staff of Campus Crusade for Christ in Europe.

The Eric who left the United States and the Eric who returned were two different persons. Every pore of his being was oozing with the passion of Jesus Christ for those who had not heard of him. It all started because I dared help Eric see other possibilities for what he could become. That is God's way. People will rise to the level of expectations. To me, trust means to believe in the people with whom I share ministry more than they believe in themselves and to help them catch God's vision for ministry.

A corollary to believing in God's people is sharing ministry with them. My written goals include the names of people whom I have recruited for training to have a significant ministry role or to direct a ministry. Martin and Debbie were a part of my regular Monday afternoon routine as we shared the leadership of a model training group to equip potential small-group leaders. Besides just enjoying being with them, I saw in them a passion and deep commitment to the value of small groups. They now feel fully prepared to become trainers of new leaders. Moreover, instead of teaching the spiritual gifts workshop by myself, I team-teach it with an elder who is a gifted instructor having particular interest in the gifts.

I have found these ministries to be stronger than ever with this approach. First, I am modeling what I am teaching about shared ministry, which speaks to the congregation as much as my words. Second, those with whom I share ministry sharpen me. I have to be prepared when we meet to plan, therefore I have less tendency to cut corners. Another's perspective opens up fresh insight when I am blinded by my own routine.

Finally, to trust people in ministry means that when we give responsibility, we must also confer authority. If a small-group leader feels that I am constantly looking over his shoulder and ready to pull the rug out from under him when I hear the first complaint from a group member, he cannot achieve his full ministry potential. One way for me to grade my effectiveness as a leader is to examine whether there is an increasing number of self-motivated people carrying out ministry in which I am not directly involved. Once people have been equipped, they need to be released.

Ministry Issues Facing an Equipping Pastor

1. *Small-group structure as a basic building block.* The best and broadest way I know to implement an equipped and mobilized people is through some form of cell or small-group structure. We

first encounter the strategy of small groups as an intrinsic building block in Jethro's advising Moses how to structure the new nation of Israel. There is no clearer model of an equipping pastor's ministry than the role that Jethro counsels Moses to have in relationship to God's people (Ex. 18:13–27).

During the time of the wilderness wanderings, immediately after the exodus of God's people from Egypt, Moses had unhealthily become the focal point of this newly liberated people. He was obviously thrust into the role of the only recognized expert in matters of justice. Moses embodied the dependency-model leader. From morning until evening the people lined up outside Moses' tent to plead their case against their neighbors, expecting Moses to settle every issue.

Enter Jethro, Moses' father-in-law. When Jethro observed the never-ending trail of humanity, he inquired of Moses, "What is this that you are doing for the people? Why do you sit *alone*, and all the people stand about you from morning till evening?" (Ex. 18:14). Moses responded like a true dependency-model pastor, "When they have a dispute, they come to me and I decide between a man and his neighbor, and I make them know the statutes of God and his decisions" (vv. 15–16). Like many pastors today, Moses perceived the role the people wanted him to play, and he lived out those expectations. If Moses were to continue in this fashion, he would always have been the focal point, and the faithful would forever have been reliant on him.

Jethro saw that this was not the way it should be. He told Moses, "What you are doing is not good. You and the people with you will wear yourselves out, for the thing is too heavy for you; you are not able to perform it *alone*. Listen now to my voice; I will give you counsel, and God be with you! You shall represent the people before God, and bring their cases to God; and you shall teach them the statutes and decisions, and make them know the way in which they must walk and what they must do" (vv. 17–20).

Jethro advised Moses that he need not lead this ministry as a lone, isolated figure. If he did, "burnout" was certain. Jethro's advice was to equip the whole nation by being a teacher of God's statutes each time a decision is rendered. Help God's people know the basis in God's Word for settling a dispute so they themselves can apply that principle to their lives. Share what you know with the people so they are educated in God's Word and can make their own decisions.

Then Jethro went into the specific strategy of implementing a shared ministry. "Moreover choose able men from all the people, such as fear God, men who are trustworthy and who hate a bribe; and place such men over the people as rulers of thousands, of hundreds, of fifties, and of tens. And let them judge the people at all times; every great matter they shall bring to you, but any small matter they shall decide themselves; so it will be easier for you, and *they will bear the burden with you*" (vv. 21–22). Jethro's counsel was to break the nation into manageable units and to entrust able people with the administration, oversight, and problem solving that would occur within these subdivisions. Moses was to take the focus of attention off himself, act as an equipper of others who were fully reliable to share the ministry load, and then set them free to do the job to which they were called. Then the burden would be shared, and a team ministry would be implemented. Jethro's plan removed Moses from the role of answer-man and raised up within the nation other leaders to whom the people could look as models of spiritual maturity.

Just as breaking the nation down into smaller units cut across the entire fabric of the life of Israel, so small groups must be viewed as an essential and basic building block of the church today. If small groups are viewed as simply another program on the list of things that successful churches have in their arsenal, we have missed the universal focus of this building block. In the church I serve we have adopted the following principle: "The primary ministry of the church is the worship service, the principal supporting ministry is through small groups." Our conviction is that face-to-face gathering of groups of three to twelve people is an essential component to our discipleship in Christ.

The small-group structure more than anything else has the potential to mobilize the body in ministry. Just as Moses entrusted those subunits in Israel to "able men," so the beauty of small groups is that they are led by equipped members of the congregation who have a call to this ministry and the spiritual gifts to carry it out. This multiplies the number of shepherds in the church and puts the pastor's focus not on being the shepherd to each and every member of the church, but particularly on those who share the shepherding responsibility.

This face-to-face ministry enables God's people to learn to tend to each other and so act as the body of Christ. Since the emphasis in an equipped congregation is not on a multigifted pastor, there needs to be a structure where the multigifted people can be the channels of God's grace gifts. In a small group one may see operating the gifts of teaching, exhortation, mercy, pastoring, prophecy, evangelism, and so on as God's people naturally interact over the study of the Word, share vulnerably their personal walk toward faithfulness in Christ, and intercede for each other to grow into full stature in the Lord.

2. *Discipling: Investment in a few.* The closing chapter in Howard Snyder's book *Liberating the Church* is entitled "Pastors: Free to Disciple." Snyder states that discipling is the primary focus of a pastor's ministry:

> Essentially, the pastor's first priority is to so invest himself or herself in a few other persons that they also become disciplers and ministers of Jesus Christ. It is to so give oneself to others and to the work of discipling that the New Testament norm of plural leadership or eldership becomes a reality in the local congregation. In other words, it is to bring the ministry of *all* God's people to functioning practical reality.[3]

Our Lord's approach to ministry serves as the model for the way we are to do ministry. Integral to Jesus' strategy was to select twelve with whom he would be in close association (Matt. 10:1–4; Mark 3:13–18; Luke 6:12–16). What was Jesus trying to accomplish by selecting a few from the larger entourage that was following him at this time in his ministry? It is estimated that Jesus had been about his public ministry for approximately a year before he clearly identified his inner core. What did Jesus think was going to be so fruitful about this approach that he was willing to risk arousing jealousy from the masses? Why not simply continue to enlarge the crowds and turn his initial popularity into a mass movement?

I believe Jesus accomplished at least two things by this strategy.

a. *Internalization.* Jesus was skeptical about the depth of devotion of the crowd that followed him. The populace was enamored by the miracle-working power of this authoritative teacher. But Jesus read the motives of their hearts. John records the thoughts of Jesus about the crowds: "Now when he was in Jerusalem at the Passover feast, many believed in his name when they saw the signs which he did, *but Jesus did not trust himself to them*, because he knew all men and needed no one to bear witness of man; for he himself knew what was in man" (John 2:23–25). Jesus knew that people were fickle; they were with you one minute and your enemy the next. As soon as the cross became the focus of Jesus' gaze and he began to instruct them in the eventuality of his own sacrifice, the crowd began to lose their infatuation. It was a short five days from Palm Sunday's shouts of "Hosanna! Blessed is he who comes in the name of the Lord!" to Good Friday's "Crucify him! Crucify him!"

Jesus didn't stake his future influence and kingdom on the ground swell of mass support. If he had he would be a footnote in history grouped with other revolutionary leaders squashed under the Roman boot. Instead Jesus had a big enough vision to think small. A. B. Bruce has stated this well in his classic work, *The Training of the Twelve.*

> The careful, painstaking education of the disciples secured that the teacher's influence in this world should be permanent; that the kingdom should be founded on the rock of deep and indestructible convictions in the minds of a few, not on the shifting sands of superficial impressions in the minds of many.[4]

b. *Multiplication.* Jesus' way to reach the multitudes was not to hold ever larger gatherings. His ministry would not have been any more successful if in Scripture we would read of the feeding of the ten thousand or a hundred thousand instead of five thousand. Robert Coleman comments, "His concern was not with programs to reach the multitudes, but with men the multitudes would follow."[5] Eugene Peterson captures this truth humorously: "Jesus, it must be remembered, restricted nine-tenths of his ministry to twelve Jews because it was the only way to reach all Americans."[6]

Jesus' model teaches pastors that one essential way to carry out ministry is to invest in a few who in turn can be equipped to invest in others. This requires vision. It requires vision to think small and to anticipate the long-term impact. In discipling we lay solid foundations in Christ in a systematic way. It entails a view of sanctification that eschews instantaneous maturity. Through discipling, people are empowered to see themselves as channels who can assist others in growing up in Jesus Christ.

In *A Disciple's Guide for Today* I define discipling as "the process of intentional modeling whereby God uses us to exhort, correct, and build up a disciple(s) in love, in order to produce maturity in Christ. This includes equipping the disciples to do the same unto a third generation." Most people do not have the confidence to assist someone toward maturity because they themselves have not been discipled. When teaching about discipling, I have repeatedly asked, "How many of you can point to someone who has acted as an intentional model and guided you through the foundation-laying stages in Christ?" People can identify models from afar or people they have respected, but fewer than ten percent can point to someone who painstakingly gave themselves week in and week out to make sure "that Christ be formed in them" (Gal. 4:19).

Anything worthy to be called "discipling" must be transferable from one generation of believers to the next. A major obstacle to moving from one generation to another is the dependency created in a one-to-one model of discipling. The dynamic itself creates a hierarchy of teacher over student. I have discovered in my discipling that triads are the most powerful context for transformation. One person invites two others into a relationship of mutual accountability for the purpose of exploring what it means to be fully faithful to Christ. This removes the discipler from the spotlight and makes him a member of the group, free to bring the natural impact of life in Christ. An interdependency develops rather than the debilitating hierarchy common in a one-to-one context. In the triad, people enter the discipling process knowing *in advance* that they are being equipped to disciple others and therefore do not enter into an exclusive, unhealthy attachment.

A pastor needs a visionary view of three to five years down the road. As the discipling network multiplies, moving out from the pastor, people will mature into self-motivated, reproducing disciples of Christ. Who wouldn't want to be pastor of a church where the people of God are self-feeders (in the Word and prayer) and self-starters (in using their gifts for ministry)? Again Robert Coleman sharpens the focus: "One must decide where he wants his ministry to count—in the momentary applause of popular recognition or the reproduction of his life in a few chosen ones who will carry on his work after he is gone."[7]

3. *"A gift-evoking and gift-bearing community."* Gordon Cosby, pastor of the Church of the Savior in Washington, D.C., believes the church is to be "a gift-evoking and a gift-bearing community."[8] The phrase "gift-evoking" suggests that a regular part of the church's ministry is calling forth gifts of the Spirit from the members of the body and challenging them to be stewards of those gifts on behalf of the body. The phrase "gift-bearing" implies that when gifts are recognized, the community must make room for them to operate.

a. *Gift-evoking*

(1) Desire. One of the pastor's responsibilities is to motivate and fan the flames of desire for people to discover their gifts and be deployed accordingly. This desire can be stirred within people when they are given a glimpse of how God has fashioned them as creatures with a unique profile of giftedness. When people catch hold of the exhilarating fact of their God-given individuality, the juices of desire begin to flow. Each person, I believe, has been created by God with the inner motivation to make a contribution or have an impact. We want to know the value for which we have been created.

Elizabeth O'Connor tells an apocryphal story in her book *Eighth Day of Creation*. Michelangelo was pushing a large hunk of stone down the street toward his sculpting studio when a neighbor cried out, "Hey, Michel, what are you going to do with that old piece of stone?" Michelangelo replied, "There is an angel in there that wants to come out."[9]

The desire to discover and use spiritual gifts can be accomplished through frequent preaching on that and related subjects. I have preached an eight-week series around such titles as "You Are Gifted," "What a Spiritual Gift Is Not," and a detailed definition of the "support," "speaking," "sign," and "service" gifts. Related preaching such as "the church as the body of Christ," "all people called to ministry," and "the ministry of the Holy Spirit" help people see where spiritual gifts fit into the theology of the church. Consistent prayer should be offered that the Holy Spirit will create a hunger in people to discover their gifts.

(2) Discover. If we are going to stir people up to find their gifts, there should be a strategy in place to funnel those people who are eager to explore the possibilities. The church, as a gift-evoking community, must provide the tools for the discovery process. There are myriad approaches and tools available to implement the discovery process. The strategy I use is a semi-annual "Spiritual Gifts Workshop" held on a Saturday. The workshop covers the essential teaching on the biblical data and includes practical exercises to help people discern their unique profile. I also teach a condensed version in the new members' classes so that people enter the church with the expectation that everyone is a minister in this congregation. Each approach is followed by individual interviews that build on the group sessions and home in on a person's own gifts.

(3) Deploy. Spiritual gifts sometimes find expression in *formal* positions within the church structure while others are expressed *informally* in the natural interchange fostered in the dynamics of service. A person who has the gift of teaching may become a teacher (formal) of a particular class of students. But other gifts are exercised in a natural (informal) process of interaction and therefore go almost unnoticed. Someone with the gift of exhortation may simply, in the course of a small-group discussion, exhort the group not to be so self-focused. The exhorter is exercising a gift, yet not occupying a formal position.

Some churches have computerized systems to assist deployment. Attempting to match people's stated profiles with identified needs can be a massive administrative task. Though some churches have been successful at this, my personal focus has been to target desire and discovery and not to attempt a formal job-placement program. This is consistent with my theology of the church, which says that our Lord, as its head, is perfectly capable of running his body. It is important that each person know his gifts and accept the responsibility of being a good steward of them. In other words, the initiative needs to be on the individual to try to plug into ministry in a satisfying way.

As I mentioned earlier, St. John's Church capitalizes on this assumed desire by holding an annual Minister's Faire. On a Sunday morning after worship the patio bustles with excitement. As people roam the patio inquiring into the opportunities for ministry, they can discover which ones fire their ministry passion. People have the opportunity to browse, converse, and sense in what context their gifts might best be used.

b. *Gift-bearing.* The church is to be an affirming community. Not only are individuals to be responsible for their gifts, but the community must be the stewards of the gifts of one another. I have mentioned that the church's leaders should have a clear understanding of the pastor's gift mix so they can be stewards of their own gifts. The same consciousness must be true among the worshiping community at large. An affirming environment allows God's people to develop and refine the use of their gifts. Permission-giving marks a community moving from a professionally focused to a body-focused ministry. People with identified gifts in teaching will not start out in full command of their materials, teaching techniques, and class presence; a supportive environment encourages fledgling teachers as they stumble, stutter, and stammer into maturity. A spirit of graciousness must pervade a community so as to create an environment of experimentation and risk.

I first encountered Karl as a guarded, self-protected individual. His self-confidence and sense of usefulness to God were at a low ebb as the result of a recent, hurtful situation in another church. Disappointed in himself, he was convinced that he had failed God. For a year we met weekly in a discipling relationship. I watched Karl appropriate the forgiveness of God and develop a heart for discipling others. As our commitment period was coming to a close, Karl expressed a growing intensity to do college ministry. The only trouble was that college ministry did not exist in our church.

As Karl's call grew into unwavering zeal, we made room for his gifts and call by validating his desire to start a college ministry. Karl and I prayed for others to come forward who might share the same vision. As a result, the Lord guided Karl to a couple who also sensed a call to college ministry. I clearly recall the excitement on a summer Sunday morning as this newly formed team read the names of the college students in our community and challenged them to be the foundation for this college ministry. Karl's call had been affirmed. To foster body ministry, the church needs to be a gift-evoking and gift-bearing community.

4. *Preaching: Stoking the fires of ministry.* If the entire body of believers is called to ministry, then the preached Word becomes the fuel necessary to keep an all-people's ministry burning. People in ministry are spending themselves; constant replenishment is necessary. The Word preached is at the heart of the central event—worship—out of which ministry flows.

So often what God's people get in preaching is not logs to keep the fire ablaze, but twigs that are barely enough to keep it flickering. Preaching must be more than an inspirational pep talk that sparks good feelings. Often worship is viewed by God's people as an opportunity to escape from the pressures of real life. People want the sermon to be simply a positive word in the midst of a world that beats on them throughout the week. "Give me something to get through another week and it better not be more than twenty minutes" is often the implicit message a pastor hears. And many preachers accommodate the notion. The sermon becomes a series of inspirational stories wrapped around a Bible passage that has been read, but not seriously dealt with. Well-told stories full of humor or pathos are not sufficient fuel for the fires of ministry.

William Diehl, a committed church member, writes:

Lord knows we desperately need relief after the drudgery and stress of the week. We need to be healed by the power of the Holy Spirit. But is that all the Christian church offers—Band-Aids for the bruises of the past week? Is our congregating Sunday morning as the people of God simply for the purpose of licking our wounds and reminding ourselves that the travail of this world will someday be ended for us in the sweet by-and-by?[10]

An equipping pastor will want to leave people with the power and substance of the Word of God. An equipping ministry is a teaching ministry. The equipper's primary tool is the Word. Paul tells Timothy the inspired Word of God makes us "complete, equipped for every good work" (2 Tim. 3:17). Paul says an elder must be "apt to teach" (1 Tim. 3:2) and to "give instruction in sound doctrine" (Titus 1:9). A style of preaching that focuses people on the inherent power and relevance of the Word and not simply the speaking ability of the preacher or the strength of his personality is essential for equipping.

As pastors we model for God's people our view of the Word every time we preach. If a Scripture passage is read and then set aside or passed over, the implicit message is that pastors think their thoughts and authority are higher than the Word of God. If our illustrations are self-focused or dominate the preaching rather than serve the written text, then the way we say it is more telling than what we say. Some form of text-centered preaching teaches people to become reliant on the Word for their source of authority and for self-feeding.

All this suggests that pastors must put a high priority on preparing to feed God's people. The ministry of prayer and study converge in the preparation time for preaching. Earl Radmacher points out that the Greek word for "scholar" includes *leisureliness* within its range of meanings. If God's people are to be fed in a timely fashion according to the stage of development of the body, then quiet reflection on the Word of God is a necessary part of a pastor's practice. Ruminating on the Scriptures with the unhurried opportunity for meditative prayer is essential for good preaching to bear fruit. More and more pastors are building into their schedules some retreat days for personal renewal. This quiet setting provides opportunity to bring the needs of God's people before the Lord. Protected study and meditation time is not stealing time from ministry—it *is* the ministry.

The repetitive themes of the New Reformation will mark the content of an equipping pastor's preaching. One role of a leader is to keep reminding the church who they are and the principles of ministry that are held in common trust. My sermons constantly reflect the themes that shape the identity of an equipped congregation: (1) all God's people are ministers; (2) the clergy-laity distinction is not biblical; we are one people of God; (3) there is one team; pastors are the coaches, but everyone is in the game; (4) each of us has a call to ministry, and ministry develops spontaneously out of the body because we are all directly connected to the Head.

The equipper uses preaching not only to remind the congregation of shared convictions about ministry, but also to paint visionary pictures of what can be. The pastor keeps alive a creative tension in creating the "gaps." The gap is the difference between what is and what can be. For the preached Word to lead the congregation into a new level of awareness, it needs to be offered in the context of the dynamic whole of the worship experience. Since the order, flow, and focus of worship may vary each week, there is a built-in element of surprise and change. Since worship is not static, there is a sense of anticipation. Visionary preaching in the context of a mood of expectancy can be received and responded to much more readily than it can in an order of worship that lacks differentiation from week to week.

Preaching is not relegated to a decreased role in an equipping congregation. If anything, a decentralized body ministry requires a central focus on the energizing word of God.

5. *Evaluating ministry effectiveness.* A church committed to equipping ministry will evaluate achievement in new terms. The pastoral staff's effectiveness is measured by an ever-increasing involvement of the body in ministry leadership. In other words, what would happen to ministry if the pastor(s) left? Are congregational members in place, fully equipped, and having the vision of particular kinds of ministry? If I left my current congregation, would the discipling network, spiritual gifts emphasis, and small-group ministry carry on? While a pastor is present, he should always be working to turn over areas of ministry to capable people while continuing to be their servant, supporter, encourager, and vision giver. The pastor's task is to bring the body's ministry to its fullness. The criteria for accountability and job performance should be measured commensurately.

6. *Building slowly, building solidly.* If an equipping philosophy

is new to the church, do not try to implement multiple equipping ministries all at once. Select one aspect of equipping like the ones already mentioned and make sure that ministry is on solid footing. This keeps a person from being spread too thin and being overwhelmed by the magnitude of equipping still to be done. This also provides a successful model to point to when other approaches to equipping are to be instituted. You can say to your leadership, "Look at this; this is the kind of ministry to which I am committed." I suggest that the place to begin is with small groups. A successful small-group ministry provides the foundation on which to build all the rest of the equipping ministry.

The whole tenor of equipping ministry is the opposite of flashy. It does not mean that we cannot have an attractive event that appeals to people's desire for pizzazz; it does mean that the real fruit of ministry will occur more in laying solid foundations, training on the job, and consistent follow-up of encouragement. Our culture's infatuation with the instantaneous has affected our view of ministry. But disciples are made through investment, and solid ministries develop over time with constant care. I train small-group leaders through a twelve-to-sixteen-week experience of a small group. Each person in the group has a chance to lead, but only after he or she has spent time with me planning the general flow of the evening. We construct the Bible study together and then the leader-trainee receives positive feedback and helpful suggestions from the other group members. Training people so ministry can expand requires the attitude of building slowly and building solidly.

THE CONGREGATION'S VIEW OF THE PASTOR

If equipping ministry is to be implemented, not only will the pastor need a different view of his role, but the congregation will need to alter their expectations of the pastor and themselves.

Know the Pastor's Gift Mix

Congregations that thrive on a whole-body ministry will release their pastors from unrealistic expectations. Instead of the guilt-producing expectation of omnicompetence, the leadership board will desire to act as stewards of the gifts and call of their pastors. There is nothing more encouraging to a pastor than for the leadership to truly know what creates joy and energy for him in the Lord's service.

A helpful exercise to these ends is to have a pastor write out an ideal job description. This should include the roles, activities, and tasks the person likes most. It should list the spiritual gifts one perceives he has and the particular way these gifts are manifest. A description of the kinds of equipping ministry to which he is drawn would also be helpful. The job description that results should then be shared with the leadership board or personnel committee, who will work with the pastor to devise a job description that is expressive of this specific purpose.

Create a Context for Support and Accountability

I have suggested that the leadership board can be a buffer group between pastors and people. The board would cushion the shocks that are bound to occur in a transition to equipping ministry. The way to identify this buffer group is for each pastor to have a support and accountability group of three to five people. This support group would offer a place where the pastor can articulate the particulars of his ministry and be fully known and appreciated. It would encourage the fulfillment of dreams in ministry wherever they might lead. It would help the pastor to see the hidden potential in his ministry, and it would give feedback as to how his particular strengths manifest themselves. In a sense, this group would hold up the mirror for the pastor's self-reflection.

The support group would also provide accountability to make sure the pastor is being a good steward of his gifts. Is the pastor operating within or outside his giftedness? Stated goals can be monitored or rejected. Accountability is not usually structured into a pastor's work as a regular thing, partly because church members may not feel qualified to evaluate his ministry. But the more the people take up roles previously held only by the pastor, the better equipped they will be for evaluating his ministry.

Receive Mutual Ministry

I believe the biggest change in a congregation's psyche will be to receive authentic ministry from one another. In chapter 4 I told the story of Pastor Jerry Cook's encounter with a disgruntled member who had been hospitalized. Mrs. White was upset because she had been in the hospital seven days and he had not paid a visit. Pastor Cook discovered that during that week an average of four persons a day had come from the church. The trouble was that Mrs. White did not see those visitors as being able to bring the presence of Christ with the same authenticity as the pastor. Only the pastor could bring "real" ministry.

For equipping ministry to reach its full promise, God's people must receive ministry from each other as genuine. It cannot be seen as "secondary" or second rate simply because the pastor is not present. People must come to know that the Holy Spirit is available to press into service the grace-gifts distributed throughout the body.

SUMMARY

Over the first seven chapters of this book, I have compared the impact of the New Reformation to dominoes falling in very different directions than we are used to. The first domino concerns seeing the church as organism from the bottom up versus the church as institution from the top down. The second domino involves a radical shift from a dependency-fostering role for the pastor to an equipping one.

The third and final domino challenges fundamental assumptions about the way we have traditionally conceived leadership. In the next chapter I will propose a way to look at leadership so we do not recreate a priesthood within a priesthood. I will also attempt to identify more objective criteria to measure those whom the body should set apart to be equippers. In chapter 9, "Servant Leadership: Empowering the Body to Its Ministry," I will challenge the generally accepted hierarchical leadership model and argue that servant leadership as modeled by Christ is the style necessary to see the body come alive to its ministry. Finally, our journey will end in chapter 10 with restyling "call" and "ordination" according to an organism view of the church.

NOTES

1. Elton Trueblood, *The Incendiary Fellowship* (New York: Harper & Row, 1967), 41.
2. Jerry Cook, *Love, Acceptance, and Forgiveness* (Glendale, Calif.: Regal, 1979), 106.
3. Howard Snyder, *Liberating the Church* (Downers Grove, Ill.: InterVarsity Press, 1983), 243.

4. A. B. Bruce, *The Training of the Twelve* (reprint, Grand Rapids: Kregel, 1971), 13.

5. Robert Coleman, *The Master Plan of Evangelism* (Old Tappan, N.J.: Revell, 1964), 21.

6. Eugene Peterson, *Traveling Light* (Downers Grove, Ill.: InterVarsity Press, 1982), 182.

7. Coleman, *The Master Plan of Evangelism*, 37.

8. Elizabeth O'Connor, *Eighth Day of Creation* (Waco, Tex.: Word, 1971), 8.

9. Ibid., 13.

10. William Diehl, *Thank God It's Monday* (Philadelphia: Fortress, 1982), x.

PART 3

Leadership in the New Reformation

CHAPTER 8

Who Are the Equippers?

SOME ARE CALLED BY GOD, in Elton Trueblood's words, "to help other men and women to practice any ministry to which they are called."[1] If this is the case, the body of Christ needs to be sensitized to identify the equippers. This chapter addresses two concerns related to this need:

1. How do we conceptualize leadership so as not to fall back into a hierarchical, top-down, institutional frame that creates a two-tiered division? How can we avoid what the Protestant Reformation in theory attempted but in practice was unable to avoid—a priesthood within a priesthood?

2. What criteria will provide a measuring stick for individuals who are pondering a call from God? Since the church is the body of ratification, how do we raise the consciousness of the Christian community so they can identify, affirm, nurture, and deploy from within their ranks the equippers God is raising up?

A FUNCTIONAL CONCEPT OF LEADERSHIP

Let me return to the image that has served as the frame for this book. To keep from creating a two-story church, we must conceive of leadership fundamentally in terms of the church as organism. The New Testament stresses function over form, operation over organization. Paul repeatedly uses functional language to describe the living organism operating under divine endowment. People are graced with the ministry gifts to affect the body. Ministry is not restricted to a professional or official position in the body. Paul focused on behaviors that motivated people instead of on authority structures and official positions.

This is not to say that the New Testament is uninterested in offices and structure. Rather, the key principle is that *function precedes position*. In other words, if authoritative leadership is translated into office, it is done only with the prior recognition that leadership has already been functioning. Office does not create authority, but is the result of authority in evidence. The following formula summarizes, as I see it, the New Testament teaching on the elements necessary for authority:

(1) Gifts/Call (Recognition) + (2) Character of Christ = Authority (Leadership)

The first criteria to identify those set apart to be equippers is the *recognition* by the body that the appropriate spiritual gifts (which we will define) are operating under the unction of the Holy Spirit. The second component essential to Christian authority is a life that reflects the servant character of Christ.[2] When leadership gifts are exercised in a manner consistent with a Christlike character, spiritual authority is the result. Members of the body implicitly validate a person's authority by "making room" for that ministry.

In what practical ways do we identify those who are called into leadership? How are leaders to be discerned in the body, and how is authority given? There is a significant contrast between the function/organism and the form/institution views of leadership.

Authority Is Rooted in the Recognition of Gifts

The starting point for authority is not title, position, office, or rank, but the endowment of the Spirit on one's life. Ideally there should be no conflict between the position one holds and the authority one exercises. David Watson writes, "The church should give official recognition to those in whom the Spirit of God is manifestly at work."[3] Let's turn again to the instructive model for selecting leaders that is recorded in Acts 6:1–6.

The apostles turned the problem of food distribution into an opportunity to recognize other gifted leaders in the body besides themselves. But note who chose the leaders! The apostles gave responsibility to the body to decide who would best serve them. "Therefore, brethren, pick out from among you . . . and they chose . . ." (vv. 3, 5). The church chose seven Greek men "full of the Spirit and of wisdom." Though I assume that the body selected people gifted with administrative skills to handle the relief program, they placed their *imprimatur* on men whom they had already recognized for their godly life and leadership qualities. In like manner, the church body at Antioch set Barnabas and Paul to heed God's call to communicate the gospel message to the Gentiles (Acts 13:1–3).

By contrast, we are aware that occupying an office cannot make up for deficiencies in personal qualities or spiritual gifts. Saul's jealousy turned into an uncontrollable rage against David. Why? The people regarded God's anointing on the new king, David, long before Saul was willing to leave his office. The women sang David's praises, and Saul fumed, "They have ascribed to David ten thousands, and to me they have ascribed thousands; and what more can he have but the kingdom?" (1 Sam. 18:8). Saul's obsession with David's prowess made him unworthy to hold the office of the Lord's anointed. Long before David was officially crowned king, he was anointed by God; but Saul, because of his personal deficiencies, was king in name only.

I have painfully observed the tragedy connected to a person who occupies the office of pastor but does not evoke the authority. Position cannot create one's identity or provide authority. There must be a congruence between person and position. One person I know struggled from day one in his new position because of confusion over what he had to bring to the church. Without a clear sense of the content of his own call or defined guiding ministry convictions, he could not get clarity on the leadership steps to take. A number of the key people in the body sensed this man's confusion and therefore had difficulty submitting to his authority, which to them appeared only positional. When there is an evident disjunction between person and position, chaos reigns in the body, as it did in Israel during Saul's latter days.

Authority is not derived from office, but bestowed from above. There could be no clearer model for this than our Lord himself. Julian Charley writes,

> The authority of Jesus during his public ministry was not an assumed role. It stemmed from the reality of who he was. When he spoke, it was recognized to have the ring of truth and the authority of God. When he healed or performed miracles, it was recognized that this was the finger of God. When he prayed, it was clear that here was a uniquely intimate relationship with God. . . . Yet his ministry all along had been one of sacrificial service and humility. Now this should be the pattern of

authority in the church, but the underlying principle has far too often been forgotten.[4]

Sadly, what we often observe in church structures is an inverse relationship between spiritual and institutional authority. When the new life of the Spirit is not being spontaneously generated from within the organism, there is a power vacuum. Anointed leaders are replaced by managers. Authority shifts from empowerment from on high to the centralization of institutional structure. There ensues the pitiful attempt to resurrect life from dry bones of institution through restructuring. The endless shuffling of committees and agencies should, it is thought, spontaneously release life. When dead institutionalism replaces the dynamics of organism authority, leaders with an institutional mindset demand that their constituents pledge allegiance to the organization. A dead institution is a skeleton bound together by wires, not sinew and muscle, flesh and blood.

We cannot do without authority. When spiritual authority is absent, it is replaced by the dry bones of bureaucratic centralization. Authority needs to be rooted in the recognition of gifts.

Authority Is Tested in the Crucible of the Body

The body of believers out of which one is called is the gatekeeper for its leaders. The community of believers ratifies or gently refutes the sense of inner call. Edmund Clowney writes, "Therefore no Christian can determine his calling in isolation from the throbbing organism in which he is called."[5] We can give a person a battery of tests to determine whether the gifts are present for ministry, but the validity of the tests can only be confirmed in doing ministry. Siegfried Schatzmann, writing about the relationship between gifts and authority, quotes Ernst Käsemann: "As charisma is only manifested as genuine in the act of ministry, so only he who ministers can have authority and that only in the actual experience of his ministry."[6] In other words, authority is not given through office, but demonstrated through action.

Once I was caught up short by a respected colleague—the youth pastor—who pointed out that I was living inconsistent with my stated views. I shared ministry with this gifted man. He clearly has a passion for Scripture, a desire to live in conformity to it, and an ability to explain its meaning in a winsome and disarming fashion. In a pointed letter to me, he said (paraphrased), "Of all the people on staff, you have trumpeted the cause that we don't need the official sanction of ordination to operate in the realm of our gifts and authority. Why then have you not gone to bat to provide me preaching opportunities when I have demonstrated abilities that have been confirmed in the body?" I could only admit it was an obvious inconsistency between my stated theology and my practice. His message to me was that for the church to be the gatekeepers, he had to have opportunities for his call to be tested in the crucible of ministry.

What some denominations have done is to bypass the local body as the place to confirm calling. Instead they have divorced authority from the community and have placed it further up in the hierarchical structures of the church. The procedure in my denomination tragically minimizes the place of the origin of call in the confirmation process. It seems that all a person needs is the personal, inward call of God, what Calvin termed the "secret" call. (It is called "secret" because the heart of a person is not open to the witness of the church, but is known only to that individual's conscience before God.) A person discloses this sense of "inner" call by making his desire to pursue vocational ministry known to the ruling body, which in turn sponsors him to the next highest level.

Thomas Gillespie, formerly a pastor and now president of Princeton Theological Seminary, has written about the ironic inconsistency that exists between the way we in our denomination select elders and deacons in contrast to pastors. Church nominating committees survey a congregation, prayerfully considering elders and deacons on the basis of godly qualities as recognized by the body. By contrast, we wait for pastors to step forward with a sense of inner "call" and assume they are right. Seldom do we survey the congregation for those who are called to equipping leadership, nor do we often provide opportunities to test gifts and cultivate ministry.

Instead of assuming that the best place to test calling is in the nurturing body, the church, we send people off to seminary and expect the test and refinement of a calling to happen there. In fact, seminaries are not the best place for this to occur, because the test shifts from a functionally demonstrated ministry in a church to academic criteria in a seminary. Passing the right courses and applying this knowledge to an academically oriented ordination exam is central to the requirements of many denominations. It is as if we expect that during seminary the *charisma*—"the gift"—

needed for ministry will be bestowed as a result of theological study. In fact, we have reversed the biblical process. Too often, people are trained for imposed leadership roles rather than being trained because they have already been identified as having an equipping function in the body of nurture.

The irony is that the final step in the development of calling is to receive "a call" (job offer) from a church that barely knows the candidate. The calling body hopes this unproven, fledgling pastor will bear fruit. How contrary this is to the New Testament model! Leadership was nurtured within the body the people served, in order to serve the body from which they came. David Watson writes, "In the early church the leaders were nearly always appointed from the area in which they served. They had the advantage of knowing the local scene intimately, and were therefore naturally placed for fulfilling an effective pastoral and preaching ministry according to the gifts given to them by God."[7]

The calling of a pastor transplanted from one locale to another is analogous to grafting skin from one body to another. Often the skin graft does not take and is rejected by the body. The reasons for a new pastor's failing to "take" are myriad. For some the cultural leap from one setting to another is greater than anticipated. Even within the United States there are enormous differences in the cultural milieu from the South to the Midwest to Southern California to New England. In the interview process both parties are putting on their best face. What you see may not be what you get. Gaining and giving accurate information in the highly competitive atmosphere of a beauty contest creates illusion, not reality. This process has led to a failure rate of about fifty percent in matches made between pastors and congregations in my denomination.

We have established such enormous institutional constraints in my denomination that it is almost impossible for someone to become ordained to serve in the body in which their calling was given birth. Between the high rate of mobility and the institutionalizing of the church through layers of regulations (e.g., no associate can become senior pastor in the church in which he serves), homegrown leadership is extinct in the denomination. We need somehow to restore the local church as the place where leadership gifts are identified, nurtured, and deployed. Authority is tested in the crucible of the church.

Authority Is Given Official Recognition in Ordination

Authority is not conferred by ordination. Ordination is the body's formal acknowledgment of authority already exercised and a setting apart of that person to serve *among* and *for* the people. Ordination is a necessary rite of passage to protect against those who would exercise the office of pastor falsely. If the institutional dimension of office takes priority over function, ordination in the minds of both pastor and people often means to be "set apart *from* and *above*." (Ordination will be examined in chapter 10.)

In an organic understanding of the church, authority for ministry originates in the sovereign God who graces a person with gifts that are confirmed through ministry in and by the body. This affects our conception of ordination. It is *charisma* that leads to office. Office is a confirmation of *charisma*.

Figure 8.1

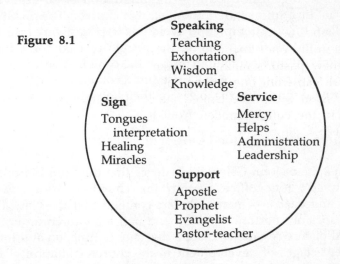

The circle represents the one people (*laos*) of God. Among a set-apart people there are those who have the important function-al distinction of helping the rest of the body reach their potential for ministry. Therefore, instead of being set apart *from* and *above*, the equippers are set apart *among* and *for* the people they serve. Ordination does not convey a sense of transcendence, but of being a minister to the ministers.

Michael Harper observes,

The Church can only authorise those whom God has author-
ised, and can only recognize those whom God has gifted and
empowered. No amount of theological training or human
pressure can bestow *charisma* on a person. It is the sole gift of
God, who gives it sovereignly to whom he wills, and when he
wills. . . . The Church is utterly dependent on the Holy Spirit,
and without *charisma*, however learned ministers may be,
however dedicated and however many of the right hands have
been laid on them, their work will be a failure. Much of the
Church has yet to learn what this means, and its failure to
honour the Holy Spirit is one of the main reasons why it has
ceased to grow. The charismatic dimension is a crucial factor in
the renewal of the ministry of the Church today.[8]

I have been attempting to answer the question, How can we
conceive of the role of leadership in the body without reverting to
the mentality of a split-level church? The Reformation was not able
to break free from a hierarchical conception because it attempted
to graft an organism doctrine—the priesthood of all believers—
onto an institutional definition of the church. The institution
prevailed. I have attempted to avoid this trap by giving priority to
function and *charisma*. Among the people of God some have a
functional call to leadership based on the combination of gifts and
call and the quality of life in Christ, just as others of the body have
their role defined on the basis of their gifts from God.

Call/Gifts Necessary for Leadership

In spite of John Calvin's insistence that the Lord himself had
"instituted" four offices within the church—pastor, teacher,
elder, and deacon—many scholars contend that the New Testament does not portray a unified and uniform church order.[9] The
biblical picture resembles more a diversity of function and form at
different stages of development in the church community. Form
had great flexibility in order to accommodate the function of the
body organism. This truth points up the difficulty of moving from
the organism nature of the church to one that invests order in
church office. How do we translate *charisma* of the Spirit into
official positions? We must return to the question I asked at the
beginning of the chapter: What criteria can a searching person use
to measure whether he or she is "called of God" to some role of
leadership in Christ's body? Equally as important, what standards
of ratification can the church community exercise to test an

individual's sense of call or to recognize someone operating under the Spirit's endowment?

If we hold a strictly organic view of the church we might conclude that leadership offices are not needed. Is there a place for prescribed leadership? A definite yes!

As the early church expanded, it became necessary to identify leadership in some way. Paul and Barnabas retraced their steps through the towns of Galatia they had visited on their first missionary tour, and they appointed "elders for them in every church, with prayer and fasting" (Acts 14:23). Paul instructed Titus to "appoint elders in every town" (Titus 1:5). By the time of the council in Jerusalem, the elders of that city had become so prominent that when the communiqué to the gentile churches went forth, it came from the "apostles and elders" (Acts 15:23). Paul held a teary-eyed meeting with the elders of Ephesus in the town of Miletus (Acts 20:17).

It is now generally agreed that the fluid terms of "elder" (*presbuteros*), "bishop" (*episcopos*), and "pastor" (*poimen*) all refer to a similar role in the church. This is all to say that there arose a need to formally identify those who would be recognized leaders in the church. The *charisma* of body functions was not enough; order demanded some structure.

The particular character of the leadership in the early church centered in two principal Greek verbs. The first is *proistēmi*.

To the Thessalonians Paul writes, "We beseech you, brethren, to respect those who labor among you and *are over you* [*proistamenos*] in the Lord and admonish you, and to esteem them very highly in love because of their work" (1 Thess. 5:12–13). Paul tells Timothy that those who *"rule well* [*proestōtes*] are worthy of double honor, especially those who labor in preaching and teaching" (1 Tim. 5:17). This is the same word used to describe a bishop who must *rule* [*prostenai*] or *manage* his own household as a prerequisite for being able to care for the church of God (1 Tim. 3:5).

It is noteworthy that this verb, which is descriptive of what leaders do, is considered by Paul to be a *charisma* of the Spirit (Rom. 12:8). The Arndt-Gingrich lexicon summarizes the intent of this word for leadership in two parts: (1) "be at the head of, rule, direct"; and (2) as if to capture the manner in which the leadership is to be exercised, "be concerned about, care for, give aid."

The second verb for leadership, *hēgeomai*, is found in Hebrews

13:7, 17, 24. This word creates a similar picture of the role of leadership and the expected response from the body as *proistēmi*. "Remember your *leaders* [literally, the "ones leading you," *hēgoumenon*], those who spoke to you the word of God; consider the outcome of their life and imitate their faith" (v. 7). Stressing the proper response to leadership, the author of Hebrews writes, "Obey your *leaders* and submit to them; for they are keeping watch over your souls, as men who will have to give account. Let them do this joyfully and not sadly, for that would be of no advantage to you" (v. 17).

From these two verbs and their rich contexts, we learn three things about biblical leadership.

1. *How leaders are to be treated.* Leaders are to receive "respect" (1 Thess. 5:12); we are to "esteem them very highly in love" (1 Thess. 5:13), "consider worthy of double honor" (1 Tim. 5:17), "remember" (Heb. 13:7), and "obey and submit" and "imitate their [leaders'] faith" (Heb. 13:17).

2. *What leaders are to do.* On behalf of God's people, leaders "are over you" (1 Thess. 5:12), "admonish" (1 Thess. 5:12), "teach and preach the word" (1 Tim. 5:17; Heb. 13:7), and "keep watch over your souls" (Heb. 13:17).

3. *How leaders are to behave.* The leader's manner must be exercised as "those who labor among you" (1 Thess. 5:12; 1 Tim. 5:17), as "those who . . . must give account . . . joyfully not sadly" (Heb. 13:17), as those who can be imitated (Heb. 13:7), and as those who exercise leadership in diligence (Rom. 12:8).

So from among the whole body of Christ some are called particularly to provide oversight, rule, discipline, teaching, and care.

We are asking how we identify those called to leadership as elders or pastors of the local church body. What distinguishes the equippers from the rest of the body? It would have been helpful if Paul and Barnabas had informed us of the basis for "appointing elders in all the towns." John Stott has written, "All God's people are priests, all are ministers or servants; but 'he gave *some* apostles, *some* prophets, *some* evangelists, *some* pastors and teachers.' "[10] The New Testament does not give us an infallible checklist. What follows is what I have deduced from Scripture and derived from experience as to the shape of the call and spiritual gifts that serve as the basis for equipping authority in the body. Remember the formula:

(1) Gifts/Call (Recognition) + (2) Character of Christ = Authority (Leadership)

Another key question: What is the shape of the call for an equipping leader, and what gifts are needed to be able to carry out that call?

Called to Be Equippers

When we speak of a "call" from God to ministry, the usual starting point is the secret or private call that resides as an inner compulsion in an individual spirit. In the *Institutes* Calvin speaks of "that secret call, of which each minister is conscious before God, and which does not have the church as witness."[11] The experience of call is a sense of the weighty hand of God that will not leave us alone. Calvin calls this "the good witness of our heart." The burning drive and desire to serve God by building up his church is known only within the individual spirit.

Little can be said about the shape of the "inner" call, first, because it is subjective, and second, because it must be confirmed by the church. It is difficult to describe the mystical yet real and transcendent dimensions of call in human language. But we need to make the matter as clear as possible.

The following definitions of equipping leadership begin to supply the content of an equipper's call.

Ted Engstrom writes,

> Leaders . . . act in order to help others work in an environment within which each individual serving under him finds himself encouraged and stimulated to a point where he is helped to realize his fullest potential to contribute meaningfully.[12]

Further building on the empowering nature of leadership, Michael Harper borrows an image from Juan Carlos Ortiz:

> The work of the pastor is not that of a watchman who takes care that no one robs the bricks as they keep piling up, but a stonemason who builds them into the edifice.[13]

Peter Wagner writes,

> An equipper is a leader who actively sets goals for a congregation according to the will of God, obtains goal ownership from the people, and sees that each member is properly motivated and equipped to do his or her part in accomplishing the goals.[14]

Finally, Gene Getz summarizes these definitions:

We are successful *only* as we are used of God "to equip the saints" to function in the body; we are successful only when the body grows and develops and ultimately manifests the "more excellent way"—the way of love and unity.[15]

The secret, or inner, call moves beyond the mystical when we see what an equipping leader is to accomplish for the body. To pull the elements together from the definitions given, ask yourself: (1) Do you have a passion and demonstrated ability to see members of the body come alive to their ministry potential? (2) Have you demonstrated specific ways whereby you have helped people reach their potential for ministry? (3) Have you managed an environment where people are encouraged and motivated to find their place in accomplishing a ministry goal?

To carry this even further, an inner call becomes more than an undefined conviction or a shapeless tug of the Spirit when we use the specifics of an equipping ministry as a grid to identify our particular focus of equipping ministry. In my experience, a "call" to be an equipper has a particular concentration. Equippers can only reproduce ministry in the areas of their precise expertise and passion. The following scheme reviews the equipping categories and the specific types of ministry that fall under each.

Mend/Restore	Establish/Lay Foundations	Prepare/Train
Healing:	Preaching	Help people find:
Emotional	(proclamation)	Spiritual gifts
Physical	Teaching	"Call" to ministry
Spiritual	Worship planning	Train for particular
Counseling	Discipling	ministry:
Discipline (correction)	Creating a nurturing	Tools
Deliverance	environment:	Skills
Hospital/Shut-in	Small groups	Mission
visitation	Education	
Crisis intervention	Evangelism	
Bereavement care		

Equippers will find themselves operating with an emphasis in one of these categories, though not exclusively so. Let me illustrate the process from my own call. The particular passion of my call is to make sure solid foundations in Christ are laid. My equipping focus straddles the "establish/lay foundations" and "prepare/train" categories.

Teaching is the gift that dominates and gives shape to my

other gifts (*establishing/laying foundations*). I am motivated to help
people understand the basics of their faith and as a result have a
transformed self-perception of who they are in Christ. I carry this
out in ministry as a teaching pastor who systematically expounds
portions of Scripture or through a thematic study of particular
topics (e.g., prayer). Careful handling of the text of Scripture is
critical for me.

I further carry out the desire to see people rooted in Christ by
having weekly discipling appointments in a triad arrangement,
meeting for the better part of the year. Those discipled are in turn
equipped to do the same to a third generation.

Central to helping create and manage an equipping environment is a commitment to small groups in multiple forms. This
decentralized ministry shifts the focus of the church from a pastor
to the body. At this point my call shifts to *prepare/train*. Small-
group leaders are given the specific tools necessary to carry out
their role. I also regularly teach about spiritual gifts in a workshop
context and assist people (through a one-hour interview) to self-
consciously be stewards of their gift mix.

A colleague's profile in ministry serves as yet another
illustration of the content of call. Joan's official title is descriptive
of her heart for ministry: Pastor for Pastoral Care and Counseling.
She is concerned for those who need to be *mended/restored* before
they can be fully useful in the Lord's ministry. She concentrates
on the wounded or stragglers who could be left behind as others
are charging ahead. This motivation takes specific expression as a
counselor with a powerful ministry of inner healing. The Lord has
given her sensitivity through imagining prayer to see how he
might be present to heal a traumatic past experience that has left
someone victimized or carrying unresolved pain.

As a way of uncovering the areas of brokenness in people's
lives, Joan leads an annual retreat, "On Becoming a Child of
God," which helps people get in touch with the hurt child within.
One result of this retreat is that many have identified themselves
as Adult Children of Alcoholics. Two ACA support groups have
evolved. Thus Joan's primary ministry focus and "call" from God
is *mending/restoring.*

I will define "call" in greater detail in chapter 10 as it relates to
the whole body, but some descriptive elements are appropriate at
this point. A call to be an equipper has the following characteristics:

1. A call comes in the form of an "inner oughtness" or burden

that says, "This I must do." By "burden" I don't mean "weighted down," but an inner compulsion to see God's people come alive to their ministry potential.

2. Call can also be identified as that place of joy where energy flows and there is deep satisfaction in service to God. I come alive when I am sharing the vision of ministry spontaneously arising out of the body or the dream of an equipped ministry. When the geyser begins to erupt from within, I know I am operating at the heart of my call.

3. A genuine call takes more energy to stifle than it does to release. Jeremiah tried to repress his call to proclaim the prophetic word, but he became more weary putting the lid on the message than he did letting it flow. He writes, "If I say, 'I will not mention him or speak any more in his name,' there is in my heart as it were a burning fire shut up in my bones, and I am weary with holding it in, and I cannot" (Jer. 20:9). An equipper's passion will be, in one form or another, to help others be living stones that find their place in the edifice that God is creating.

GIFT MIX FOR EQUIPPERS

In our quest to provide some objective criteria by which "call" can be tested, we have looked at (1) how to conceive equipping leadership, and (2) the focus of equipping ministry. The third criterion I propose is spiritual gifts. God's call to leadership in the body is directly related to the means or tools given leaders to carry out the call. Gifts and call are related to each other as means to ends.

Unfortunately we cannot draw a direct correlation biblically between sovereign organism gifts and institutional offices in the church. Discernment of God's will would be much simpler if there was a one-to-one relationship between equippers' leadership gifts and those who would be professionally set apart to occupy an official position such as pastor, elder, or missionary. But I believe there is a cluster of gifts that could generally be subsumed under the category of leadership gifts for the body. In other words, there are gifts that would need to be present for someone to hold an office. Hans Küng holds this view: "The Pauline charisma cannot be subsumed in the clerical office, but the clerical offices can be subsumed under the charisma."[16] The Pauline perspective moves from charisma to recognition to commission. Organism always precedes institution.

Peter Wagner offers a helpful explanation of a spiritual gift mix, which I draw on here. Instead of seeing one gift as dominant or the primary way a person functions, I believe most leaders have a cluster of gifts that interact with each other to form the person's unique profile. For example, my profile includes the gifts of pastor-teacher, visionary leader, and exhorter. Within my gift mix, teaching tends to give shape to the way I pastor, exercise leadership, and exhort. I want people to understand and see things as they have not seen them before.

The following descriptive list of equipping gifts serves as a self-test for personal examination:

Support Gifts	Others
Apostles	Leaders
Prophets	(a) Visionary
Evangelists	(b) Administrative
Pastor-teachers	Exhorter
	Wise

What is your gift mix as an equipping leader?

Support Gifts

The obvious place to begin is to define the gifts already specifically stated in Scripture as given to the body to prepare it for ministry. "And his [Christ's] gifts were that some should be *apostles*, some *prophets*, some *evangelists* and some *pastors* and *teachers*" (Eph. 4:11). These gifted members of the body bear in common the tool of God's word. They wield the sword of the Word, but each with a different focus. Michael Harper has helpfully identified a key *verb* that captures the motivation of each of these gifted ones.[17]

1. *Apostles (Go).* The apostolic ministry is a constant reminder that each local church's parish extends to the ends of the earth. Though I do not believe there are apostles in the restricted sense of the original disciples called to be unique and authoritative witnesses and interpreters of the redemptive events of Christ, I do believe their spirit continues to be embodied in certain members of the church. In a general sense, the term "apostle" means "messenger" or "emissary," "one who represents another." The apostolic spirit is a missionary spirit. Paul expressed this spirit when he wrote that it was his "ambition to preach the gospel, not

where Christ has already been named, lest I build on another man's foundations, but as it is written, 'They shall see who have never been told of him, and they shall understand who have never heard of him'" (Rom. 15:20–21).

Those who embody an apostolic spirit have the passion to "go." There is a desire for an adventure and living on the edge in order to take the gospel to new territories like the unreached people groups identified by the U.S. Center for World Mission. Missionaries adapt well to another culture and can use their gift mix in a cross-cultural setting. Apostles are filled with compassion for those who have never had the opportunity to be exposed to the living God. Our God is a seeking and sending God, and an apostle is captured by his spirit to go in his name.

Missionaries equip the church through the constant reminder that God's heart encompasses the whole world. If we are to be faithful disciples, we must be "world Christians," even if we ourselves are not called to "go." Missionaries stretch us beyond our self-focus.

2. *Prophets (Hear).* Listening to God's Word for a particular time and place marks the prophet's ministry. A prophet is literally one who speaks for another, as Aaron spoke for Moses. The Greek word *prophētēs*, when broken down into component parts, conveys a prophet's role: *pro*, "before," and *phētēs*, "cause to shine." So a prophet is one who stands before the word of God and causes it to shine. A prophet's ministry can take various forms, such as a biblical exegete with a passion for truth, or a person who spontaneously inspired by the Spirit has a word for a local body of believers.

Prophets hear a message from God and are inwardly compelled to deliver it. Truth is an obsession with prophets. They tend to see things in broad strokes with the instinctive sense of knowing what is right for a whole group of believers. Prophets paint in two colors, black and white, for they see things more incisively than the rest of us who muddle around in the shades of gray. A prophet intuitively understands the spirit of our times or the cultural drift so that his message cuts through those things that dull the spirit of Christian community, such as the comfort of wealth.

A prophet equips the body by inciting them to action or holding up the mirror image so they can see what they have become. Like the head sending the signals through the electrical impulses of the nervous system to stimulate it for action, so the prophet passes on what he hears.

3. *Evangelists (Grow)*. The fact that "evangelists" are rarely mentioned in Scripture may be indicative of the role they played to equip the saints. Paul exhorts Timothy, "Do the work of an evangelist" (2 Tim. 4:5). Philip embodied the gift of evangelism. When he encountered the Ethiopian eunuch on the road to Gaza and observed the eunuch's struggle with the scroll of Isaiah 53, Philip, "beginning with the Scripture, told him the good news of Jesus" (Acts 8:35). An evangelist is a person with a particular passion and facility to tell of the overwhelming love of God individually or publicly so that people take the initial steps of Christian discipleship.

Perhaps the reason not many are identified with the gift of evangelism is that evangelism is a responsibility of the entire body of believers. Evangelists remind the body that it is natural for organisms to grow. Evangelists keep the body alive through a steady influx of new babes in Christ. It is then the responsibility of the church through a multigifted body to nurture them toward maturity in Christ.

4. *Pastor-Teachers (Care and Know)*. Though "pastor" and "teacher" are listed as two separate gifts in the Revised Standard Version, the Greek structure indicates these are to be placed together as one gift. As evangelists are the obstetricians presiding at the birth, pastor-teachers are the pediatricians who provide the care and knowledge for growth toward maturity. Therefore pastor-teachers function with a sense of protective care for the long-term spiritual welfare of the flock and teach the Word of God as the primary means to feed, nurture, and shepherd.

A pastor's heart is evidenced by a concern for the spiritual health of God's people. Positively this is expressed by a desire to teach the Word of God so there are proper nutrients for growth to occur. This suggests that those who enter pastoral ministry should have the characteristics of a teacher.

Teaching ministry comes into focus when we contrast this gift with preaching (Acts 5:42). Preachers announce and proclaim like trumpets in an orchestra, while teachers explain and expound like the violins that fill in the broader nuances. A preacher presses for a decision, appealing to the heart, but a teacher addresses the mind and desires understanding. Preachers stir up the troops to action; teachers are concerned with long-term change. You can be a teacher without being a pastor, but you cannot be a pastor without being a teacher.

The gift of pastor-teacher may have a direct correlation to the office of elder, or bishop. When Paul refers to "elders who rule well . . . especially those who labor in preaching and teaching" (1 Tim. 5:17), it is difficult to see any difference between the office of elder and the gift of pastor-teacher. The only gift Paul seems to identify with those qualified to be elders is "apt to teach" (1 Tim. 3:2); an elder "must hold firm to the sure word as taught, so that he may be able to give instruction on sound doctrine and also confute those who contradict it" (Titus 1:9). Pastors are to be teachers.

As one having the ministry of oversight of the local body of believers, a pastor-teacher has perhaps the most relevant gift to an equipping ministry. Pastor-teachers manage an environment and set a tone for equipping.

Other Equipping Gifts

There are other equipping gifts that are important supplements to the essential, support gifts.

1. *Leadership.* One word for leadership mentioned earlier is identified with Paul as a *charisma* (Rom. 12:8). *Proistēmi* can be translated to "stand before" or "be out in front." The gift of leadership thus has to do with helping the body reach its potential and arrive at its God-appointed destination. There are two types of leadership biblically. Some people are gifted with both these abilities, but most are not.

a. *Visionary leadership.* I link the gift of faith (1 Cor. 12:9) to leadership and come up with "visionary leadership." People with the gift of faith have the ability to apprehend the promises of God for a particular body of believers and become convinced that these dreams will be a reality. A visionary is someone who "sees before." He has the ability to know what can be and then articulate those dreams in such a way that people come to see the possibilities they could not see on their own.

Visionary leaders are transforming leaders. They help people to see themselves differently and identify their roles in accomplishing the dream. Visionaries throb with a sense of urgency and intensity. Since the dream is from God, leaders will call God's people to account and cause them to examine the cost to accomplish a goal worthy of the sacrifice.

I view this entire book as an expression of my gift of visionary leadership. My hope is to lift our sights to the horizon of a biblical vision of the church as organism. If this vision has been sufficiently clear and is caught, then you have been lifted onto a higher plane accompanied by the energy that a vision unleashes.

The famous jurist Oliver Wendell Holmes once boarded a train, but was unable to find his ticket. After watching Holmes fumble through his pocket in growing dismay, the conductor politely said, "That's all right, Mr. Holmes, I am sure you have your ticket somewhere." Looking the conductor straight in the eye, Holmes replied, "Young man, that is not my problem at all. I don't care about giving my ticket to the railroad, I just want to find out where in the blazes I'm going." Visionary leadership helps chart the course in the body of Christ.

b. *Administrative leadership*. We discover the word *"administration"* in 1 Corinthians 12:28. Translated "governments" in the King James Version, the Greek word literally means "helmsman." This is the person who charts the course, steers the ship, and makes sure it arrives at the proper destination. Note that the administrator differs from the visionary, as the helmsman differs from the owner of the ship. The ship's owner determines its destination; the helmsman is responsible for getting it there. I repeat, the two gifts may exist in a single person, but this is rare.

Often the administrator is a person who will accomplish someone else's vision. Thus this gift could be defined as the ability to make decisions on behalf of others that result in the efficient operation and fulfillment of goals.

The gift of administration is integral to managing in an equipping environment. Administrators have the ability to see the big picture as well as the necessary steps needed to reach the goal. They often have the insight into the kinds of gifted people needed for the task. They will identify who has the gifts of pastoring, exhortation, or teaching long before others will, and they will urge them to play their God-given roles.

Administrators are the planners, strategists, and delegators of the body. They are good at decision making and excellent problem solvers when the gift of wisdom is also present. Their leadership is best exercised when they help a group accomplish its goals by encouraging maximum participation so that the mind of Christ is corporately discerned. Administration is one of the most underrated gifts in the body because it does not sound supernatural. But when the gift is properly functioning, the other members of the body will be flourishing as well.

2. *Exhortation.* The word "exhort" commonly suggests confrontation. It may conjure up images of ranting or gushing individuals with flailing arms. Exhortation reminds me of the cartoon of a pastor shaking his finger at his congregation from his lofty perch and saying, "Naughty, naughty, naughty!" But biblically the gift of exhortation (Rom. 12:8) is derived from Jesus' word for the Holy Spirit: *paraklētos* (John 14:16; 16:7). Far from having the sense of standing over another in judgment, the word literally means "to be called alongside to help" or "to speak to someone by being at his or her side." An exhorter is one who is essentially a motivator.

Biblically there are two nuances of exhortation.

a. *Encouragement.* Barnabas was called a "son of encouragement" for doing such deeds as selling property in order to support those in need in the early church. His heart walked alongside those in the church who had little. The ministry of counseling in its various forms captures the spirit of Barnabas in today's church. Counselors tenderly "come alongside," providing an atmosphere of acceptance in which someone can learn to be safe. In an atmosphere of safety, hurts, wounds, and fears can be exposed and hope for wholeness instilled.

b. *Challenge.* Exhortation also comes in the form of challenge. Barnabas paved the way for the new convert, Saul, to be accepted among the apostles, who were justifiably suspicious (Acts 9:27). Barnabas saw the genuine change in Saul and challenged the apostles to see it also.

Exhorters are the cheerleaders of the body. They are able to stir up joy and enthusiasm for the Lord's work. They could be called spark plugs, inciters, and promoters. Exhorters call people to be their best, much like a coach at halftime igniting his team for action for the second half through a rousing pep talk. Exhorters are the motivators who bring out the best in others because they fervently believe in the God-given potential of every person.

3. *Wisdom.* Another gift needed in a leader is the ability to apply Holy Spirit-given insight to specific needs. The gift of wisdom is like the doctor who is a skilled diagnostician; he draws incisive conclusions from specific symptoms.

When Solomon became king he was rewarded by God because he prayed for an "understanding mind to discern between good and evil" (1 Kings 3:9). This "understanding mind" was immediately tested by the dilemma of the child claimed by two mothers. Solomon's command to divide the child in two revealed the compassionate heart of the true mother. So the story concludes, "And all Israel heard of the judgment which the king had rendered and they stood in awe of the king, because they perceived that the wisdom of God was in him, to render justice" (1 Kings 3:28).

We have stood in awe when a striking solution is suddenly proposed to a complex and seemingly insoluble problem. People with wisdom seem to be able to penetrate the heart of the matter. They are able to separate the wheat from the chaff. I have sat in meetings that have been hopelessly polarized until someone who has listened quietly offers a solution that both sides immediately see as a way out of the dilemma. Wisdom carries inherent authority and power. Truth knocks down dividing walls. Leaders with the gift of wisdom are perceived as fair and judicious without an axe to grind. Their word can be received.

DISCERNING CALL

In summary, people who sense a call to professional leadership in the body should measure that call against their own and others' perception of their gifts. Leaders should have at least one dominant and one subordinate leadership gift in their gift mix.

In this chapter we have interpreted leadership so as not to create de facto another clergy-laity split. By emphasizing the functional role of leadership within the one people of God, we have said that leaders are set apart from *within* and *for* the body. We have examined the shape of "call" and the gifts that might give some objective criteria whereby a person and the whole body of Christ can discern a call to leadership. In the next chapter we will examine the leadership style necessary to empower the body to its ministry. We will see how this applies to relationships among staff, between staff and the leadership core, and between the leadership core and the congregation.

NOTES

1. Elton Trueblood, *The Incendiary Fellowship* (New York: Harper & Row, 1967), 41.

2. The range of character qualities a leader should exemplify is not within the purview of this book. These qualities are examined elsewhere, notably in *Sharpening the Focus of the Church* by Gene Getz (Wheaton, Ill.: Victor, 1984).

3. David Watson, *I Believe in the Church* (Grand Rapids: Eerdmans, 1978), 262.

4. Quoted in Watson, *I Believe in the Church,* 262.

5. Edmund P. Clowney, *Called to the Ministry* (Chicago: InterVarsity Press, 1964), 34.

6. Quoted in Siegfried Schatzmann, *A Pauline Theology of Charismata* (Peabody, Mass.: Hendricksen, 1987), 97.

7. Watson, *I Believe in the Church,* 268.

8. Quoted in Watson, *I Believe in the Church,* 263–64.

9. Thomas Gillespie, "Our Ministerial Roots" (Unpublished paper, Princeton Theological Seminary), 12.

10. John R. W. Stott, *One People* (Downers Grove, Ill.: InterVarsity Press, 1968), 45.

11. John Calvin, *Institutes of the Christian Religion* (Philadelphia: Westminster, 1960), 4.3.11.

12. Ted W. Engstrom, *The Making of a Christian Leader* (Grand Rapids: Zondervan, 1976), 20.

13. Michael Harper, *Let My People Grow* (Plainfield, N.J.: Logos International, 1977), 214.

14. Peter Wagner, *Leading Your Church to Growth* (Glendale, Calif.: Regal, 1984), 79.

15. Gene Getz, *Sharpening the Focus of the Church* (Chicago: Moody Press, 1974), 121.

16. Quoted in Schatzmann, *A Pauline Theology of Charismata,* 86.

17. Harper, *Let My People Grow,* 44.

CHAPTER 9

Servant Leadership: Empowering the Body to Its Ministry

WE HAVE NOTED some specific touchstones by which we might identify the people called to be equipping leaders in the church. We noticed that authority biblically defined is not the result of a position occupied, but the natural by-product of the anointing of God. This authority is recognized by the body when call and gifts are reflected in and are consistent with godly character. Although there is one ultimate manager of the body, Jesus Christ, human leaders are necessary within the organism of the church.

How is leadership to be exercised? Is there a leadership style that is consistent with an all-members-are-ministers view? Are there leadership styles that inhibit the release of the giftedness of the body and by contrast styles that promote this? The following principle helps us to answer these questions: *The goal of leadership in an equipping ministry is for all believers to accept before God their responsibility to be stewards of their gifts and call in order to make a contribution to the health of the whole body of Christ.*

In dealing with leadership styles I hope to move beyond the vague generalizations that often mark discussions of this subject. We will look at authority, accountability, and role expectations associated with senior pastors, staff members, leadership boards, and members of the congregation. We need to ask, How does ministry originate in the local church? Who has authority to initiate new ministries or determine when old ones no longer serve their purpose?

We will again compare the institutional view of leadership and the organism view. Our starting point greatly affects our conception of the exercise of authority, accountability, and role definition.

THE INSTITUTIONAL MODEL

Figure 9.1

The Institutional Model
Hierarchical (Centralized authority)

Characteristics:

- Authority—Flows from top down
- Accountability—One way
- Roles—Determined by relative position in hierarchy

In the institutional or hierarchical model, authority is concentrated, if not by design, then in practice, in the pastor, the head of staff. Pastors are the ones who "run things around here," people will say. If you want to get anything done, somewhere along the line it is assumed the pastors must at least give their blessing. All roads eventually lead to the pastor's office. Let's examine the pastor's role as head of staff in the hierarchical conception.

1. *Senior Pastor.* The following picture seems to be a generally accurate description of much of the American church:

a. *Chief executive officer.* The following is held up as the ideal for the senior pastor in the Church Growth Movement: "In these days of illustrated success stories, the Senior Pastor is usually shown ensconced in managerial splendor, oozing charm and self assurance from a black leather swivel chair in his lavishly appointed executive suite."[1] Though few will be multigifted pastors of megachurches, all senior pastors are perceived to be the administrative heads of the organization. They should have the skills to run an efficient operation. This usually means that all job descriptions are clearly delineated and all persons know precisely the tasks they are to perform for the organization. As CEO, the executive is the one who assigns responsibilities.

b. *Team ministry.* There is much talk today about "team" ministry, but the phrase is applied to two very different concepts. In the hierarchical structure the senior pastor's role is very much like the football coach who assigns the players to their position and calls the plays that are going to be run on the field. The staff knows clearly that their roles are defined for the efficient operation of the organization according to the senior pastor's perceived needs of the congregation.

c. *Initiation of ministry.* The responsibility for initiating ministry ultimately resides in the senior pastor as the primary visionary. This is the trickle-down view of ministry. The vision for the church originates at the top and is carried out by the staff, who are called to fulfill that vision. The senior pastor is the primary goal setter, since he is the one who has access to the power position of the pulpit. Authority centers in preaching. A ministry that is not declared from the pulpit is not seen by the congregation as important or valid. The senior pastor is given the privilege and responsibility of articulating and supporting from the pulpit the full range of the church's vision for ministry. This leaves the validity of the ministries of other staff members subject to the senior pastor's stamp of approval.

d. *Control.* In a hierarchical model, control begins at the top and moves downward. Thus the senior pastor will want to know and approve any initiative in ministry. For any ministry to begin, permission must be granted by "the boss." Control or the need to know is often a response to the fear that something might occur which will upset people. I once served with a pastor who would allow no committees to meet without his being present. In his mind, the pastor's role meant having one's finger in every aspect of church life.

e. *Accountability.* Accountability flows only in one direction— from the top down. In a hierarchical structure a clear chain of command is intended. The senior pastor will review the work of subordinates and so on. Associates and assistants feel the same pressure to please their "bosses" and fulfill their expectations that is typical in any business hierarchy. To think that subordinates might also be able to hold their superiors accountable is inconceivable. A Christian attorney friend did the unthinkable when he told the partners of his law firm that he had asked those whom he supervised—paralegals and secretary—to review his work as a manager. Needless to say, the partners would never have considered allowing themselves to be in that position. Moreover, the subordinates who were asked to evaluate their boss were equally flabbergasted. This approach would very likely draw the same response in the church.

f. *Hierarchical language.* Perhaps our terminology is as clear an indication of our institutional framework as anything. We confer titles to identify a person's rung on the authority ladder and to clarify his position relative to the pinnacle of power. From the top down it may look something like this: senior pastor, associate pastor, assistant pastor, assistant to the pastor, director, assistant director, executive secretary, and secretary. The church has adopted language that communicates power via position, not via the call or function of persons. Therefore we tend to make value judgments about the relative worth of individuals based on a pecking order.

I recall conversations with other pastors at a conference where the inevitable question would be asked, "What is your role in the church?" When I replied that I was an associate, I often sensed them sizing up my relative worth and deciding how much time they should invest in this conversation with me.

2. *Staff and Leadership Board.* The role of the leadership board is usually an extension of the structure of the pastoral staff. If the staff is hierarchically and task focused, the leadership board will follow suit. The church is heavily influenced by a secular, business model and tends to adopt the latest philosophy of management. Richard Hutcheson sees this managerial emphasis as one element that is stifling the life of the Spirit in the church.

> As useful as these tools (i.e., management by objective, etc.) may be for specific purposes, however (and they are), they have not proved to be the answer to the kind of decline exemplified by membership losses. Indeed the managerial revolution within the church, with widespread adoption of the assumptions as well as the technologies of management science and organizational sociology, may have been one of the reasons for the decline.[2]

As in the secular world, "management by objective" took the church by storm. This is what I would call a centralized, trickle-down approach to running the church. The central body establishes the specific objectives for the organization that are to be implemented by its various program entities, usually called committees. Flowing from the staff to the administrative board and out through its working groups will be the objectives that originate at the top. As a result, a church board will often have the following characteristics:

a. *Rubber stamp or obstacle.* In a staff-centered ministry the church board often serves as a rubber stamp that unquestionably approves the staff's dreams and goals. One pastor I know called the church board together four times a year to receive new members and fulfill other denominational requirements only. In some denominations where board leadership is invested with considerable authority, the board sees its role as blocking the unnecessary or is so thoroughly entrenched in tradition that anything new is automatically suspect. Such a board is viewed by the staff as an obstacle to ministry. So the leadership style adopted by the senior pastor is one of persuader or salesman; an adversarial relationship exists between staff and board.

b. *Administrators.* Because the board's primary function is to handle the organizational business of the church, it oversees programs through committees. The board has an agenda and moves through it, making decisions that cover the entire gamut from starting new programs to replacing a cabinet in a particular room. This process can be particularly frustrating to those who find decision making and administration foreign to their gift mix and distinct from the way they want to serve the church.

c. *Committee focused.* Committees are the administrative bodies used to carry out the program emphasis and oversight. Usually acting as conceptualizing and decision-making groups, they are not the ministry implementers. Frank Tillapaugh describes well the layered approach to administration represented by committees. The first thing a committee does is decide whether something should be done. This often involves considerable research and information gathering. One characteristic of Presbyterians (of which I am one) is that people are never ready to make a decision until all points of view are considered. This can consume considerable time and energy, which would not be so bad if that were the end of the process. It isn't. Committees are not usually the direct implementers. They must next ask, "Who can we get to do it?" So even if a committee finally decides to have a college ministry or church softball team, it must then recruit another level of structure to carry out what has been decided.[3] Thus a committee functions as a think tank and oversight body, not doers of hands-on ministry. It expends great amounts of time and energy, but is usually one step removed from the actual fulfillment of ministry.

d. *Task focused.* We tend to do the work of God without being the people of God. By that I mean we may serve on committees, task groups, or leadership boards without really knowing or ministering to the people with whom we serve. All eyes may be focused on the task to be accomplished, as if it can be done without serving each other simultaneously. People may be

experiencing a crisis of faith, turmoil in their work, disillusion-
ment with their home life, loneliness, and so on, but this
information is rarely known to the other committee members,
because with the hierarchical program orientation, they value
getting the job done rather than attending to each other while
doing the job.

3. *Congregation as a whole.* How does the hierarchical, top-
down, centralized approach to ministry affect the congregation as
a whole?

a. *Passivity.* In general, concentrating power and initiative in
the hands of a few creates passivity in those who are not a part of
the leadership structure. The people wait for the vision of the
church to be "delivered from on high." While Moses was meeting
with God on the mountaintop, the people were deciding what to
do in their leader's absence. People sense that they are the
recipients of someone else's work and feel little ownership of the
vision, for they receive it as *fait accompli.* Persons who are
motivated in ministry but are not a part of the hierarchy may feel
stifled; anything they propose must have the official approval of
the church board. What significant role can a member have if he is
not a part of the church hierarchy?

I believe the hierarchical structure creates a consumer mentality in the church. And the 20-80 principle applies. It takes only
about ten to fifteen percent of the membership to run the
administrative machinery. Is it any wonder that the 20 percent
provide for the 80 percent in most churches?

b. *Value judgment.* In a hierarchical structure those in the
upper echelon are considered to be of greater value to the
organization. If people decide that their value is determined by
their position, they will hear the call to serve as leaders as a call to
power, a call "to be somebody." This sets up an unhealthy
dynamic in the church. Some may agree to serve for the wrong
reasons, while others refuse to serve in order to avoid work.

Once an elder confessed to me that his motivation for
accepting the call was to be seen as a part of the "in" group of
movers and shakers. He felt this would overcome his low self-
esteem. Instead I watched his zeal for being an elder flag as the
reality of the work required set in. Since he felt no "call" to serve,
he lacked energy for the task. Often people are willing to let
someone else do the work and not accept their share of responsibility. For them, the hierarchical approach creates a built-in excuse
not to get involved.

The church in general has adopted a leadership style that is at odds with an organism view. The institutional, hierarchical approach to leadership stifles the ability of God's people to see themselves as initiating centers of ministry.

Much more consistent with body ministry is Jesus' model of servant leadership designed to empower others to reach their potential. Before I sketch an organism model of leadership, let us examine servant leadership as taught and modeled by our Lord. From him we can distill several principles from which an organism model of leadership can be derived.

THE PHARISEE MODEL: A STYLE TO AVOID

Jesus tells us, first, what servant leadership is not. Comparing the behavior he expected of his followers with the model of both gentile and Jewish leadership, Jesus describes the prevailing concept of greatness and then calls his disciples to walk away from the only model they had known. He calls them to be immersed in a radically different model he has lived out before them.

The gentile leaders' style is captured by the word "over." "You know that those who are supposed to rule *over* the Gentiles lord it *over* them, and their great men exercise authority *over* them" (Matt. 20:25; Mark 10:42; Luke 22:25). Gentile leaders gloried in their control over their realm. Their subjects felt the caprice and whim of a potentate's arbitrary desires. Rulers expected to be catered to, because they were at the top of the pyramid, with everyone else finding his place somewhere along the slippery slope.

The word translated "lord it over" (*kurieuō*), though it can refer to the authority of God (Rom. 14:9), is almost always used in the New Testament to mean "negative control." Paul uses it three times in Romans 6 to refer to the negative hold of death, sin, and law. Referring to Christ's resurrection and triumph over death, Paul concludes, "Death no longer *has dominion over* [lords it over] him" (v. 9). Since a believer in Christ is under grace and not law, "sin will have *no dominion over* [lord it over] you" (v. 14). Finally, Paul makes the point "that the law *is binding on* [lords it over] a person only during his life" (Rom. 7:1).

A different form of the word (*katakurieuō*) appears when Peter exhorts the elders to exercise their role with a servant spirit "not as *domineering* [lording it] over those in your charge but being examples of the flock" (1 Peter 5:3). J. B. Phillips captures the haughtiness of this phrase: "Don't act like little tin gods."

But Jesus reserves harsher condemnation for the Jewish leaders. They were supposed to be models the populace could follow. In Matthew 23:1–7 Jesus verbally undresses the scribes and Pharisees and exposes their shame for all to see: "Then Jesus said to the crowd and the disciples, 'The scribes and the Pharisees sit on Moses' seat'" (vv. 1–2). "Moses' seat" was a stone chair permanently placed in the synagogue on which a teacher would sit to expound the law. Jesus holds the scribes and Pharisees up before the disciples as the very model of leadership they were to avoid. By "sitting on Moses' seat," they positioned themselves as authoritatively carrying on the traditions of the law as given by Moses. The name "Pharisee," meaning "the separated ones," tells us that they thought highly of themselves. Their holiness was to be observed. They expressed their holiness through *separation* from anyone or anything that could be considered unclean and by *purification* through ceremonial washing and keeping the laws that governed all aspects of life. They demonstrated their zeal for law keeping by fasting twice a week, although it was only required by law once a year, on the Day of Atonement.

What was the negative model the disciples were to avoid?

1. *Hypocrisy: Disjunction between teaching and doing.* Jesus exhorts his listeners, "So practice and observe whatever they tell you, but not what they do; for they preach but do not practice" (Matt. 23:3). Jesus says essentially that these leaders have good things to say, but their lives contradict their words. They are not examples of their teaching. There is an incongruity between words and deed, and therefore these leaders cannot be trusted.

The result was that the populace was weighted down by the words of the scribes and Pharisees. "They bind heavy burdens, hard to bear, and lay them on men's shoulders, but they themselves will not move them with their fingers" (Matt. 23:4). The Pharisees prided themselves on keeping the 613 laws that ordered every aspect of life from personal piety to social relationships. At the same time they looked down their noses at the common person, especially those pejoratively called the *am aaretz*—"the people of the land." The burden placed on the shoulders of the people was a legalism that says you are made right before God by law keeping. Their heavy backpack contained only condemnation, guilt, and fear.

2. *Spiritual pride.* Underlying the behavior of "saying and not

doing" is spiritual pride. "They do all their deeds to be seen by men" (Matt. 23:5). A characteristic of spiritual pride is that it is never content to remain secret in one's heart. What good is the knowledge that you are better than everyone else unless everyone else knows it as well! Pride cannot be kept under wraps; it must find expression.

Jesus exposes three forms this pride takes:

a. *Religious piety.* "They make their phylacteries broad and their fringes long" (Matt. 23:5). What are phylacteries and fringes? Taking literally the injunction of Deuteronomy 6:8 to bind the word of God on their wrists and foreheads, the Pharisees attached little leather boxes containing four portions of God's Word by cords to their wrists and foreheads. Fringes, which reminded them of the many commandments, edged their prayer garments, similar to the frills on a woman's shawl. A pious Jew rocks back and forth, as a part of the ritual of piety, tossing the phylacteries and fringes rhythmically. This was how the scribes and Pharisees sought public recognition for their devotion to God and their favored status before him.

b. *Honor.* "And they love the place of *honor* at feasts and the best seats in the synagogues" (Matt. 23:6). In the Pharisees' minds, special people deserved special perks. At a feast they wanted the positions of honor near their hosts. In the synagogue, which was carefully graded on the basis of worth, the Pharisees placed themselves in the front for all to see, while women and children were safely hidden behind a screen in the back.

c. *Titles.* "And salutations in the market place and being called rabbi by men" (Matt. 23:7). "Rabbi" literally means "O Great One" or "O Lord." The Pharisees and scribes loved this title of esteem. Like them, too often we seek titles as a measure of our greatness and spirituality.

What Servant Leadership Is Not

What principles can we derive from Jesus' teaching about what servant leadership is *not?*

- Leadership is not measured by how many people serve you.
- Leadership is not exercising control over a chain of command.
- Leadership is not using coercion to get what you want.

- Leadership is not receiving deference or being treated in a separate category of specialness.

- Leadership is not receiving honorary, positional titles.

I mourn for the church because we seem to display so many of the characteristics that Jesus said, "Not so among you" (Mark 10:43). Shameful arrogance and haughtiness have reached epidemic proportions among church leaders. Recently I attended a conference where five platform presenters shared their expertise as leaders of growing churches. Only one impressed me as winsome and self-effacing with a contagious enthusiasm for our Lord. Typical of the other four was the pastor of a congregation of 2,400 members who exuded bravado and emitted a sense that he was God's gift to the church. He wanted us to know that his church had a net growth rate of 200 a year and that he was the reason why. Another Christian leader was quoted as saying, "The board does not run these organizations. Legally it has the final say. If they said, 'You can't build a Bible college,' I couldn't build one. But you know what I'd do? I'd fire the board, because I am the spiritual head of this organization. It can't run without me."[4] Jesus says, "Not so among you."

We get the kind of leaders we deserve. It often seems that the world's view of greatness is the standard we use when we select our leaders. We have allowed arrogant, unaccountable, and self-professed channels of the Spirit to shoot off like loose cannon. We sometimes have a penchant in the Christian community for holding up the proud and arrogant as our ideal because "they get the job done." Using the world's view of power, we want leaders to exercise influence, work their way into positions of power, and throw their weight around. We therefore get what we ourselves honor—Christian leaders who act like potentates rather than self-sacrificing servants of Jesus Christ. Our actions show that we do not believe that real power is expressed through servanthood that leads to a cross.

The Church Growth Movement has identified strong pastoral leadership as a key ingredient in the growth of a congregation. I will grant that leaders must lead. But what gets passed off as leadership often has no resemblance to servant leadership as modeled and taught by our Lord. In the Church Growth Movement even autocrats may be considered servant leaders if they produce results, that is, members. Stating that we cannot prejudge leadership style because it must be an expression of the cultural milieu, Peter Wagner writes, "When a church is established within that culture, to a large degree the form which effective church leadership patterns will take is determined by that culture."[5]

Wagner tells of Pastor Kim, the pastor of Kwang Kim Methodist Church in Seoul, Korea, the largest Methodist church in the world. Pastor Kim senses no tension between servanthood and leadership. He showed Peter Wagner the conference room where he meets with the elders. At one end of this long table are two chairs. Standing behind the chair on the right side, Pastor Kim said, "This is my chair." Pointing to the one next to it, he said, "No human sits there—it is for Jesus Christ." The implication was that Jesus talks to the pastor, and the pastor tells everyone what Jesus has said. So even autocratic leadership is transformed into servant leadership.

Does this mean we simply accept whatever cultural expression is in vogue if it is expedient? Jesus apparently did not think so. What was he doing if he was not undressing the dominant cultural expression in both the gentile and Jewish worlds? Our natural tendency is to concentrate power at the top, but Jesus modeled and taught a different way of life.

THE JESUS MODEL: WHAT SERVANT LEADERSHIP IS

Jesus calls for a radical change in leadership models with phrases such as "But you are not" (Matt. 23:8) and "but it shall not be so among you" (Matt. 20:26; Mark 10:43). Far from being swept along by the prevailing currents of greatness, Jesus says we must walk into the force of the gale and not be carried away by it. The subject of greatness was a topic of discussion among the disciples on more than one occasion (Mark 9:34; Luke 22:24). Luke writes, "A dispute also arose among them, which of them was to be regarded as the greatest." "Dispute" literally means "rivalry." It does not mean an accidental falling into an argument, but a habitual, contentious spirit. Because of the disciples' fondness for power, they verbally attacked each other, evidently marshaling arguments as to why each should be considered the greatest.

On occasion a disciple moved beyond words to a power play. James and John jockeyed for the top position, preparing to take over the seats of power when Jesus began his earthly reign. Apparently they had an aggressive mother, for Matthew tells us that she was the one who initially approached Jesus on behalf of her sons (Matt. 20:20–28; Mark 10:35–45). Surreptitiously James and John asked Jesus, "Grant us to sit, one at your right hand and one at your left, in your glory" (Mark 10:37).

It was in this context that Jesus turned the world's view of greatness upside down. First, he redefined greatness. Jesus said:

"Whoever would be great among you must be your servant" (Mark 10:43; Matt. 20:26).

"Whoever would be first among you must be a slave of all" (Mark 10:44).

"If anyone would be first, he must be last of all and servant of all" (Mark 9:35).

"Whoever humbles himself will be exalted" (Matt. 23:12).

"Let the greatest among you become as the youngest, and the leader as one who serves" (Luke 22:26).

"For he who is least among you all is the one who is great" (Luke 9:48).

A direct implication of Jesus' servant stance was his obliteration of titles. What else could Jesus have intended by the following than to wipe out gradations of worth and value: "But you are not to be called rabbi, for you have one teacher, and you are all brethren. And call no one your father on earth, for you have one Father, who is in heaven. Neither be called masters, for you have one master, the Christ" (Matt. 23:8–10).

We have refused to take Jesus' words at face value. Jesus' obvious intent was to remove any basis for "lording it over" others by dispensing with titles that give people an elevated place in the "pecking order." We all occupy the same level ground at the foot of the one Teacher, Jesus Christ. We are not "great ones" or "lords." We are not "fathers" with spiritual authority like Abraham, Isaac, or Jacob. In this context Jesus was most likely using "father" as a reference to those who occupied positions of spiritual authority such as the patriarchs or a distinguished scribe of historic significance.

Finally, do not accept the designation "master" or "leader." No human can usurp the position of the head of the body, Christ. Our tendency seems always toward idolatry, to make someone larger than life. Never forget: Jesus alone is Lord.

Jesus added another dimension to his picture of true greatness with a simple object lesson. He and the disciples were traveling one day, and the disciples were having an intense discussion when they arrived at Capernaum. Jesus asked what they had been talking about. Embarrassed because they had been debating who was the greatest, they remained silent. But Jesus intuited their discussion (Luke 9:47). To make sure they did not miss the reality of the values in the kingdom, Jesus said,

> "If anyone would be first, he must be the last of all and servant of all." And he took a child, and put him in the midst of them; and taking him in his arms, he said to them, "Whoever receives one such child in my name receives me; and whoever receives me, receives not me but him who sent me" (Mark 9:35b–37).

So servant leadership—true greatness—is demonstrated by a heart for the powerless, unprotected, and exploitable. Jesus displayed, through the tenderness of touch and caressing arms, his care for such as children.

To "receive" someone into your home meant to embrace them into your life and state that your house was blessed by their presence. To "receive" means to welcome into friendship and to enfold into your heart. Greatness is to make children, the weak, powerless, and needy, the honored guests in your life. Why? Because our Lord's heart went out to these little sheep who needed a shepherd.

The poignant account of Jesus' washing of his disciples' feet appropriately adds the final touch to Jesus' model and interpretation of servant leadership. Jesus had an other-worldly view of power and authority. He is the king who stoops to conquer. Or as someone has said, "Jesus is the king whose scepter is a towel and whose crown is a wash basin."

The lesson of Jesus' model is that servanthood comes out of the security of knowing we are God's children. That security sets us free to be servants. Jesus' strength is that he knows who he is. No one and nothing can take that away. His identity is firmly rooted in his position before the Father. John introduces Jesus' act of servanthood with these words: "Jesus, knowing that the Father had given all things into his hands, and that he had come from God and was going to God, rose from supper, laid aside his garments, and girded himself with a towel" (John 13:3-4). Servanthood, far from being the result of a vacuous ego, is possible only when we are absolutely secure about our worth and value. Jesus embodied "self-emptying" (Phil. 2:7) because he knew he would never lose his eternal standing before his Father. He was willing to play the role of a household slave, whose task it was to wash the day's grime from between the toes of a master's guests, because his status with the Father could never be shaken.

Afterward Jesus instructed the disciples on the meaning of what he did. Notice that Jesus returned to the issue of his identity. "Do you know what I have done to you? You call me teacher and Lord; and you are right, for so I am" (John 13:12–13). It is as if Jesus were saying, I have every right to command you to wash my feet because of who I am. But I never have used my position to secure my rights. My whole pattern has been to give up what I could justly claim. "If I, then, your Lord and Teacher, have washed your feet, you also ought to wash one another's feet. For I have given you an example that you also should do as I have done to you" (John 13:14–15).

Only as we know who we are as children of the King can we be secure enough to lead from our knees. People will then recognize an authority that comes from above and will call us "blessed."

Principles of the Organism–Servant Model

Having examined Jesus' model and instruction on servant leadership, we must ask, How can this be translated into an organism-servant model of leadership in the church today? Several principles of application emerge from our discussion:

1. People in the highest positions of authority have the greatest obligation to serve. Senior pastors exist to serve associates, the leadership board, and ultimately the congregation. The upper echelon of denominational structures exists for the purpose of enhancing the grass-roots ministry of the local church.
2. Servant leadership is rooted in relationship, not coercion. Motivation is generated by modeling and intimacy, not the force of fear or judgment.
3. Servant leadership naturally seeks to support, not to control. A servant leader is able to come alongside to help someone realize their potential, whereas hierarchical leaders attempt to suppress those who might outshine them.
4. Servant leaders shine the spotlight of recognition on those with whom they share leadership. Far from being concerned that they will be diminished if the focus is diverted from them, servant leaders glory in the accomplishments and growth of colleagues.

5. Servant leaders are embarrassed by titles and the trappings of status. They will attempt to remove the hierarchical, status language of "senior," "associate," and "assistant" and to put in its place functional language that simply describes what one does (e.g., "pastor for proclamation and evangelism," "pastor for youth," "pastor for senior adults").
6. Servant leaders' authority is recognized on the basis of their character in Christ, not on the position or office that is held. Spiritual authority is reflective of others' awareness of the presence of Christ in the one who is a model. When E. Stanley Jones got it straight who was in fact the ultimate authority, he wrote, "I have resigned as the general manager of the universe."[6] Then Christ's authority was able to shine through.

How then do the principles derived from Jesus' model of servant leadership express themselves through human leaders?

Figure 9.2

The Organism Model
Egalitarian (Decentralized authority)

Characteristics:

- Authority—Plural leadership
- Accountability—Mutual
- Roles—Determined by gifts and call

PRINCIPLES OF AN ORGANIC CHURCH

The organism model of the church is rooted in a theology of the church as the living, animated body of Christ. The principles for our understanding of the way the church functions are as follows:

1. The church functions properly only when Jesus Christ is the acting Head of the body. He is not its honorary head; he is its leader. Paul states clearly that Jesus Christ is fully capable of directing the life of his body if we let him (1 Cor. 12). The church must be structured to reflect this truth. (See chapter 7, "Implementing the Equipping Model of Ministry," and chapter 10, "Call and Ordination in the New Reformation," as further illustration of what this looks like.)

2. What enables the church to function as an organism under the direction of the Spirit of Jesus Christ? It is the direct

relationship that each person has to Jesus Christ. R. Paul Stevens has captured this truth:

> There is a direct and living connection between the Head and every member of the body. . . . No church leader in the New Testament is ever called the head of a local body. That title is reserved for Jesus. The head does not tell the hand to tell the foot what to do. The head is directly connected to the foot. Therefore, people find their ministries not by being directed by the leaders but by being motivated and equipped and directed by the Head himself.[7]

3. These ministries are not discovered in isolation—me and Jesus. They develop within the body. It is within the body that ministry is discovered, affirmed, equipped, and commissioned. Ministry is done within community. This principle is facilitated through our "mission communities," where a shared ministry occurs in response to a common call. To keep this principle before us at the church I serve, we have reduced it to a catchy phrase: "We are to be the people of God as we do the work of God."

4. In the church organism every person makes a valuable contribution to the health of the whole. All service is honorable to the Lord. This being the case, we should avoid positional language that would elevate some and demean others. Using descriptive or functional language gives honor to all the parts.

Team Ministry: Plural Leadership

Biblically, ministry is predicated on plural, not solo, leadership. One-person ministry violates the body concept because it views the pastor as the solitary leader. In the Bible, elders in the local church are always referred to in the plural, with the exception of reference to the function and qualifications of a bishop (1 Tim. 3:2; Titus 1:7). David Watson adds,

> Although there might have been a presiding elder, there is never the slightest hint of a solitary leader (such as the pastor) even in the smallest and youngest churches. Always it was *a shared responsibility*, thereby giving much mutual encouragement, protection and support.[8]

Therefore I define a leadership team as *a group of people working cooperatively to accomplish a common mission through the exercise of their gifts and call in the context of mutual accountability*. The assumption is that the whole is greater than the sum of its parts.

Wisdom of the group is greater than the wisdom any individual brings to problem solving and vision setting. "For in the abundance of counselors there is victory" (Prov. 24:6).

Let us examine team ministry from the varied perspectives of authority, accountability, and roles. In addition to these tangible qualities, there are intangible qualities necessary for a team to gel.

Authority

Pastor, Head of Staff

1. *First-among-equals*. The organism model stresses contributions without value judgments. The first-among-equals approach places the head of staff in a servant mode with a stress on *equal* rather than on *first*. The head of staff then becomes a servant to fellow servants on a ministry team. Instead of the staff's being an alter ego, the head of staff gives his life away to see that those with whom ministry is shared are encouraged to be all they are meant to be. This will require a considerable investment of time by the head of staff in order to know the passion or calls of each individual and the gifts God has given as the means to carry out the call. Permission is given in an atmosphere of freedom to pursue the dimension of the call wherever that may lead.

My role model for a pastor as head of staff is Jerry Kirk, former pastor of the College Hill Presbyterian Church in Cincinnati. Jerry had a shared ministry with his staff, giving away ministry to the gifted ones with whom he served. Instead of holding the reins tightly, he allowed others to share roles heretofore exclusively associated with the head of staff. Recognizing that Gary Sweeten was gifted by God as a process person and facilitator, Jerry made him the presider at staff meetings. The ministry of pastoral care often associated with the "priestly presence" of the senior pastor was directed by Mel Steinborn, who in turn equipped members of the body to do what usually remained the province of the professionals.

The true test of shared ministry is the ability to open up the power center—the pulpit—to others. Over a period of time Ron Rand came to share the preaching ministry equally with Jerry. At the staff level, Jerry created an atmosphere in which members of the team functioned according to their calls and giftedness. Jerry permitted an organism view of the church to become an operational reality among the professional staff.

2. *Leadership.* It is a truism that when everyone is responsible, then no one is responsible. There must be a place where the buck stops and ultimate accountability resides. A ministry team can have a shared accountability, but there must be someone designated with the responsibility to enforce the accountability.

The person who is first-among-equals must have one of two kinds of leadership abilities.

a. *Visionary leadership.* Visionary leaders dream dreams or visualize where the church needs to go in the future. James MacGregor Burns, writing in *Leadership,* defines visionary leaders as transformational leaders.[9] Visionary leaders are so able to articulate a picture of the future that others can grasp it and see their part in helping to fulfill it. In a shared-ministry approach, however, vision setting is not the sole province of one person.

The vision of the head of staff can be shaped and qualified in two ways: (1) Once a vision is shared with a staff and leadership board, it should become community property to be reshaped by the wisdom of the whole. For a vision to become shared, people must feel they have a stake in its formulation if they are to put energy into its implementation; (2) the staff and members of the leadership board carry portions of the vision for ministry that can add to the vision of the head of staff. For staff and leaders to feel fully invested, they must believe that they can affect the direction of the church. Maximizing the tributaries flowing into the vision creates a corporate dream with broad-based ownership.

b. *Administrative leadership.* Some senior pastors are not themselves visionary leaders, but are capable of managing people resources so that a vision can be drawn from those with whom ministry is shared. An administrative leader creates an environment in which staff and leadership can formulate direction together on a particular ministry.

I observed administrative leadership at its finest during a weekend retreat of our board of elders (the session). An outside consultant had been hired to help the staff and the session work in harmony toward a reinvigoration of purpose, goals, and objectives. The consultant was not there to set an agenda for the church or impose his sense of vision, but simply to draw from the twenty participants their sense of the crucial issues facing the church.

Using the nominal-group method, which places each person's concerns on a par, the consultant asked us to write down the four key issues facing our church. We were instructed to tend to the concerns within our spheres of responsibility. We then took several hours for each person to communicate his concerns to the group, posting them for all to see. From there we identified the high-priority items on the basis of their repetition in the lists. We all had the opportunity to influence the group, but we also agreed to submit to the will of the whole. The agenda for the church arose out of a corporate mind, not the vision of a single authority. Moreover, the pastoral staff was included on an equal basis with the board of elders. So the pastor as head of staff can function as an administrative coordinator, drawing on the vision arising from the group. In essence the first-among-equals then becomes a consensus builder.

If visionary leadership gifts are not present, it seems to me that the gift of administrative leadership must be. Otherwise what is left is a caretaker approach to pastoral ministry that sees the church as a family tending to its internal needs, but not as a mission that is ever evolving and developing.

There is a need for someone to keep an eye on the big picture and survey the landscape. Staff members and individuals on the leadership board tend to focus on small plots of ground. Often this means tending to their territories without much thought of how it fits into a master plan. In contrast, the head of staff coordinates the whole so that people resources and ministry fit together in a comprehensive direction.

Staff

Members of staff, who have responsibility in specialized areas of ministry, are fully vested with the authority to dream and implement a vision. In the hierarchical model, congregational members look to the head of staff to articulate positions on ministry direction while the staff acts as gofers for his wishes. In our organism model, authority and responsibility are shared, and this creates an atmosphere for staff to grow and evolve. As an associate I received permission to develop the discipling ministry to the full extent of my dreams. I was allowed to be an experimenter. I was given the opportunity to write a guide for implementing discipling relationships. A test group of "disciples" fed back their observations on both the content and the dynamics of the discipling process. The result was a field-refined tool that passed through the furnace of actual ministry. This created an atmosphere of shared ministry between pastor and people. The dross and impurities were removed in this approach to discipling ministry as the lives of both pastor and disciples were enhanced and enabled by mutual contribution.

Accountability

The traditional, hierarchical model is based on a one-way flow of accountability from the top down. But in an organic team ministry, accountability is mutual. Submission is not exclusively up the ladder, but one to another. A head of staff sets the standard. He must strike a balance between, on the one hand, being the one with whom the buck ultimately stops, and, on the other, submitting to fellow team members. The head of staff must courageously permit the others to require accountability of him.

Mutual accountability impinges on two areas:

1. *Ministry.* As the team members articulate their desired goals and God-inspired accomplishments in ministry, other team members encourage the fulfillment of these goals and monitor their completion. After a particularly anxiety-producing season of ministry, I decided that I needed a thorough rearranging of my out-of-control schedule with a narrower focus on immediate goals. I submitted a detailed plan to the staff for their information and feedback. Though fellow staff members appreciated the information and were impressed by my self-reflection, I encountered a reluctance to intrude into my life at the level of accountability. I sensed that this was foreign territory to the staff. Our usual approach is to exist somewhat autonomously in our specialized areas, only reporting information to each other but not placing our ministry design on the table for each other's shaping.

To be mutually accountable means to have a stake in the success of fellow partners in ministry. I have had the privilege of being on a couple of teams where I received such encouragement and confidence from respected team members that I discovered potential I had never seen in myself. A dear friend and respected colleague, Darrell Johnson, became my "head of staff" for a brief period of eighteen months. He would say to anyone who would listen, "More than anyone I know (or know of), Greg has grasped and lived the radical implications of the biblical doctrine of the priesthood of all believers. There is much 'talk' about this . . . but little 'walk.' Greg walks every bit of this talk." This book is a direct result of the encouragement of Darrell, who saw in me what I could never have seen in myself.

Mutual accountability is not only encouragement, but also correction. This involves speaking hard words to each other. Gordon MacDonald has written, "One solid and loving rebuke is worth a hundred affirmations."[10] We must allow teammates to offer a word of rebuke and to tell us where they see our giftedness. I referred earlier to the model of the College Hill Presbyterian Church. There, more than any other place I know, the staff have taken mutual submission seriously. They entered into a process in which they gave each other feedback on their spiritual gifts and then defined their roles on the basis of the composite picture. As a result, the preaching ministry was shared more equitably among these staff, one of whom was not ordained. Decisions about accepting speaking engagements and even future career opportunities were submitted for prayerful consideration and mutual decision.

2. *Personal growth.* In shared ministry, program development is not kept separate from personal growth. Public ministry cannot be separated from the model of Christ's life in us. To foster personal integrity in Christ, accountability means to open our lives to our teammates. Staff meetings regularly need to deal with questions like (a) what is the Lord teaching us in our devotional life? (b) what is the cutting edge of our discipleship? (c) how much attention and time are we giving to family? (d) where is the pressure of the world squeezing us into its mold? and (e) where are we feeling like a failure in ministry?

I have a tendency to get so wrapped up in what I am doing in ministry that I am not aware of what's going on elsewhere. When that happens, I neglect building relationships with team members. I need to balance task orientation with the personal tending to relationships. I can schedule out of my life the relaxed moments in the office in order to catch a casual conversation or an impromptu dialogue in the hall. I need people to call me away from the treadmill of task and productivity and toward caring for each other.

Time to build relationships is important. So is regular time to review and evaluate goals. I find quarterly two-day retreats a necessity for effective ministry team building. This block of time is essential for building stronger personal relationships and for opportunities to refine the staff's vision and goals. Likewise, weekly staff meetings include a balance of ministry strategy and personal concerns.

What God's people see modeled in staff relationships will affect the way ministry is fulfilled throughout the church. We decided to organize the staff as a mission community. By "mission community" I mean a group of three to twelve people who share a common heart for ministry. We wrote a covenant together that stated our purpose and the specific activities we agreed to accomplish together. This provided a basis for clear expectations, mutual ownership of ministry goals, and a standard for accountability.

Roles

Roles or job descriptions are fluid in an organic model. Positions are defined on the basis of the spiritual gifts and the call of God on the individual. Unfortunately, job descriptions are often so tightly written that they become a straitjacket. What they provide in clarity they lack in flexibility. They may articulate the church's need for a particular job to be done, but are not able to take into account the unique profile of the person who has filled the position. There needs to be room in the job description both to provide for the identified needs of the church and to encourage development of the gifted individual hired to accomplish the desired goals. The person hired should certainly have the abilities required to do the job, but from then on the church needs to set that person free to arrive at these goals in the way he or she is particularly motivated to carry it out.

Fluidity means not only freedom to carry out a responsibility, but the opportunity to grow into new dimensions of ministry. As people follow their hearts, develop approaches to ministry, and refine the dimensions of their gifts, they discover new vistas. When the discipling network was growing from one generation to another, an inner compulsion began to develop within me that was matched by an outward call to spread the discipling vision. In support of this vision our leadership team began to set me apart for defined periods of time to take this ministry beyond the church. They also allowed me a three-day block each month to put on paper my vision for ministry. Such a relationship is symbiotic. It is a mutually advantageous sharing of life. It is the church organism acting together in ministry.

Flexibility within staff means that roles are defined among the team according to the giftedness. In the institutional model it is assumed that the head-of-staff pastor will be the primary administrator, visionary, pulpiteer, pastoral care-giver, and so on. Though some abilities are essential to operate as a head-of-staff pastor, the organic model says that the roles on the team should be defined by the gifts each person brings to it. The key role of head of staff is to make sure the ministry is given away to those who are gifted and in turn get themselves out of the way so it can go forth.

Qualities Needed for a Team

We can hold an organism view of authority, accountability, and role definition, but if the intangible qualities of a team are lacking, all goes for naught. These intangible qualities are the glue that holds a team together.

Head of Staff

In my experience the most important quality for a head of staff is personal security. If ministry is shared with others who will receive the spotlight, the senior pastor must not be easily threatened. Insecurity about one's abilities in a leadership position leads to control of the other team members. Ministry jealously guarded, rather than graciously given away, will stifle associates.

Frank Tillapaugh, the pastor of Bear Valley Baptist Church in Denver and a modeler of shared leadership, articulates the internal struggle that will periodically raise its ugly head.

> I thought I had settled the shared leadership issue long ago. Yet all of a sudden I felt this tremendous need to be visibly appreciated. I knew that I was appreciated and people continually expressed their appreciation, but it wasn't enough for my hungry ego. I frequently thought about those pastors who had built their ministries differently and who had received all kinds of trips and material things. I began to dwell on how good those pastors really had it.
>
> A pastor in a shared ministry has a price to pay. . . . When the poor-little-old-me blues strike, you may wish you had done it another way.[11]

When your self-worth is rooted in God's love and acceptance, then you are freed to herald gladly the graces of fellow pastors.

Staff Team

1. *Mutual respect.* One ingredient in the glue for team ministry is the ability to respect the competence of teammates. If you question a team member's abilities to do the job, you may tend to hold back what you give or feel overwhelmed or resentful because you are covering for his deficiencies. This is obviously destructive of the very spirit of trust and interdependence essential for ministry together.

2. *Work ethic.* Properly functioning teams share a similar degree of intensity and work ethic. I once headed a college ministry team of five full-time staff, all of whom had a passionate commitment to reach and disciple the university for Christ. Our staff meetings felt like military strategy sessions plotting a conspiracy to win the war for Christ on campus. It was a supercharged atmosphere with students coming to Christ weekly. We were willing to pay the price of battle because we were equally committed to our goal.

3. *Positions that fit.* A fluid and functioning team will place its members in positions that fit their gifts and calls. When all members are doing what they love, the whole team is energized. Individual satisfaction makes for group satisfaction. If a person is not functioning because he or she does not "fit" the position, the rest of the team will be thrown out of balance trying to cover deficiencies, helping that person to learn or to do the job, or fielding the congregation's complaints.

4. *Servant spirit.* The call to ministry is the call to serve, not to be served. Yet people in ministry who are tempted to be known as "great" servants or superstars stifle community and camaraderie. They engender jealousy and resentment. They fear they will diminish their own stature if they praise the talents of others. In contrast, a genuine desire to see others succeed and become all God intended them to be will foster esprit de corps. What a delight to be a part of a group where you cheer for and rejoice in the way you see God using another! True servants are thrilled by others' successes.

When these qualities of team ministry are combined with an organism understanding of authority, accountability, and roles, the result can be dynamic ministry unleashed and the New Reformation realized in our lives. When it all works, there is a freeing of energy for ministry that makes it feel as if we are working in God's powerhouse.

In the concluding chapter I will address a redefinition of "call" and ordination in the New Reformation conception. If all God's people are ministers, then our exclusive designation of "call" and "ordination" for professional believers needs to be reexamined.

NOTES

1. Philip Greenslade, *Leadership, Greatness and Servanthood* (Minneapolis: Bethany House, 1984), 7.

2. Richard G. Hutcheson, *Mainline Churches and the Evangelicals* (Atlanta: John Knox, 1981), 119.

3. Frank Tillapaugh, *The Church Unleashed* (Ventura, Calif.: Regal, 1982), 71.

4. Jimmy Swaggart, as quoted in *Time* magazine.

5. Peter Wagner, *Leading Your Church to Growth* (Ventura, Calif.: Regal, 1984), 83.

6. As quoted by Gordon MacDonald, *Ordering Your Private World* (Nashville: Thomas Nelson, 1985), 91.

7. R. Paul Stevens, *Liberating the Laity* (Downers Grove, Ill.: InterVarsity Press, 1985), 36.

8. David Watson, *I Believe in the Church* (Grand Rapids: Eerdmans, 1978), 271.

9. James MacGregor Burns, *Leadership* (New York: Harper & Row, 1978), 4.

10. Gordon MacDonald, *Restoring Your Spiritual Passion* (Nashville: Thomas Nelson, 1986), 191.

11. Tillapaugh, *The Church Unleashed*, 108.

CHAPTER 10

Call and Ordination in the New Reformation

THROUGHOUT THIS BOOK I have been shaping a view of the church as an organism. Implicit in the discussion is a challenge to the traditional views of call and ordination. We are led to ask, How does the truth that all God's people are called to ministry affect our conceptions of call and ordination? Is it fair to assume that if all have a ministry, then *all are called?* And if that is the case, what "rite of passage" might there be for the members of the body that sets them apart for their call?

Again, we will approach answers to these questions by comparing the institutional and organic views of the church.

CALL AND ORDINATION THROUGH THE INSTITUTIONAL LENS

Since the institutional lens views the church from the top down, the call has been restricted to a few who go into vocational ministry. Phrases like "heard . . ., sensed . . ., or received a call" automatically conjure up an image of either missionary or pastor or perhaps seminary professor. Those who receive a call enter some form of professional Christian service. A private or "secret" call is prerequisite to pursuing a vocation in the church. It is secret precisely because it is known only to the inaccessible heart of the individual on whom God has placed his hand or quickened his Spirit.

Thomas Gillespie wrote that when we examine the biblical view of call, we must begin where the New Testament begins. This is not where we are accustomed to beginning.

In our ordinary church parlance, the call of God *is limited to* those among us who bear ordination to professional ministry. . . . I cannot ever remember ever hearing either an elder or a deacon saying that he or she serves because of the call of God. Neither have I heard a church member say that his or her life vocation is the result of a divine calling.[1]

Our theology of ministry will lead directly to our conception of call and ordination. Gillespie goes on to say that the reason we have limited call to a restricted few is that our starting point for understanding the nature of ministry is wrong. Traditionally, he states, our theology of ministry has begun with a doctrine of ordained offices. This starting point leads to a clericalism and therefore an elitist understanding of call and ordination. Our theology of ministry is wrong precisely because our point of departure is wrong.

The inevitable result is a split-level living arrangement with the clergy "upstairs" and the laity "downstairs." A theology of ministry turns into a sociology of status. No matter how much we push for the laity to be involved in ministry within this framework, they will have a second-class value. A "trickle-down" theology, just as in economics, results in the "haves" and "have nots."

Since a hierarchical theology of ministry has been our worldview, we have implicitly operated out of a hierarchy of call. Challenging this corruption of the Reformed tradition, Donald McKim writes,

The Reformed tradition, it is true, has put some special emphasis on the calling to "Word and Sacrament," to the position of pastor in the church. But it is a perversion of the tradition and diversion from the New Testament if we conclude from this that called Christians who are preachers, or evangelists, or missionaries (or even seminary professors!) are somehow blessed by a special calling that puts them head and shoulders above the rest of the called body of Christ.[2]

We implicitly pigeonhole people into categories of seriousness along a rating continuum of call. The base of the pyramid is labeled "secular" and its pinnacle is the "sacred." At the base are those who do not take their faith too seriously. Their vocational pursuits are invested in the temporal. Then, as we move up the pyramid, there are those who are just "homemakers" who perhaps have a little more serious sense of call in terms of the family. Further up are those who go into the caring professions, such as the medical field or some form of "people" work. But serious Christians demonstrate their commitment by becoming professional Christians—that is, pastors or missionaries or seminary professors. Devoting one's whole life to God means to pass into the realm of the sacred.

Figure 10.1

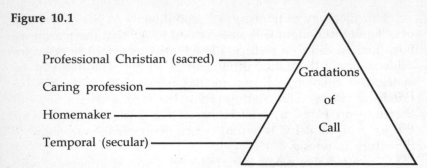

Professional Christian (sacred)

Gradations

Caring profession

of

Homemaker

Call

Temporal (secular)

Although the Reformation theologically laid the groundwork to erase the line between the secular and sacred, this false distinction is still the predominant paradigm. The secular is associated with the temporal, is connected to the realm of the public, social order, and is therefore profane. The sacred, in contrast, is concerned with the eternal, is connected to the realm of personal family values, and is therefore spiritual.

As long as this is the framework that affects our view of call, we will *de facto* remain mired in a hierarchical, sacerdotal, and clerical view of call.

Under this view of call, ordination becomes a rite of passage into the sacred. Ordination not only implies the right of the church to set standards and tests to recognize and order its leadership, but also conveys a mystical entrance into a realm off-limits to "ordinary" Christians. It is not surprising to read the following view of ordination in a report of the Anglican-Roman Catholic International Commission: "Christian ministers . . . share through baptism in the priesthood of the people of God. . . . Nevertheless their ministry is not an extension of the common Christian priesthood but belongs to *another realm* of the gifts of the Spirit. Ordination denotes entry into this apostolic and God-given ministry."[3] But what is disturbing is that this same language was adopted in *The Report of the Churches' Council for Covenanting*, an alliance of Protestant denominations exploring structural union.

We have not fully realized the priesthood of all believers

because we have created a priesthood within a priesthood. On the one hand we affirm that a "minister" participates as every Christian does in the priesthood of all believers, but in the next breath we list special responsibilities that are marked "ordained only." We cannot have it both ways. What is affirmed one moment, is taken away the next. What is the difference between "the ministry" and "lay ministry"? Ordination. Anthony Harvey asks, "What is it that makes a Christian minister what he is?" His answer: "We shall, of course, regard one qualification as essential. The man [sic] must have been ordained."[4]

Ordination has its sacerdotal perquisites. First is the exclusive right to preside at the Lord's Supper. What was originally a matter of church order has been turned into a mystical rite for the ordained. In chapter 4 I quoted Thomas Torrance, who views ordination as completed at the time the ordinand takes up the bread and wine for the first time and thereby enters into the sphere of the self-consecration of Christ. Deny it as we may, this is nothing less than a New Testament veneer placed over an Old Testament priesthood. We could also question why baptisms, weddings, funerals, preaching, and the like are off limits to the nonordained. The results have been deadly.

> Where this ordering of ministry results in a class or caste system, where it divides the community into "clergy" and "laity," where it separates those who have "a part" in the ministry from those who have no part in it, there *the theology of ministry authorized by the New Testament is forsaken.*[5]

The prevailing practice of ordination is a denial of the New Testament theology of ministry.

CALL AND ORDINATION FROM A "NEW REFORMATION" PERSPECTIVE

Each member of the people of God stands under God's call. Each is accountable to God for his or her response to it. Ministry is rooted in a prior call of God upon every believer. A hierarchy of call is foreign to the New Testament. Martin Luther challenged the conception of a "special" calling, which had been fully entrenched in the Roman Catholic tradition.

> Monastic vows rest upon the false assumption that there is a special calling, a vocation, to which superior Christians are invited to observe the counsels of perfection, while ordinary Christians fulfill only the commands; but there is simply *no*

special religious vocation, since the *call* of God comes to *each* at
the common tasks.[6]

"The Report of the Special Committees on the Theology of Call"
from the Presbyterian Church, U.S.A., gives us the proper angle
to begin our discussion of call: "There is one call of God to all the
people of the earth, to the whole Church, and to every member of
the Church, to the one ministry of God's word and work in Jesus
Christ." Ministry is accomplished through the *whole* church, not
just a part of it. To quote Thomas Gillespie again, "The membership becomes the medium of God's ministry. Through the
distribution of the Spirit's ministry, every member becomes a co-
worker with God. To each for the sake of all."[7]

The call of God incumbent on all Christians has several levels.
Basically, call can be divided into two overall categories with
subdivisions under each. First, there is a general call, which
relates to *who* we are (our personhood). Second, a particular call
upon all believers relates to *what* we do.

General Call

The designated roles between God and humans become
clearly defined around call. God calls, and people respond. The
New Testament verb for call is *kaleō* and the noun is *klēsis*,
meaning "call" or "calling." The verbal form has the sense of "to
invite" or "to summon." These ordinary words take on special
significance when it is God in Christ who issues the call. Donald
McKim has said, "God's call is to all who believe *to be* Christian."

This general call breaks out to three levels: (1) a call to Christ,
(2) a call to community, and (3) a call to transformation.

1. *Call to Christ.* A disciple is one who responds in faith to the
gracious call of Jesus Christ. It is a call to *relationship* and *salvation*.
Jesus met Simon and Andrew, James and John working as
fishermen by the Sea of Galilee. He summoned them to follow
him. These disciples left the predictable, secure trades their
families had followed for generations in response to the magne-
tism of the Son of God (Mark 1:19–20). Call fundamentally means
to enter into *relationship* with God in Jesus Christ. "God is faithful,
by whom you were called into the fellowship of his Son, Jesus
Christ, our Lord" (1 Cor. 1:9).

Jesus came to seek and to save the lost. When the religious
leaders questioned him about the questionable company he was

keeping, Jesus said that he "came not to *call* the righteous, but sinners" (Mark 2:17). Paul sketches in broad strokes the panoramic plan of God's eternal salvation. When the plan of salvation intersects individual humans in history, God sends forth an "effectual" call. Paul writes, "And those whom he [God] predestined he also *called*" (Rom. 8:30).

That call has its origin in a call to the person of Christ is made painfully clear to the Galatians, who were rapidly turning from the source. "I am astonished that you are quickly deserting him who *called* you in the grace of Christ" (Gal. 1:6). The call of Christ is a claim upon us that is so radical and uprooting, it means being *"called* out of darkness into his marvelous light" (1 Peter 2:9). Therefore God's call in Christ is first and foremost a call to *salvation.*

2. *Call to community.* Donald McKim has described the church as the *locus* out of which we live the *focus* of our particular call. The *locus* of the church is the base of operations from which your particular ministry is launched. It is the supportive place where we find our identity, nurse our wounds, and are held accountable. A call to Christ is simultaneously a call into community. Is it any wonder that the Greek word for church, *ekklesia,* is derived from the verb "to call forth"? The Second Helvetic Confession defines the church as "an assembly of the faithful called or gathered out of the world; a communion, I say, of all saints, namely of those who truly know and rightly worship and serve the true God in Christ" (chap. 17, 5.125). Writing to the Corinthians, Paul greets them with this description of their identity: "To the church of God which is at Corinth . . . *called* to be saints *together* with all those in every place who call on the name of our Lord Jesus Christ" (1 Cor. 1:2).

The "called out" people are both a local assembly in a particular locale and the church universal, "in every place." There is no call to Christ without a call to the body of Christ. To be in Christ is to be in the church. Paul substitutes the image of baptism for call in 1 Corinthians 12:13, but certainly "call" is implied in his meaning: "For by one Spirit we were all baptized into one body." The church community is the indispensable *locus* or center. It is within the church that our particular call is discerned, supported, and refined.

3. *Call to transformation.* When we respond to Christ, we enter a lifelong process of change. Gordon Cosby describes the call to transformation as a call to inward development. "We are to

overcome those obstacles in ourselves which hold us back and keep us from growing up into the full stature of Christ. The call of Christ is a call to die to the old self in order to become the new creation."[8] Paul states that "God has . . . called us . . . in holiness" (1 Thess. 4:7). Addressing the character and qualities of the Christian community that make for unity, Paul pleads, "I therefore, a prisoner for the Lord, beg you to lead a life worthy of the *calling* to which you have been *called*" (Eph. 4:1).

The Scriptures use a number of different images to capture the goal of transformation. All these metaphors assume that there must be an inward change of heart that will then be reflected outwardly. Jesus taught us that *fruit-bearing* will be the result of our abiding in the life that flows through the vine, an image Jesus uses to describe our relationship with him (John 15:1–11). Good fruit cannot occur unless the tree producing the fruit is also good (Luke 6:43–45). Good works are a product of our "inner being." Paul's image of *being led by the Spirit* conveys the same truth. Those who relinquish their life to the Spirit's control will produce as the natural by-product the fruit of the Spirit (Gal. 5:16–26).

In another place Paul shifts to the picture of *maturity* as the goal for Christian living. "Him we proclaim, warning everyone and teaching everyone in all wisdom, that we might present everyone *mature* in Christ" (Col. 1:28). Though "mature" is rendered "perfect" in the King James Version (*teleios* does not convey sinlessness but is closer to "complete"), a mature Christian is one who has passed through the stages of birth, childhood, and adolescence, and is now an adult. Adult Christians are those who take full responsibility for and are self-disciplined in their growth in Christ.

Yet I believe the image that summarizes all that has been stated so far is simply that we are to grow to *Christlikeness*. Paul Tournier describes growth in Christ as an increasing congruence between our "person" and our "personage." One result of the fall of Adam and Eve was a disjunction between the inner and outer persons. Clothes covered up the shame of nakedness. Humans were cut off from themselves. The image of God in humans was marred.

When the relationship with God was severed, so was knowledge of self. The "person" is the hidden inner being; the "personage" is the façade or public image presented to the world.[9] When Christ comes to live in us, he begins restoring our fractured inner image. So Paul writes that the goal of salvation is "to be conformed to the image of his Son" (Rom. 8:29). The more we relinquish our life to the indwelling Christ in our person, the more our personage becomes a reflection to the world of a divine life within. "Christ . . . through us spreads the fragrance of the knowledge of him everywhere" (2 Cor. 2:14). "And we all, with unveiled face, beholding the glory of the Lord, are being changed into his likeness from one degree of glory to another" (2 Cor. 3:18).

The general call of God is a call for our character to be transformed individually and corporately so that we reflect Christ's life in us and among us. No one has said this better than C. S. Lewis:

> The more we get what we now call "ourselves" out of the way and let Him take us over, the more truly ourselves we become. There is so much of Him that millions and millions of "little christs," all different, will still be too few to express Him fully. He made them all, He invented—as an author invents characters in a novel—all the different men [and women] that you and I were intended to be. In that sense our real selves are all waiting for us in Him. . . . It is when I turn to Christ, when I give myself up to His personality that I first begin to have a real personality of my own."[10]

The general call to Christ, community, and transformation places a priority on the inner life of being that undergirds and gives direction to the outer life of doing.[11]

Particular, or Concrete, Call

When we move from the general call to all to be Christian to the particular call also placed on all, we are moving from being to doing. Donald McKim notes this shift by adding a phrase to his definition: "God's call is to all who believe to be Christian *in all we do.*" Paul reflects this balance of being and doing when he states the intended results of salvation: "For we are his workmanship, created in Christ Jesus for good works, which God prepared beforehand, that we should walk in them" (Eph. 2:10). We are called to ministry or service.

In the Reformed tradition we speak of the call that takes shape in the various spheres of our lives as "the Christian vocation." Vocation is an all-encompassing term for Christian obligation or duty derived from the Latin *vocatio*, which in turn comes from the Greek for calling, *klesis*. Though vocation is

equivalent in contemporary usage to "profession" or "occupation," this historically is only one of the spheres of our vocation or
"calling for service." Our calling is the response to the summons
that God has laid claim to us in Christ in absolute terms—our life
is not our own (1 Cor. 6:19).

For each of us, this calling takes on a specific shape
depending on the particular sphere of our call. The chart on page
197 is an attempt to capture the biblical conception of our
particular or concrete call.

Before turning to the specific sphere of call, let me reveal a
conviction I hold about "the called person." There is a core built
into our beings by the God who has made us. There is an
essential, unchanging design that forms the fabric of our inner
world. This unchangeable you is carried into the various spheres
of our call. Far from entering this world as a *tabula rasa* on which
our specific cultural milieu etches its design, I believe that all
people are unique and therefore order their environment at least
as much as the environs order them.

Any attempt to describe the central motivating thrust of our
life remains somewhat illusive. Arthur Miller and Ralph Mattson,
Christian vocational counselors, have discovered that there is an
inner governor, which we might call the "motive" or "will," that
gives shape to everything we do. They believe this is part of what
it means to be created in the image of God. They conclude that
"people begin with a specific design that remains consistent
through life and that design cannot be changed."[12]

Contrary to the *me-ism* of our culture that suggests that each
day brings unlimited possibilities, we cannot wake up each
morning and say, "What do I want to be today?" Overnight the
molecules in our bodies do not rearrange themselves so that we
greet the new day with a vastly different temperament, set of
abilities, and set of desires. This does not exclude alterations in
our lives. Skills can be taught; character can be molded. Rather,
we are amazingly consistent so that over time others become
aware of a unique personality.

What is this consistent inner self of which we speak? It is not
just talents and abilities, but something that lies behind them.
According to Mattson and Miller, "We seek a description of a
central pattern that resides behind a person's talents and determines how and when they are used. We aim at knowing that
fundamental part of us that needs to be fulfilled before we can
believe our talents have value."[13] This is the stuff of inner drive or

Figure 10.2

CALLED TO MINISTRY
(Sphere of Our Call)

Church: Ecclesia Ministry
"Called Out People"

Shape of call:

1. Gifts—Ministry abilities

2. Sphere—Particular focus of use of gifts

Key questions:
1. In service where/and when is joy/excitement/energy flowing?
2. What particular concern for or need do you observe in your church?

Family: The Ministry of Home

Shape of call:

1. Protector—Provide a safe haven
2. Teacher of values

3. Development of self-worth and value

World: Diaspora Ministry

"Sent Out People"

Shape of call:

1. Witness in word and deed to the kingdom of God

2. Expression of the compassion of Jesus Christ
   a. Ministering to felt need
   b. Standing for justice

Key question:
Where does the compassion of Christ in you intersect the brokenness of the world?

THE CALLED PERSON

"Much of the will of God for us is written in us."

Key questions:
1. What gifts and motivated abilities has God given to you which are an expression of your inner design?
2. What contribution has God given you to make?

Sabbath Rest: The Ministry of Rest

Shape of call:
1. Restoration—Refilling the reservoir of joy

2. Worship

3. Recreation

Key question: What activity restores your soul?

Work: The Ministry of Work

Shape of call:
1. Inherent identity in the created order

2. A place to express inner design or motivated abilities
3. A place of witness to the kingdom of God

Key question: As you review your life, what achievements have given you the greatest satisfaction?

motivation—in a word, the will. The will is what Miller and
Mattson call "the dictator within"; it gives shape to thoughts,
intention, and attitudes. "To know the pattern of motivated
abilities is to know the shape of a person's will."[14]

As I look back over fifteen years of professional ministry, I am
amazed by how consistent my own sense of who I am has been.
At the heart of all that I do is the desire to *influence*, to leave a
transforming mark on people's lives. The role of equipper and
trainer has fit me ever since the beginning of my ministry. My
desire has been to help others discover the unique contribution
they have to make to Christ's kingdom. As I grew in this self-
understanding, the image of coach became appropriate. The *coach*
designs the strategy for the game and sees how each player can
make a contribution to the winning effort. A commitment to be a
discipler comes out of the desire to influence people's growth in
Christ. Finally, as a *teacher* I want to inform minds so people's
views are transformed. All these labels describing the core of my
motivation spring from the same desire: I want to leave an imprint
for Jesus Christ on people's lives. That unchangeable part of me
directs all the various spheres of my life.

Much of the will of God for us is "written" in us. God has
created us to live lives that are complete only when directed by his
purposes. Yet, in our evangelical subculture we are often pro-
grammed to seek God's will in the outward circumstances of our
lives. We tend to equate God's will with the discovery of the right
marriage partner or a career. But the will of God is a far more
dyi.amic, lifelong process of being a steward of our inner design in
the context of the specific demands of the various spheres of our
call. "God's call [will] is to all who believe to be Christian in all we
do."

The call of God takes particular forms according to the sphere.
Figure 10.2 identifies five spheres of call: family, sabbath rest,
church, world, and work. I will concentrate here on the last three
of these.

CALL TO THE CHURCH: ECCLESIA MINISTRY

Figure 10.3

Call to the Church
Focus:
1. The exercise of our spiritual gifts
2. A sphere of our call
Discernment questions:
1. Where and when are joy, excitement, and energy flowing in service to the church?
2. What particular burden or concern do you have for the church?

The "called out" people, the church, constitute one sphere in which we do ministry. In terms of *general call*, the call to community is the *locus* of all our ministry. But the church is also the *focus* of ministry. It is the call of every Christian to upbuild, edify (1 Cor. 14:3), strengthen, and work for the common good (1 Cor. 12:7).

The central clue to discovering our spiritual gift mix is to get in touch with the spheres of service that produce a flow of inner joy, excitement, and energy. For me doing the study necessary for teaching, developing a strategy for presentation, and engaging in the classroom dynamic of give and take excite and energize me. When I help people discover their spiritual gifts, I ask them to complete the following statement: "In my work (job) or church ministry I find myself most fulfilled when . . . " The assumption is that when we operate consistent with our inner motivation there is a spontaneous, yet deep release of joy that says, "This is what I was made for."

Yet our call is not to be equated with discovering our gifts. The gifts are tools like those in a workman's kit; we use them, but they do not tell us what type of project we are to work on. Among the synonyms for spiritual gifts in Paul's parallel structure in 1 Corinthians 12:4–7 we discover the word *diakonia*. This word translated "service" or "ministry" not only tells us the *manner* in which gifts are to be exercised, but following the insight of Ray Stedman, also conveys the idea of *sphere*. The sphere is the particular locale within the church where our gifts are best used.

Our call to *ecclesia ministry* is complete when we discover both our spiritual gifts profile and the place where those gifts are best used. For example, I may know that I have a gift of teaching, but that doesn't tell me how it is to be exercised. Is my gift of teaching most beneficial to children, adolescents, or adults? Am I to be a classroom teacher, or would I function better in a small-group or discipling atmosphere?

How do we identify a sphere of service? It is best uncovered by identifying the weight of concern we bear for the church. Call comes with a sense of positive burden. Since all members of the body view the church through their own eyes, they will identify vastly different needs. I help people get in touch with their burden for the church by asking them to complete the following statements: (1) I believe God has given me the responsibility of _____ in my congregation. (2) My biggest concern for this church is _____.

Each of us has a contribution to make in the church. The call is not static. The call God places on our life evolves as we grow in our own gifts and willingness to own what God has placed in us, all of which interacts with the particular needs of a congregation at any given time.

CALL TO THE WORLD: DIASPORA MINISTRY

Martin Luther said that every Christian should experience two conversions. The first conversion is to respond to God's call to come out of the world. Unfortunately, many of us never hear the second call, which is to be sent back into the world to penetrate it with the message and model of the kingdom of God. It is not so much that we refuse to experience the second conversion; rather, many of us have an inaccurate understanding of the first one.

Many Christians live a schizophrenic existence. We have divided our life experience of reality into two nonbiblical categories. We have two separate realms; the *sacred*, the church, and the *secular*, the world. We have two separate sets of values. We have become adept at moving from the sacred to the secular and vice versa without conscious recognition. In matters related to family values, personal ethics, and church we wear the sacred hat. Yet we imperceptibly exchange the sacred hat for the secular one when it comes to matters of the prevailing social order (e.g., business, politics, economics). We often act as if we need to be Christian only in the sacred realm.

The Bible teaches that there is never a time when we step out of this sacred arena. There is no distinction between the "sacred" and "secular" realms of society, no gulf between the personal and social, the private and public, or individual and corporate sin. The biblical distinction is between the kingdom of God and the kingdom of darkness. In professing the Christian faith we were transferred from the dominion of darkness to the "kingdom of his beloved Son" (Col. 1:13). We owe allegiance to King Jesus in all that we do. Everything we do requires a kingdom consciousness.

God's kingdom is an invading force, and we are the shock troops. This kingdom penetrates the darkness. Jesus calls us to pray it into being and to be a part of the answer to the prayer, "Thy kingdom come, they will be done, on earth as it is in heaven" (Matt. 6:10). When Jesus said, "You are the salt of the earth . . . the light of the world" (Matt. 5:13–14), he was speaking of our being infused with life from God as a mark of the kingdom's presence that has come through Jesus. We are penetrating salt and light when we are connected with Christ the King.

As shock troops we are called to be diaspora—scattered— ministers, sent from the *locus* of the community of believers into the world. In Scripture, "world" is a technical word. It refers to the created order shattered by sin. Humanity's rebellion against God's authority resulted in brokenness. The "world," therefore, is corporate life organized and functioning without reference to God. Jesus calls us to go into this needy, hurting world. "As thou didst send me into the world, so I have sent them into thy world" (John 17:18). This is the Christian's "second" conversion, the mandate of which Luther spoke.

What is our call to the world?

Figure 10.4

Call to the World
Focus:
1. Declaration of the gospel (witness of words)
2. Compassionate acts of service (witness of deeds)
• Sympathy
• Outrage
Discernment question:
Where does the compassion of Christ in you intersect the brokenness of the world?

We are to be witnesses to God's invading kingdom of love and justice in word and deed.

1. *Witness of words.* We have been entrusted with the message of reconciliation. The means by which God has chosen to call people to him is our articulation of the gospel. The gospel is the power of God unto salvation. As we faithfully share the good news that God has taken the initiative to reconcile us to him by ransoming us through the costly death of his Son, God's Spirit penetrates the darkness of people's hearts, drawing and wooing them into a life-changing relationship. God has no other plan. He has tied the accomplishment of his purposes to save mankind to our willing cooperation to proclaim the good news that we are the "visited planet." (I refer the readers to the numerous discussions of the biblical imperative for the Great Commission and the tools needed to carry it out.)

2. *Witness of deeds.* We live in a "post-Christian" age in which the Western world is indifferent, apathetic, or hostile to the biblical God. We need other forms of witness to build bridges of contact to the unbelieving world. To be witnesses to the kingdom of God in deed means that we touch people's lives at the point of their felt need. There are gaping wounds in people's lives that need the healing touch of Christ's compassion through the Christian community.

We live in a casualty society. People are weighed down by the baggage of guilt from abortions, the wreckage of divorce, and the aftereffects of alcoholism and substance abuse. The more we can enter into the pain of people's lives, the more we win the right to share the gospel. To be kingdom people penetrating society means that *we enter the spiritual battle against the forces of darkness that oppress and do violence to people's lives.*

Our attitude toward this world can be captured by one word: compassion. Compassion, as exemplified by our Lord, has two components: sympathy and outrage.

Sympathy

After Jesus had ministered among the villages of Palestine, Matthew recorded the following: "When he saw the crowds, he had *compassion* on them, because they were harassed and helpless, like sheep without a shepherd" (Matt. 9:36). What did Jesus see as he walked among his errant creation? He saw people who were harassed and helpless. These people were living without knowledge of the Father, though they were beings created for fellowship with him. Jesus, the agent of creation, slipped incognito among them. What was Jesus' response? He had compassion.

Our call is to show the lost world the compassion of Jesus. "God so loved the world that he gave . . . " (John 3:16). Yet what I often see in myself and other Christians is not a servant spirit of graciousness, but judgment and anger toward the world. With red-faced belligerence, we castigate the world for having values that are anti-Christian. We seem to build walls, not bridges to a world in need. We appear more repulsed by the world than compelled by God's great love to show the compassion of Christ.

For our Lord, compassion meant sympathy. Its origin is a Greek word, *sympatheō,* meaning "to feel with." Jesus had a deep feeling for humanity. In the incarnation Jesus identified with us in our weakness. That is sympathy. The letter written to the Hebrews captures the *sympathy* of compassion: "Since therefore the children share in flesh and blood, he himself likewise partook of the same nature, that through death he might destroy him who has the power of death, that is, the devil, and deliver all those who through fear of death were subject to lifelong bondage. . . . For we have not a high priest who is unable to *sympathize* with our weaknesses, but one who in every respect has been tempted as we are, yet without sinning" (Heb. 2:14–15; 4:15).

For Jesus, sympathy meant he would himself bear the penalty for our sin. His sympathy extended to being our substitute, to stand in the way of and to take the full brunt of God's fury toward sin. Isaiah predicted that a servant was coming who would absorb the wounds and bruises we deserved for our transgressions and iniquities. Our wholeness would come at the price of his punishment; he would be "smitten by God" (Isa. 53:5–6). Os Guinness writes, "As God became man in Jesus, he was no White Hall or Pentagon Chief, making quick flying inspections of the front lines, but one who shared the fox holes, who knows the risks, who felt the enemy fire. Ours is the only God with wounds."[15]

As followers of Jesus into the world, we too are called to identify with the pain. I believe that for the church to restore credibility with the world, we must both be and be seen as suffering servants ourselves. The world is able to recognize that true sympathy is much more like Mother Teresa's service to those dying on the streets of Calcutta than the show-biz glitz of some Christian ministries. Our call is to costly service.

Outrage

But we get only a partial picture of compassion if we stop with sympathy. Compassion is sympathy laced with outrage. One of the Greek words that means "compassion" even sounds as if it might indicate righteous anger: *splagnizomai.* The Hebrews thought that emotions emanated from the bowels. When someone was particularly pained by a life circumstance, a person would say, in effect, "you are cutting up my intestines." This is how the father felt when he saw his prodigal son returning in rags. The Scripture says he "had compassion" on him (Luke 15:20). It is also Jesus' response to the leper who threw himself at the Master's feet, pleading, "If you will, you can make me clean" (Mark 1:40).

Mark records that Jesus was "moved with pity." The word "pity" in no way captures the intensity of Jesus' emotion. He did not simply feel sorry. His reaction to the leper and the father's response to the broken prodigal is a gut-wrenching, visceral clutch at the stomach. To have compassion means to simmer at a low burn with a controlled anger against the forces that trap individuals and reduce them to a quality of life far less than God intended. Compassion was Jesus' agonized cry against leprosy and a disheveled youth: "This is not the way it is supposed to be!"

Another graphic term, though not translated "compassion," reveals Jesus' reaction to the ultimate human enemy. It is used when Jesus dramatically stood before the tomb of his friend Lazarus, who had been four days in the grave. Emotions were intensified by the gawking onlookers anticipating Jesus' next move and the grieving of Mary and Martha over the loss of their brother. John says of Jesus, "When Jesus saw her [Mary] weeping, and the Jews who came with her weeping, he was *deeply moved in spirit.* . . . Then Jesus, *deeply moved again,* came to the tomb" (John 11:33, 38).

"Deeply moved" does not do justice to the depth of Jesus' intensity. This is the same word used to describe a powerfully trained Greek stallion ready to charge into battle. The stallion would rear back on its hind legs with muscles rippling, paw the air, and in controlled fury "snort" before hurling itself at the enemy. As Jesus stood at Lazarus' graveside, death for him symbolized the culmination of evil, pain, sorrow, suffering, injustice, cruelty, and despair: "This is not the way it is supposed to be!!" As Jesus stood face to face with death, he "snorted in spirit" and let loose an inner fury against the final enemy. In compassion, Jesus cried out from the depths of his being, "Lazarus, come forth!"

The compassion of Jesus incarnated in us is *sympathetic identification with and outrage against the world.* Christians can identify their calls to the world by sensing where the compassion of Christ in them intersects the brokenness of the world. Where does your heart go out to the victims of the world ravaged by sin? Where do you feel controlled fury against forces of oppression and dehumanization that wear the countenance of Satan? The answer to these questions identifies your compelling call. For example, people active in St. John's Central American Refugee Mission Community identify with the pain of individual, political refugees from El Salvador, Guatemala, and Nicaragua. They are outraged by the political forces and systems of injustice that create death squads and economic exploitation.

Often our heartfelt compassion is buried under layers of fear. To penetrate our carefully constructed defenses, I ask people to listen to their hearts. To penetrate the fear, people are invited to complete this statement: "If I could be assured of not failing in ministry, I would . . ." The responses to this statement have been like a geyser spouting forth from an untapped well.

Janet tried to respond to this statement without losing control. Her moist eyes were an indication that we had struck a deep reservoir. Sobbing, she told me of the pain she bore for teens who threaten suicide. Her dream was to run a church-based ministry that reached out to desperate youth in the impersonal city. This was the first time she had allowed her passion to emerge into the light. In the years since we had that conversation, Janet's life has been a steady progress toward living out this call.

Our call to the world is at the intersection of the world's pain.

THE MINISTRY OF WORK

One of the great legacies of the Reformation was the rediscovery of the dignity of work. Martin Luther stated, "There is simply no special religious vocation, since the call of God comes to each at the common tasks."

Luther identified "calling" with occupation, or profession. In his exposition and translation of 1 Corinthians 7:20, he used the

German word *Beruf*. "Every one should remain in the state [*Beruf*] in which he was called." Luther assumed this meant vocational immobility. In the highly authoritarian, stratified German society, one's vocation was the inherited family trade and was predetermined. Parental authority was to be obeyed. It is ironic that Luther did not take his own advice. Hans Luther, Martin's father, wanted him to be a lawyer, but Martin wanted to dedicate his life to God, which in his mind meant pursuing the highest call, being a monk.

Figure 10.5

Call to Vocation

Focus:

1. Declaration of the gospel (witness of words)
2. Vocation as an expression of our motivated abilities (cultural mandate)

Discernment question:

As you examine your life at various stages, what achievements have given *you* greatest satisfaction?

Most biblical scholars today believe Luther's interpretation of 1 Corinthians 7:17–24 was off the mark. Paul's concern in the passage was broader than occupation. He instructed the Corinthians not to attempt to change the life circumstance in which they received the gospel. The two life situations he mentions are (1) circumcision/uncircumcision, and (2) slavery/freedom. It makes no difference whether we are circumcised or uncircumcised, or whether we are slaves or freedmen. "Only, let everyone lead the life which the Lord assigned to him, and in which God has called him. . . . So, brethren in whatever state each was called, there let him remain with God" (vv. 17, 24). In other words, don't attempt to change your life circumstances, but serve Christ in whatever situation you find yourself.

Calvin's commentary on the same passage speaks of "calling" as life duties that govern our life action. Vocation keeps us from wandering aimlessly through life, Calvin says. Calvin was more flexible than Luther and felt that one's vocation could change. "It would be asking too much if a tailor were not permitted to learn another trade, or a merchant to change to farming."[16]

The importance of Luther's and Calvin's rediscoveries for our purposes is simply stated, "Work is a place to serve God." Our life situation is the locale of responsible calling. Therefore work is not merely the way we earn a living, but the way we give expression to our Christian life. Our job, according to Calvin, is "the post at which the Lord has placed us." In other words, vocations are not hierarchically graded on a religious-secular continuum.

Although this rediscovery of the value of work can be stated simply, it is no simple matter for Christians. Our workplace is often the single greatest source of tension. Dual realities that tug us in different directions converge on our jobs. On the one hand, work is the place where we are immersed in the world; on the other, it is the place where we are called to reflect the light of the gospel. Work is for many the focus of their call to the world. Everything I have written about call in regard to a verbal witness and compassionate deeds applies to the workplace.

Yet, as Luther and Calvin have suggested, work is also an expression of "the cultural mandate." We were created in the image of God and delegated the responsibility by God to have dominion over the living things and the created order (Gen. 1:26, 28). Work is a means whereby we live out the dignifying call to be co-workers with God. We are called to serve together in the creative process to structure justice in the social order. Miller and Mattson have said of this role, "What a pleasure it must have been for Adam to cultivate the ground for the pleasure of God."[17]

But the Fall contaminated work along with everything else. Although "creation and order cooperated in pre-fall days, now we labor as the means to take care of the necessities of life."[18] At its worst, work can become a task to be endured. Yet even under the curse, work can provide an environment to express the creativity God has placed in humans. While work was cursed, it is not in itself a curse. The "Genesis principle"[19] is still in place—the world was created by God as good. Though marred by sin, work is still to be the context for dignifying activity.

The workplace is not just the locale for Christians to witness to the gospel or minister to human need, but also an avenue to express their unique abilities. Work is an expression of being. Being good stewards of the abilities God has placed in us is also a fulfillment of the call to work. In other words, we are free to seek a vocation that expresses the inner design God has given to us. God receives no glory by our laboring in frustration in jobs that are inconsistent with our motivated abilities. The cultural mandate exists alongside the Great Commission.

Study after study has shown that human resources are

tragically wasted and many people live in frustration because
there is a mismatch between their skills and the jobs they hold.
Conservatively these studies show that three or four out of every
five people have jobs for which they are not suited. One person
expressed his frustration this way: "I think most of us are looking
for a calling not a job. . . . Jobs are not big enough for people."[20]
When there is congruence between one's abilities and inner
motivation, in a position that facilitates the inner design, a sense
of call is a natural by-product.

Consider Joyce, who uses her administrative abilities to
manage the office of our church. She could be using these same
talents in private industry and earn twice the income. But she
remains where she is because, she says, "When I use my gifts here
I know this is where I belong." The rest of us benefit from an
efficiently run office and are amazed that she is able to keep track
of the details in a very complex system of volunteers, programs,
committees, mailings, phone calls, and scheduling. Yet it is all
done with grace and joy. She fits. Joyce is fulfilling her call
through her work.

This book is not the place for an exhaustive theology of work
or a thorough discussion of the complexities and tensions of the
workplace for Christians in the fallen world. My aim in dealing
with the ministry of work is to focus on work as one place where
the call of God to us is fulfilled. For Christians, work need not be
only an unwanted job that puts food on the table or a place of
evangelizing the lost. Though we recognize that in a fallen world
there are no perfect jobs, as Christians we are called to express our
individual inner design as a means of producing societal wholeness. The workplace provides the context for this to happen.

The call of God originates in our being. Being precedes doing.
Our unique self gives the fundamental shape to our call. What
God places in our heart from birth, releases through the grace of
Christ, and enhances by the anointing of the Holy Spirit is
fundamentally an inside job. So we can say that much of the will
of God for us is written in us. All believers have a particular,
concrete call on them. The various spheres of church, world,
work, family, and Sabbath all have the particular demands of
faithfulness I have outlined. These spheres are the context for
doing what flows from our being.

Characteristics of Call

The following characteristics of call serve as criteria to help us as individuals get in touch with the call that is experienced deep within us. I believe God's voice to us can be heard in the following ways:

Figure 10.6

Characteristics of Call
1. Inner oughtness
2. Bigger than ourselves
3. Satisfaction/joy

1. Call has a sense of *inner oughtness*. Call is an "I must do." It is a compelling, inner force that drives us with an energy of its own—like an alien force rather than mere willpower.

The apostle Paul spoke the language of call when he wrote, "For if I preach the gospel that gives me no ground for boasting. *For necessity is laid upon me.* . . . For if I do this of my own will, I have a reward; but if not of my own will, *I am entrusted with a commission"* (1 Cor. 9:16–17). "Necessity is laid upon me." This I must do. It is not my own choosing, but I am compelled by the hand of God. A call cannot be possessed, because we are not the owners of a call but the custodians of it. A person who takes credit for the call of God destroys it. Paul is aware that he must be a faithful steward of a commission.

The inverse of "this I must do" is "this I *cannot* not do." If we are called, it takes more energy to suppress the call than to release it and be carried by the inner energy that comes with it. Paul writes, "Woe to me if I don't preach the gospel." He is saying that judgment is on him if he does not do what he has been specially selected to do. Yet he is also saying that he cannot *not* preach the gospel—it burns within him.

The prophet Jeremiah attempted to squelch the call to preach because of the consequences of personal terror. What happened to Jeremiah when he attempted to curtail his proclamation? "If I say, 'I will not mention him or speak anymore in his name,' there is in my heart as it were a burning fire shut up in my bones, and I am weary with holding it in, and I cannot" (Jer. 20:9). With call comes an inner oughtness.

2. Call is *bigger than ourselves*. The call of God on us is to accomplish something we could never imagine doing or fulfilling with our own resources. For this reason, our call is often buried. God's call on us is pushed into the recesses of our inner being because a fearful inner voice says, "I could never do that." For some time I have felt that God has set me apart to influence the next generation of pastors in their understanding of the pastoral role. Each time the thought dared to surface, I would squelch it with an opposing thought: "Who do you think you are?" Two things needed to happen for me to respond to this call: (a) I had to recognize that the accusing voice was the Evil One attempting to cut me off at the source. I am nothing, but the call of God is everything. If God has something for me to do, I am simply the custodian of his purpose; and (b) fear is opposed to love. Only when I experienced the love of God poured out in my heart through the Holy Spirit (Rom. 5:5) was I able to embrace the call of God.

Fear riddles our being and buries the dreams God would grow in us for his kingdom. Fear was the first emotion of fallen mankind and continues to be the greatest hindrance to the release of the power of the Holy Spirit. When I am helping people to discern their spiritual gifts, I ask them to complete one statement, "If I could be assured of not failing in ministry I would . . ." This response gives people permission for just a moment to get behind the stifling inner fears to listen to their dreams. Putting these dreams on paper and sharing them with others brings them out of our closets of hiddenness into the light that gives them power.

The call of God is always greater than anything we could ever do in our strength or by ourselves.

3. The call of God gives us *the greatest satisfaction and joy*. Jesus concluded his remarks on abiding in the vine by saying, "These things I have spoken to you, that my joy may be in you, and that your joy may be full" (John 15:11). Abiding in Christ leads to obedience. When we do the will of the Father, we are in touch with our reason for being. When we operate according to the particular call on us, a flood of joy is released in us. Then we know in our deepest being, "For this I was created." Even when I am most tired and depleted, the quiet contemplation of God's call issues forth new life. Call is tapping into a fresh, underground stream. Even if life above ground is chaotic, there is a place of stability and rooting in the call of God.

Gordon Cosby summarizes the characteristics of call:

Vocation [calling] has the elements of knowing that if you respond to the call, you are faithful to your own inner being and you are enhanced by it. Your own awareness converges with some need out yonder and intersects with it in such a way that you have the sense that you were born to this.[21]

IS THERE A SPECIAL CALL?

In the New Reformation redefinition of call, I have stressed the general and particular call that is incumbent on all the members of the body. Conspicuous in its absence has been any mention of a "special call" associated with ordained ministry. Is there a qualitatively different call to leadership that is of a nature not experienced by the ordinary members of the body of Christ? Or does the New Testament conceive of the call to leadership as a particular call among other particular calls? My bias is toward the latter. From within the one body of Christ some have the function of helping the members of the body discover their ministry to upbuild the church and be deployed to the world. Any view of call that debilitates and devalues the ministry of the whole body of Christ is contrary to the New Testament conception of the church.

The traditional roles of clergy and laity must be reversed: The laity become the troops in the front lines and the clergy, with the gathered church, help to support *them*. Until this revolution occurs, the Protestant "concept of the priesthood" of all believers remains vague and unrealized.[22]

Figure 10.7

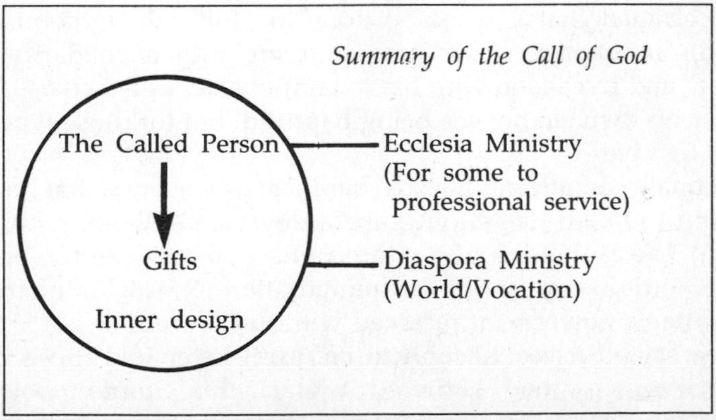

Summary of the Call of God

The Called Person ——— Ecclesia Ministry
(For some to
professional service)

Gifts ——— Diaspora Ministry
(World/Vocation)

Inner design

Ordination in the New Reformation

A study in the United Presbyterian Church, U.S.A., raised the pertinent question, "Is ordination, as it is now practiced, consistent or in conflict with the understanding of the common ministry of all Christians?"[23] I have already argued that ordination traditionally serves as the great divide that creates the class consciousness between clergy and laity. It is the "essential difference" between two peoples.

James Dunn proposes a radically different application of ordination:

> Until we count "ordination" of Sunday School teachers and distributors of church flowers as no different in essence from "ordination" of an elder or bishop, we cannot claim to be functioning as the body of Christ.[24]

Ordination, a setting apart, is conferred through a symbol. If we apply ordination to *all* the ministries within the body, what might be the symbol of an every-member ordination?

My suggestion is that we rediscover the significance of baptism. Baptism as it is now commonly practiced is an initiation rite into the body of Christ that represents the washing of regeneration and the newness of life in Christ. But who associates baptism with ordination for ministry? I urge a reclaiming of baptism, to fill this symbol with content associated with the entrance of all into Christ's ministry.

We look to Jesus' baptism as the prototype. Jesus inaugurated his ministry in the waters of John's baptism (Matt. 3:13–17). John recoiled at the thought of baptizing Jesus, the Sinless One. Yet Jesus claimed that it must be done to "fulfil all righteousness" (v. 15). In baptism Jesus was entering into a solidarity with sinners and foreshadowing his redemptive act in the cross. It was not for his own sin he was being baptized, but for those whom he came to save.

Equally significant in Jesus' baptism, however, is that "he saw the Spirit of God descending like a dove, and alighting on him" (v. 16). We cannot miss here the connection between the descent of the Spirit in baptism at the inauguration of Jesus' ministry and the same empowerment received with the descent of the Spirit at Pentecost and its connection to baptism. Peter told those under conviction who had gathered to hear his Spirit-emboldened message, "Repent, and be baptized everyone of you in the name of the Lord Jesus Christ for the forgiveness of your sins; and you shall receive the gift of the Holy Spirit" (Acts 2:38). The Faith and Order Report on "the Meaning of Baptism" states, "The outpouring of the Spirit at Pentecost is the counterpart of what happened to Jesus at his baptism. . . . The same Spirit who remained on Jesus for his messianic ministry has ever since Pentecost dwelt in the church, which is the temple of his body."[25]

The apostle Paul also makes a connection between the Holy Spirit and baptism as a sign of entrance into ministry of the whole body. In 1 Corinthians 12 he wrote that the Holy Spirit apportions gifts of ministry to the whole body for the building up of the church. "For by one Spirit we were baptized into one body" (v. 13). It is this baptism of the Spirit that inducts a person into the one ministry of Jesus Christ.

Historically our emphasis in baptism has been on the benefits received, and not on the claim of Christ on the one baptized. We have stressed our entrance into the covenant community of God's people, the forgiveness of sin and cleansing from guilt symbolized in the water, but we have failed to instruct the candidate for baptism that in that rite, the Holy Spirit empowers us to give our life away in service to Christ. Every service of baptism should be a service of ordination for ministry and an opportunity for the gathered people of God to recommit themselves to living out the implications of their baptismal vows.

Therefore, whether or not we believe in the rite of ordination to a "special" ministry for pastors, we must not forget that there is only one people of God—all are baptized Christians. All have the same identity in Christ no matter the particular form of ministry to which we may be called. This means that ordination should never create a class distinction where a group of people is set apart *from* and *above* the rest of the members of the body. Leaders from *among* the body are set apart from *within* and *for* the body, to equip them so the body may arrive at the fullness of its ministry.

Ordination of the Membership

Instead of limiting ordination to a few, a more fruitful approach consistent with the church as organism is to conceive of ways to affirm the calls within the body. George Peck opens up our thinking by proposing a five-step process whereby ministries can be confirmed.[26] To have a ministry means we are:

1. *Called*—have a sense of God's hand upon us for a particular task.
2. *Prepared*—enter a regimen of training necessary to carry out this task
3. *Recognized*—be affirmed publicly by the congregation and appointed for a ministry
4. *Supported*—done in the context of community, rarely in isolation
5. *Held accountable*—establish a standard to which a person submits

This pattern could function both for those called to a specific ministry within the church or to the world. For example, in our church, small-group leaders are recruited (1) from within the existing groups after demonstrating gifts to lead a group and passing through a discernment process to test call. There is a course of training (2) that includes formal classroom sessions and on-the-job apprenticeship. There is a means to publicly recognize (3) their role in the church. A small-group leadership team meets regularly to provide relational and prayer support (4) and to uphold the standards of accountability mutually agreed upon (5).

Peck urges a similar model for vocation-call as Christians respond to serve where they are planted in the world. Why do we not have structures of support and accountability for Christian doctors, lawyers, nutritionists, builders, social workers, and the like?

The traditional view of call and ordination restricts ministry to a few. But the New Reformation view throws open the door of concrete call to all who have responded to the summons of Jesus Christ. There are not a few who have important things to do for God's kingdom, but it is the privilege and responsibility of all to cultivate God's voice in order to hear the inner promptings of the Holy Spirit. What ministry can be released if only we believe in the full empowerment of all of God's people!

NOTES

1. Thomas Gillespie, "The Call and Ordination in a Reformed Theology of Ministry" (Unpublished paper), 10–11.

2. Donald McKim, "The 'Call' In the Reformed Tradition" (Unpublished paper), 7.

3. "Anglican–Roman Catholic International Commission, Final Report" (CTS/SPC, 1982), 36.

4. Quoted by James D. G. Dunn, "Ministry and the Ministry: The Charismatic Renewal's Challenge to Traditional Ecclesiology" (Unpublished paper), 11.

5. Gillespie, "The Call and Ordination," 10 (emphasis mine).

6. As quoted in Roland H. Bainton, *Here I Stand: A Life of Martin Luther* (New York: Mentor, 1950), 156.

7. Gillespie, "The Call and Ordination," 7.

8. Gordon Cosby, *Handbook for Mission Groups* (Waco, Tex.: Word, 1975), 27–28.

9. Paul Tournier, *The Meaning of Persons* (New York: Harper & Row, 1957), 9.

10. C. S. Lewis, *Mere Christianity* (New York: Macmillan, 1952), 189.

11. This balance is captured by the title and is the subject of Elizabeth O'Connor's book *Journey Inward, Journey Outward* (New York: Harper & Row, 1968).

12. Arthur F. Miller and Ralph T. Mattson, *The Truth About You* (Old Tappan, N.J.: Revell, 1977), 17.

13. Ibid., 19.

14. Arthur F. Miller and Ralph T. Mattson, *Finding a Job You Can Love* (Nashville: Nelson, 1982), 97.

15. Os Guinness, *The Dust of Death* (Downers Grove, Ill.: InterVarsity Press, 1973), 387.

16. John Calvin, *Institutes of the Christian Religion*, trans. John McNeil (Philadelphia: Westminster, 1936).

17. Miller and Mattson, *Finding a Job You Can Love*, 46.

18. Ibid., 46.

19. Ibid., 47.

20. As quoted in Frank Tillapaugh, *The Church Unleashed* (Ventura, Calif.: Regal, 1982), 199.

21. Cosby, *Handbook for Mission Groups*, 28.

22. Ernst Klein, "A Christian Life Style in the Modern World" (Unpublished pamphlet).

23. *Report of the Task Force to the General Assembly Mission Council Executive Committee*, 1978.

24. Dunn, "Ministry and the Ministry," 26.

25. From the Faith and Order Report on "the Meaning of Baptism," in *One Lord, One Baptism* (London: SCM Press, 1960), 53ff.; as quoted in *Theological Foundations for Ministry*, ed. Ray S. Anderson (Grand Rapids: Eerdmans, 1979), 432.

26. George Peck and John S. Hoffman, eds., *The Laity in Ministry* (Valley Forge, Pa.: Judson, 1984), 88–89.

General Index

Scripture Index